# THE COMIC BOOK STORY OF
# PROFESSIONAL WRESTLING

# THE
# COMIC BOOK STORY OF
# PROFESSIONAL WRESTLING

A Hardcore, High-Flying,
No-Holds-Barred History
of the One True Sport

**Aubrey Sitterson**
AND **Chris Moreno**

Colors by Len O'Grady, Brad Simpson,
Allen Passalaqua, and Jay Moreno
Letters by Rus Wooton

TEN SPEED PRESS
California | New York

Check out aubreysitterson.com/wrestlingresources for detailed chapter notes, additional material, news, recommendations for further reading, and more.

Text copyright © 2018 by Aubrey Sitterson
Illustrations copyright © 2018 by Chris Moreno

All rights reserved.
Published in the United States by Ten Speed Press, an imprint of the
Crown Publishing Group, a division of Penguin Random House LLC, New York.
www.crownpublishing.com
www.tenspeed.com

Ten Speed Press and the Ten Speed Press colophon are registered trademarks
of Penguin Random House LLC.

Library of Congress Cataloging-in-Publication Data
Names: Sitterson, Aubrey, author. | Moreno, Chris, author.
Title: The comic book story of professional wrestling / Aubrey Sitterson and Chris Moreno.
Description: New York : Ten Speed Press, 2018. | Includes index.
Identifiers: LCCN 2017036338 |
Subjects: LCSH: Wrestling—History—Comic books, strips, etc. | Lucha libre—History—
    Comic books, strips, etc. | National Wrestling Alliance—History—Comic books, strips, etc. |
    World Championship Wrestling, Inc.—History—Comic books, strips, etc. | World Wrestling
    Federation—History—Comic books, strips, etc. | World Wrestling Entertainment, Inc.—
    History—Comic books, strips, etc. | Graphic novels.
Classification: LCC GV1195 .S57 2018 | DDC 796.812—dc23
LC record available at https://lccn.loc.gov/2017036338

Trade Paperback ISBN: 978-0-399-58049-9
eBook ISBN: 978-0-399-58050-5

Printed in China

Design by Chloe Rawlins
Art layouts by Dennis Culver, Luke Malone
Color assists by Dee Canniffe, Juan Castro
Illustration page vi by Amitofo

10 9 8 7 6 5 4 3 2 1

First Edition

**AUBREY:**

To Queenie, who endures all my wrestling chit-chat.

**CHRIS:**

To Mel, without whose support (and patience), I wouldn't have finished this book.
And to Dad, the original manager of the Flying Moreno Brothers.

ONE:
**Carnival Origins and the Early Days**
1

TWO:
**The Gold Dust Trio and Becoming Entertainment**
17

THREE:
**A National Wrestling Alliance**
34

FOUR:
**The Masked Men and Women of Lucha Libre**
53

FIVE:
**All-in in the U.K.**
69

**SIX:**
**Puroresu, Strong Style, and King's Road**
82

**SEVEN:**
**The Golden Age**
102

**EIGHT:**
**The Monday Night Wars**
123

**NINE:**
**The New Millennium**
147

**Acknowledgments**
171

**Index**
172

PROFESSIONAL WRESTLING IS THE **ONE TRUE SPORT.**

WHILE **OTHER** SPORTS HAVE THEIR SHARE OF INTENSE, **DRAMATIC** MOMENTS, NONE CAN COMPARE WITH **PROFESSIONAL WRESTLING.**

THAT'S BECAUSE, FROM THE **GROUND UP,** WRESTLING HAS BEEN DESIGNED...

...TO GET A **REACTION.**

WRESTLING ISN'T THE **ONE TRUE SPORT** IN **SPITE** OF BEING FIXED, BUT RATHER... **BECAUSE OF IT.**

IT'S THE **ONE TRUE SPORT** BECAUSE IT'S NOT **REALLY** A SPORT AT ALL.

OF COURSE, THAT WASN'T **ALWAYS** THE CASE.

AS LONG AS THERE HAVE BEEN THINGS TO **FIGHT** OVER, HUMANS HAVE SETTLED THOSE DISAGREEMENTS THROUGH **WRESTLING.**

WORLD RELIGIONS ARE **FULL** OF WRESTLING **REFERENCES** LIKE THE BIBLICAL **JACOB'S** BOUT WITH AN **ANGEL.**

OR **BHIMA** VS. **JARASANDHA** IN THE **MAHABHARATA.**

OR **GILGAMESH** VS. **ENKIDU** IN **THE EPIC OF GILGAMESH,** WRITTEN ALL THE WAY BACK IN 2700 BCE.

IT'S EVEN BEEN **SUGGESTED** THAT THE FOREFATHER OF **WESTERN** PHILOSOPHY WAS CALLED **PLATO,** MEANING "**BROAD**"...

...ON ACCOUNT OF HIS IMPRESSIVE **SHOULDERS** AND **WRESTLING ABILITY.**

IN **ICELAND,** COMPETITORS PLACED **MAGICAL SYMBOLS** IN THEIR SHOES TO IMPROVE THEIR PERFORMANCE IN THE **VIKING** MARTIAL ART OF **GLÍMA.**

AND IN **CENTRAL ASIA,** A COUSIN OF **KUBLAI KHAN** NAMED **KHUTULUN** DECLARED SHE WOULD ONLY MARRY A MAN WHO COULD **BEAT** HER IN A **WRESTLING** MATCH.

SHE WAS SO **SKILLED** THAT SHE WON **TEN THOUSAND** HORSES FROM HER **VANQUISHED** SUITORS.

CULTURES ACROSS THE GLOBE DEVELOPED THEIR **OWN** WRESTLING STYLES AND RULES FOR **COMPETITION,** MANY OF WHICH **ENDURE** TODAY.

BUT WHILE **SIMILAR** TO PROFESSIONAL WRESTLING, THESE WERE **LEGIT** CONTESTS, AND ONLY DISTANT RELATIONS TO THE FOLK COMPETITIONS THAT GAVE RISE TO THE **ONE TRUE SPORT.**

TO **UNDERSTAND** THE ORIGINS OF PROFESSIONAL WRESTLING, IT'S **BEST** TO START WITH THE **NORTH AMERICAN** COLONIES.

PRIOR TO THE FOUNDING OF THE **UNITED STATES** OF AMERICA, BEFORE THE PROLIFERATION OF **GUNS** AND **KNIVES**, COLONIAL MEN WOULD OFTEN SOLVE DISPUTES IN ONE OF TWO WAYS...

FIGHTING **FAIR** WAS BASICALLY **BOXING**. FIGHTS WERE WON BY KNOCKOUT OR A FAILURE TO **STAND** BY A COUNT OF THIRTY. ATTACKING A DOWNED FIGHTER WAS **FORBIDDEN**.

BUT UNDER **ROUGH-AND-TUMBLE** RULES...THERE **WEREN'T** ANY RULES.

A **FAIR** FIGHT?

**ROUGH AND TUMBLE!**

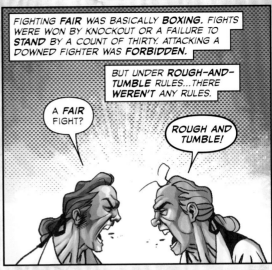

THOUGH THIS EARLY FORM OF **DUELING** WAS LARGELY **RELEGATED** TO **RURAL** AREAS OF THE SOUTH, WHERE HONOR CULTURE REIGNED **SUPREME**...

...IMMIGRANTS--LARGELY FROM **WESTERN EUROPE**--BROUGHT THEIR OWN DISTINCT STYLES WITH THEM, BEGINNING TO CREATE A **HYBRID** FORM OF WRESTLING.

BUT NO MATTER **WHERE** A FIGHTER CAME FROM, IN **ROUGH-AND-TUMBLE** DUELS, THE OBJECTIVE WAS ALWAYS THE SAME: **DISFIGURE** OR **MUTILATE** YOUR OPPONENT.

THAT COULD MEAN TEARING OR BITING OFF **EARS, LIPS, FINGERS,** EVEN **GENITALS**. BUT THE MOST **POPULAR** WAY TO WIN GAVE THE FORM ITS **OTHER** NAME...

DAMN YOUR...

...EYES!

**AGGGGGH!**

...GOUGING.

BUT THOUGH **GOUGING** OVERLAPS WITH THE **ONE TRUE SPORT** AS A FOLK COMPETITION, IT WASN'T **WRESTLING** BECAUSE IT HADN'T YET EMBRACED **SPECTACLE**.

THAT **ALL** CHANGED IN THE WAKE OF THE **AMERICAN CIVIL WAR**, WITH THE RISE OF **TRAVELING CARNIVALS** AND THEIR **ATHLETIC SHOWS**.

COME **ONE**, COME **ALL!** WHICH OF YOU **FARM BOYS** CAN LAST **FIVE MINUTES** WITH...

THE MEN IN CHARGE SOON **REALIZED** THAT THE MORE **IMPRESSIVE** AND **SPECTACULAR** THEIR WRESTLERS WERE, THE MORE PEOPLE WOULD **PAY** TO SEE THEM...

...BIG BILLY CLAYTON?!

...AND, JUST AS **IMPORTANTLY**, THE MORE THEY'D **BET** ON THEM.

**THREE-TO-ONE** ODDS THE KID DOESN'T LAST **TWO** MINUTES!

SOMEWHERE ALONG THE LINE, A **DECISION** WAS MADE TO **CONTROL** THE **OUTCOME.** THERE WAS TOO MUCH **MONEY** ON THE TABLE **NOT** TO.

AS FOR HOW THEY **DID** IT... THERE WERE A **FEW** OPTIONS:

DING! DING-DING!

SOMETIMES, THE WRESTLER'S **OPPONENT** WAS IN ON IT, DIRECTED TO **LOSE**...BUT ONLY AFTER AN **AGREED-UPON** LENGTH OF TIME.

NNNGH! EASY, BILLY!

THE CARNIVAL WOULD RAKE IN THE **CASH** VIA THE **BOOKIE,** WITH WHOM THEY WERE TYPICALLY IN **CAHOOTS.**

AND IF THE GUY **WASN'T** IN ON IT? OR JUST DIDN'T **GO ALONG?** THAT'S WHERE **HOOKS** CAME IN.

**LITTLE-KNOWN** HOLDS THAT WERE OFTEN **BANNED** IN ORGANIZED COMPETITION, **HOOKS** COULD END A MATCH **INSTANTLY.**

AGGGGH! I GIVE **UP!** GET HIM **OFFA** ME!

AND IF THINGS STARTED TO LOOK **REALLY** BAD FOR THE TRAVELING **WRESTLER?**

THE CARNIVAL WOULD TYPICALLY HAVE SOME OTHER **TRICKS** UP THEIR SLEEVES.

KRAKT!

THIS PERIOD WAS THE **TRUE** BEGINNING OF PROFESSIONAL WRESTLING, THE **BEAUTIFUL** MOMENT WHEN A **SPORT** GAVE UP SOME OF ITS **LEGITIMACY...**

...FOR THE SAKE OF **ENTERTAINMENT** AND THE **MONEY** IT BROUGHT **IN.**

AND THE PEOPLE **WATCHING?** THEY **LOVED** IT. EVEN IF THEY WEREN'T YET **IN** ON IT.

OUT OF THIS CARNIVAL MILIEU EMERGED ONE OF THE MOST **IMPORTANT** AND **INFLUENTIAL** WRESTLERS OF ALL TIME: **MARTIN "FARMER" BURNS**.

BORN IN CEDAR COUNTY, IOWA, IN **1861**, BURNS BEGAN WRESTLING AS A **CHILD**, LATER TAKING A **SCIENTIFIC APPROACH** TO THE THEN-NEW BRITISH STYLE OF **CATCH-AS-CATCH-CAN** (OR JUST **CATCH**) WRESTLING.

**CATCH WRESTLING** EVOLVED IN BRITAIN IN PARALLEL WITH **AMERICAN** WRESTLING AND SHARES MANY TRAITS WITH IT.

THEY BOTH MAKE USE OF A **VARIETY** OF REGIONAL STYLES, RELYING MORE ON **SUBMISSIONS** AND **HOOKS** THAN SHEER **POWER**, WHICH WAS **PERFECT** FOR THE 165-POUND BURNS.

IN 1895, BURNS BEAT **EVAN "STRANGLER" LEWIS** TO BECOME THE **AMERICAN HEAVYWEIGHT CHAMPION**.

HE HELD THE TITLE FOR **TWO YEARS** AND CLAIMED TO--OVER THE COURSE OF HIS CAREER--WRESTLE MORE THAN **SIX THOUSAND** MATCHES, ONLY LOSING **SEVEN**.

BUT EVEN AMID ALL THOSE MATCHES-- WHICH WERE, AT MOST, **SEMI- LEGITIMATE** --BURNS STILL UNDERSTOOD THE VALUE OF **SPECTACLE**.

USING HIS IMPRESSIVE **TWENTY-INCH NECK**, BURNS WOULD ALLOW HIMSELF TO BE DROPPED **SIX FEET** AND **HANGED** AT FAIRS, WHISTLING **YANKEE DOODLE** ALL THE WHILE.

Farmer Burns School

Les

Wrestling

Ph

OM

AS **PHENOMENAL** A TALENT AS HE WAS, WHAT MAKES BURNS **TRULY** IMPORTANT TO THE HISTORY OF **PROFESSIONAL WRESTLING** IS WHAT HE GAVE **BACK**:

HIS **WILDLY** POPULAR *"LESSONS IN WRESTLING AND PHYSICAL CULTURE"* AND A PLETHORA OF GRAPPLERS THAT TRAINED UNDER HIS **TUTELAGE**.

IN ADDITION TO THE **COUNTLESS** STUDENTS WHO RECEIVED HIS LESSONS IN THE MAIL, BURNS **PERSONALLY** TRAINED MORE THAN 1,600 WRESTLERS.

CINCH IT **IN**, FRANK.

THESE INCLUDED **JAMES ERVIN "TOOTS" MONDT**, RUDY DUSEK, EARL CADDOCK, AND MORE. HOWEVER, **FRANK GOTCH** STOOD ABOVE ALL THE REST.

IN 1899, AT THE AGE OF **TWENTY-TWO**, GOTCH LOST A WRESTLING MATCH TO BURNS IN ONLY **ELEVEN** MINUTES...

...A DECISIVE VICTORY IN A TIME WHEN **COMPETITIVE** MATCHES COULD GO ON FOR **HOURS**.

BUT BURNS SAW GOTCH'S **POTENTIAL**, AS WELL AS HIS ALREADY INFAMOUS **TOE-HOLD**, SO HE OFFERED TO **TRAIN** THE YOUNG GRAPPLER.

UNDER BURNS'S **INSTRUCTION**, GOTCH FOUND INCREASING SUCCESS IN HIS NATIVE **IOWA**, AS WELL AS DURING A **STINT** FIGHTING IN YUKON WORK CAMPS.

IN 1904, GOTCH WON THE **AMERICAN HEAVYWEIGHT CHAMPIONSHIP**, THE SAME TITLE THAT BURNS HAD WON FROM **EVAN LEWIS**.

GOTCH'S STAR WAS **RISING**, AND SO WAS **WRESTLING'S**. MOSTLY SEEN AS **LEGIT** AT ITS HIGHEST LEVELS--FAR REMOVED FROM ITS **CARNIVAL ORIGINS**--WRESTLING BECAME **MASSIVELY** POPULAR.

AND IT WAS GOING TO GET EVEN **BIGGER**, AS GOTCH SET HIS SIGHTS ON BECOMING THE FIRST AMERICAN **WORLD HEAVYWEIGHT CHAMPION**.

BUT **FIRST**, HE'D HAVE TO GET PAST THE **ONLY** MAN THAT HAD EVER HELD THAT TITLE...

...*"THE RUSSIAN LION"* **GEORGE HACKENSCHMIDT.**

*EUROPE FELL IN LOVE WITH THE* **SPECTACLE** *OF PROFESSIONAL WRESTLING SOMEWHAT* **EARLIER** *THAN AMERICA DID.*

*AS IN* **AMERICA,** *THE TRANSITION CAME VIA* **CARNIVALS,** *WHERE MEMBERS OF THE AUDIENCE COULD CHALLENGE* **MONSTROUS** *WRESTLERS IN PURSUIT OF A* **PRIZE.**

## MICHEL, LE MONSTRE!

*BUT IN 1848, EUROPEAN WRESTLING BECAME MORE* **FORMALIZED,** *AS FRENCHMAN JEAN EXBROYAT POPULARIZED A STYLE CALLED* **FLAT HAND WRESTLING,** *WHICH DIDN'T ALLOW STRIKES OR* **HOLDS** *BELOW THE* **WAIST.**

*IN AN ATTEMPT TO EVOKE WRESTLING'S* **CLASSICAL** *ORIGINS, ITALIAN GRAPPLER BASILIO BARTOLETTI LATER BEGAN CALLING FLAT HAND THE NAME BY WHICH WE KNOW IT TODAY:* **GRECO-ROMAN.**

*GRECO-ROMAN WRESTLING SWEPT WESTERN EUROPE, AS WELL AS* **RUSSIA,** *IN CONTESTS THAT, BY* **SOME** *ACCOUNTS, REMAINED AT LEAST* **PARTIALLY** *LEGITIMATE.*

*AND IN 1898, FRANCE'S* **"COLOSSUS,"** **PAUL PONS,** *DEFEATED RUSSIAN* **WLADISLAUS PYTLASINSKI** *TO WIN THE FIRST WORLD CHAMPIONSHIP, CONTESTED UNDER* **GRECO-ROMAN** *RULES.*

BORN IN 1877, IN **DORPAT**, A CITY IN WHAT IS NOW **ESTONIA**, BUT WAS THEN PART OF THE RUSSIAN EMPIRE, **GEORGE HACKENSCHMIDT** WAS A **STUNNING** PHYSICAL SPECIMEN.

HE WAS CAPABLE OF **TREMENDOUS** FEATS OF STRENGTH FROM A **YOUNG AGE**, INCLUDING LIFTING **HORSES** OFF THE GROUND!

THE RUSSIAN LION'S **PRODIGIOUS STRENGTH** MADE HIM A NATURAL FIT FOR GRECO-ROMAN WRESTLING, WITH ITS EMPHASIS ON **POWER**. HE EVEN CREATED THE **BEAR HUG**.

IN APRIL OF 1898, HACKENSCHMIDT MADE HIS PROFESSIONAL DEBUT BY DEFEATING **PAUL PONS**, ONLY **EIGHT MONTHS** BEFORE THE COLOSSUS WOULD WIN THE WORLD CHAMPIONSHIP.

**COMPETING** WORLD TITLE CLAIMS BEGAN TO POP UP, BUT **HACKENSCHMIDT** WAS **UNSTOPPABLE**, WINNING MANY OF THEM.

IF I WASN'T **PRESIDENT** OF THE UNITED STATES, I WOULD LIKE TO BE **GEORGE HACKENSCHMIDT**.

THE RUSSIAN LION MADE GRECO-ROMAN WRESTLING AN **INTERNATIONAL** SENSATION, WITH EVEN **WORLD LEADERS** STANDING IN AWE OF HIS ACCOMPLISHMENTS.

IN 1903, HACKENSCHMIDT WENT TO **ENGLAND**, WHERE THE NEWER STYLE OF **CATCH-AS-CATCH-CAN** WAS ALL THE RAGE.

CATCH WRESTLING ALLOWED HOLDS **BELOW** THE WAIST, MITIGATING THE RUSSIAN LION'S **POWER**, BUT HE PROVED **INDOMITABLE** AND WAS SOON RECOGNIZED AS WORLD CHAMPION IN **ENGLAND**.

IN 1904, HACKENSCHMIDT FIRST DEFEATED **AMERICAN** CATCH-AS-CATCH-CAN CHAMPION **TOM JENKINS** UNDER GRECO-ROMAN RULES.

BY THE **FOLLOWING** YEAR, THE RUSSIAN LION HAD GROWN **ACCUSTOMED** TO THE NEWER STYLE, AND HE ALSO BEAT JENKINS UNDER **CATCH** RULES IN NEW YORK'S **MADISON SQUARE GARDEN**.

HACKENSCHMIDT WAS RECOGNIZED AS THE FIRST **WORLD HEAVYWEIGHT CHAMPION**, IRRESPECTIVE OF **STYLES**. BUT HE HADN'T YET FACED THE MAN WHO WOULD BE HIS **GREATEST** RIVAL.

GOTCH AND HACKENSCHMIDT WERE A STUDY IN **CONTRASTS**--GOTCH, AN HEIR TO THE CARNIVAL TRADITION, TRAINED BY **FARMER BURNS;** HACKENSCHMIDT A PRACTITIONER OF THE MORE "REFINED" GRECO-ROMAN STYLE.

ADDITIONALLY, THE AMERICA OF THE EARLY 1900S WAS **NOT** THE AMERICA OF TODAY. IT WAS SEEN AS A **YOUNG UPSTART** IN MANY WAYS, INCLUDING **PROFESSIONAL WRESTLING.**

AS SUCH, THIS FEUD BECAME ONE OF **INTERNATIONAL** INTEREST BY THE TIME THE TWO **FINALLY** SQUARED OFF IN CHICAGO IN **1908.**

UP UNTIL THAT POINT, HACKENSCHMIDT HAD ALWAYS RELIED ON HIS **RENOWNED** STRENGTH TO PUT OPPONENTS AWAY **QUICKLY.**

BUT GOTCH, EMBODYING THE **SLIPPERY** NATURE OF **CARNIVAL WRESTLING,** WAS ABLE TO **EVADE** HACKENSCHMIDT.

AND **GOTCH,** ONCE AGAIN, SCHOOLED IN THE **ROUGHER** ASPECTS OF THE ONE TRUE SPORT, ALSO MADE LIBERAL USE OF **HEADBUTTS** AND OTHER **QUESTIONABLE** TACTICS.

**THE RUSSIAN LION** EVEN SPOKE OUT MID-MATCH ABOUT THE EXCESSIVE AMOUNT OF OIL ON GOTCH'S SKIN (A COMPLAINT THAT WENT **UNHEEDED** BY THE REFEREE).

THE TWO GRAPPLED ON THEIR FEET FOR A FULL **TWO HOURS** BEFORE GOTCH DROPPED A WANING HACKENSCHMIDT AND WENT FOR HIS **INFAMOUS TOE-HOLD.**

HACKENSCHMIDT **SURRENDERED** THE FALL--CHAMPIONSHIP MATCHES OF THE ERA WERE **TWO OUT OF THREE FALLS**--AND **RELINQUISHED** HIS TITLE INSTEAD OF CONTINUING THE MATCH.

AS **WORLD CHAMPION,** GOTCH WAS AN AMERICAN **HERO,** ELEVATING WRESTLING TO EVEN GREATER HEIGHTS AT HOME AND **ABROAD.**

HE **SUCCESSFULLY** DEFENDED HIS TITLE AGAINST **STANISLAUS ZBYSZKO, DR. BEN ROLLER,** AND THE AFOREMENTIONED **TOM JENKINS.**

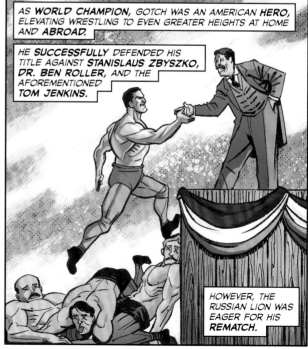

HOWEVER, THE RUSSIAN LION WAS EAGER FOR HIS **REMATCH.**

THOUGH HACKENSCHMIDT HAD **INITIALLY** TAKEN HIS LOSS **GRACIOUSLY**, BY 1911, WHEN THE TWO MET AGAIN AT CHICAGO'S **COMISKEY PARK**, THAT WAS **NO LONGER** THE CASE.

WHEN THE RUSSIAN LION RETURNED HOME TO **EUROPE**, HE HAD CHANGED HIS TUNE, **BAD-MOUTHING** GOTCH AND ACCUSING HIM OF **UNSPORTSMANLIKE** BEHAVIOR.

BUT THE HOPE THAT THEIR **REMATCH** WOULD CLEAR UP ANY **CONTROVERSY** WAS IN VAIN, DUE TO A PURPORTED **INJURY** SUFFERED BY HACKENSCHMIDT WHILE TRAINING WITH **DR. BEN ROLLER**.

THIS **ACCIDENT** AGGRAVATED THE RUSSIAN LION'S **RIGHT KNEE**, IN WHICH HE HAD SUFFERED A CASE OF **BURSITIS** SEVEN YEARS EARLIER.

BUT PRIOR TO THE MATCH, THIS INJURY DIDN'T CONCERN **ROLLER**, THE **REFEREE**, OR EVEN **HACKENSCHMIDT**, WHO DECLARED HIMSELF "**FIT TO WRESTLE FOR MY LIFE**."

AND SO, THE MATCH WENT ON AS **SCHEDULED**, THOUGH IT WAS A VERY DIFFERENT **CONTEST** THAN THEIR FIRST MEETING.

GOTCH WON THE **FIRST** FALL AFTER ONLY **SIXTEEN MINUTES**, AND THEN, COURTESY OF HIS **TOE-HOLD**, SECURED A **VICTORY** OVER THE VANQUISHED RUSSIAN LION.

THE **ENTIRE** CONTEST LASTED LESS THAN **THIRTY MINUTES**, SUCH A **SHORT** PERIOD OF TIME THAT IT GARNERED ACCUSATIONS OF **FIXING**.

HACKENSCHMIDT **RETIRED** SOON AFTER HIS SECOND LOSS TO GOTCH, BUT HE STAYED IN THE **PUBLIC EYE,** REVERED FOR HIS CONTRIBUTIONS TO BOTH **WRESTLING** AND **BODYBUILDING.**

THROUGHOUT IT **ALL,** HE AND THOSE CLOSE TO HIM CONTINUED TO **HARP** ON GOTCH, HIS **QUESTIONABLE** TACTICS, AND THE **KNEE INJURY** THAT LED TO HACKENSCHMIDT'S **LOSS** AND **RETIREMENT.**

DECADES LATER, THE **KNEE STORY** GAINED ANOTHER WRINKLE, AS **AD SANTEL** TOLD FUTURE WORLD CHAMPION **LOU THESZ** THAT GOTCH'S CAMP PAID HIM **$5,000** TO INJURE HACKENSCHMIDT.

WHILE THE CLAIM IS **UNSUBSTANTIATED,** WITH **NO** PROOF THAT SANTEL WAS EVEN **TRAINING** WITH THE RUSSIAN LION AT THE TIME, THE ACCUSATION **STILL** CARRIED WEIGHT.

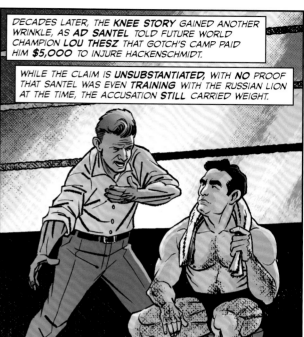

IN THE YEARS FOLLOWING GOTCH'S **EARLY DEATH** IN 1917, **MORE** STORIES EMERGED THAT TWEAKED THE PERCEPTION OF HIS TACTICS AS GOING FROM **ROUGH** TO **UNETHICAL** TO **ILLEGAL.**

**THESZ** EVEN CLAIMS IN HIS AUTOBIOGRAPHY, **HOOKER,** THAT THERE WERE RUMORS THAT GOTCH WOULD GET REFEREES IN HIS **POCKET** PRIOR TO MATCHES.

**UNORTHODOX** METHODS OF **QUESTIONABLE** LEGALITY, **COLLUSION** BETWEEN WRESTLERS AND OFFICIALS... PERHAPS THE STORIES SHOULDN'T BE **SURPRISING** GIVEN GOTCH AND BURNS'S CARNIVAL PEDIGREE.

OR PERHAPS IT WAS THAT **CARNIVAL PEDIGREE** ITSELF THAT GAVE RISE TO THE **RUMORS?**

THERE'S A **TEMPTATION** TO LOOK BACK AT THE FIRST **GOLDEN AGE** OF WRESTLING AS AN ERA WHEN THE **ONE TRUE SPORT** WAS, FOR LACK OF A BETTER TERM, A **REAL** SPORT...

...ONE **REVERED** BY **POLITICIANS,** AND WHOSE CONTESTS TOOK PLACE IN VENUES LIKE **ROYAL ALBERT HALL, MADISON SQUARE GARDEN,** AND **RESPLENDENT** OPERA HOUSES AND CONCERT HALLS.

BUT THE **SPECTACLE** THAT WAS POSITIONED AS A **LEGITIMATE SPORT** IN THOSE VENUES...

...WAS THE **DIRECT DESCENDANT** OF THE **FIXED** ENTERTAINMENT FOUND AT **TRAVELING CARNIVALS** AND **FAIRS.**

ONE THAT SAW GRAPPLERS--THOUGH THEY WERE **LEGITIMATELY TALENTED**--TAKE PART IN MATCHES THAT WERE...SOMEWHAT **LESS** THAN LEGITIMATE.

THIS PATTERN **REPEATS** THROUGHOUT WRESTLING'S HISTORY: SOMEONE WILL ACKNOWLEDGE THE **FIXED** NATURE OF CURRENT WRESTLING AS A WAY OF **ROMANTICIZING** THE REALITY OF THE PAST...

BACK IN **MY** DAY...

...WHEN THE **REALITY** IS THAT FOR AS LONG AS PROFESSIONAL WRESTLING HAS **EXISTED,** IT'S NEVER BEEN **REAL.** AT LEAST NOT **FULLY.**

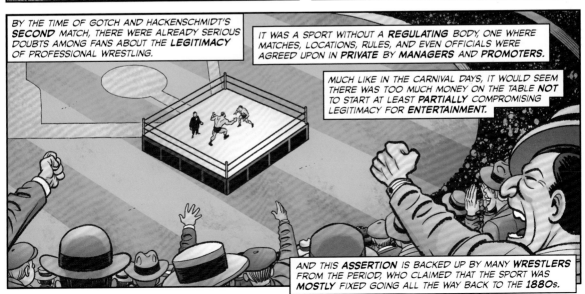

BY THE TIME OF GOTCH AND HACKENSCHMIDT'S **SECOND** MATCH, THERE WERE ALREADY SERIOUS DOUBTS AMONG FANS ABOUT THE **LEGITIMACY** OF PROFESSIONAL WRESTLING.

IT WAS A SPORT WITHOUT A **REGULATING** BODY, ONE WHERE MATCHES, LOCATIONS, RULES, AND EVEN OFFICIALS WERE AGREED UPON IN **PRIVATE** BY **MANAGERS** AND **PROMOTERS.**

MUCH LIKE IN THE CARNIVAL DAYS, IT WOULD SEEM THERE WAS TOO MUCH MONEY ON THE TABLE **NOT** TO START AT LEAST **PARTIALLY** COMPROMISING LEGITIMACY FOR **ENTERTAINMENT.**

AND THIS **ASSERTION** IS BACKED UP BY MANY **WRESTLERS** FROM THE PERIOD, WHO CLAIMED THAT THE SPORT WAS **MOSTLY** FIXED GOING ALL THE WAY BACK TO THE **1880s.**

BUT WHILE WRESTLING WASN'T **TOTALLY** LEGITIMATE--AND IN CERTAIN WAYS, PROBABLY **NEVER** WAS--THE APPEARANCE OF LEGITMACY WAS STILL A **HUGE** PART OF ITS APPEAL.

**JOURNALISTS** WOULD WATCH **TRAINING SESSIONS** TO REPORT ON **TECHNIQUES,** PROGRESSION, **INTENSITY,** AND MORE.

AND THE MATCHES **THEMSELVES**--EVEN IF AND WHEN THEY **WEREN'T** LEGIT--WERE ALWAYS **WRESTLED** AS IF THEY **WERE.**

00:04:32

WHICH **TYPICALLY** MEANT A SLOW, METHODICAL PACE...

...AND MATCHES THAT LASTED FOR **HOURS,** WITH SUDDEN, **ANTICLIMACTIC** FINISHES.

01:53:02

PROFESSIONAL WRESTLING HADN'T YET BEEN **OPTIMIZED** FOR **MAXIMUM** ENTERTAINMENT VALUE.

BUT THERE WAS A **PROBLEM.** IF THE COMPETITION WASN'T **LEGITIMATE** OR **ENTERTAINING**...

...WHAT WAS THE **POINT** OF WATCHING TWO GUYS GRAPPLE ONE ANOTHER FOR **HOURS** ON END?

FRANK GOTCH **RETIRED** AS WORLD HEAVYWEIGHT CHAMPION IN 1913. BUT IN THE **FIVE YEARS** THAT HE HELD THE TITLE, NO **NEW STARS** HAD ARISEN TO TAKE HIS PLACE.

IN FACT, IT WOULD BE ANOTHER **TWO YEARS** BEFORE A NEW **WORLD HEAVYWEIGHT CHAMPION**, JOE STECHER, WAS EVEN **RECOGNIZED.**

AND EVEN THEN, THE TWENTY-TWO-YEAR-OLD GRAPPLER REMAINED IN THE SHADOW OF **GOTCH,** WHO HAD NEVER ACTUALLY **LOST** THE TITLE.

WITHOUT A **NEW STAR** AND WITH INCREASING **QUESTIONS** ABOUT WRESTLING'S LEGITIMACY, IT WAS ONLY A MATTER OF TIME BEFORE PREVIOUSLY **PACKED** VENUES...

...BEGAN TO CLEAR **OUT.**

THEN IN 1917, THE **UNITED STATES** ENTERED **WORLD WAR I,** DEPRIVING PROFESSIONAL WRESTLING OF FUNDS, INTEREST, AND THE **ATHLETIC YOUNG MEN** THAT IT NEEDED TO **THRIVE.**

TO **SURVIVE,** THE ONE TRUE SPORT NEEDED TO **EVOLVE.**

# WRESTLING IS MAGIC

AS A WAY OF **EVANGELIZING** TO THE **UNCONVERTED,** FANS WILL OFTEN DESCRIBE WRESTLING AS A LIVE-ACTION **SUPERHERO** FIGHT OR A MUSCLE-BOUND **SOAP OPERA.**

WHILE NOT **WRONG** PER SE, THESE CHARACTERIZATIONS MISS OUT ON WHAT THE ONE TRUE SPORT **TRULY** IS...

...A **CON.**

LIKE A **CARNIVAL BARKER** TRYING TO GET YOU TO PLAY A GAME YOU **KNOW** IS **RIGGED,** WRESTLERS WANT YOU TO **CARE** ABOUT A FIGHT YOU **KNOW** IS **FIXED.**

OFTEN, WRESTLERS **ACCOMPLISH** THIS THROUGH THE SHEER **INTENSITY** OF A MATCH. FANS ARE DRAWN IN BY THE **DRAMA** AND **ACTION** BETWEEN THE ROPES.

AND AS WITH A **MAGICIAN'S** AUDIENCE, THE ILLUSION **WORKS** BECAUSE ON **SOME** LEVEL, PEOPLE **WANT** TO BELIEVE IT'S REAL.

BUT AGAIN, LIKE A **MAGIC TRICK,** WRESTLING ALSO MAKES **LIBERAL** USE OF WHAT FANS **KNOW,** AND JUST AS IMPORTANTLY, WHAT THEY **THINK** THEY KNOW.

THIS CAN INCLUDE WRESTLERS' SHARED **HISTORY, REAL WORLD** EVENTS, OR EVEN **RUMORS.**

THE ONE TRUE SPORT TAKES IT **ALL** INTO ACCOUNT; IT **ACKNOWLEDGES** YOUR EXPECTATIONS, AND THEN WORKS TO **DENY, SUBVERT,** OR MAKE **GOOD** ON THEM.

AND IN THE **BEST** MATCHES, WITH THE **BEST** WRESTLERS? YOU GET ALL **THREE.**

WRESTLING STORIES, LIKE **ALL** STORIES, ALTERNATE BETWEEN **SURPRISING** AUDIENCES AND GIVING THEM **EXACTLY** WHAT THEY WANT.

BUT WHAT MAKES IT **MAGICAL** IS THAT UNLIKE A BOOK OR A MOVIE, WRESTLING HAS NO BOUNDARIES, AND IT ALWAYS PROMPTS A SINGLE, **ALL-IMPORTANT,** UNANSWERABLE QUESTION:

HOW **MUCH** OF THIS IS **REAL?**

DURING THE 1910s, IN THE WAKE OF GOTCH'S **RETIREMENT**, WITH WORLD WAR I TIGHTENING **PURSE STRINGS**, PROFESSIONAL WRESTLING **STRUGGLED**.

HOWEVER, CLIMBING THROUGH THE **CARNIVAL** RANKS WAS A **TRANSCENDENT** TALENT, WHO WOULD BE AT THE CENTER OF WRESTLING'S **BIGGEST** EVOLUTIONARY LEAP.

BORN **ROBERT HERMAN JULIUS FRIEDRICH**, THE GRAPPLER TOOK THE NAME **ED "STRANGLER" LEWIS** WHEN HE BEGAN WRESTLING AT **FOURTEEN**.

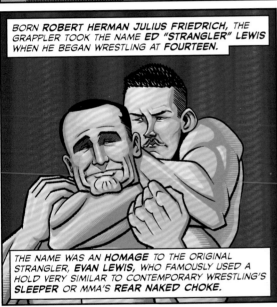

THE NAME WAS AN **HOMAGE** TO THE ORIGINAL STRANGLER, **EVAN LEWIS**, WHO FAMOUSLY USED A HOLD VERY SIMILAR TO CONTEMPORARY WRESTLING'S **SLEEPER** OR MMA'S **REAR NAKED CHOKE**.

LEWIS, HOWEVER, USED A **DIFFERENT** MOVE, ONE MUCH **MORE** SIMILAR TO WHAT WRESTLING NOW CALLS THE **SIDE HEADLOCK**.

THESE DAYS, IT'S SEEN AS A **TRANSITIONAL** MOVE, ONE USED ON THE WAY TO SOMETHING MORE **INTERESTING**.

BUT IN **LEWIS'S** DAY, WHEN VICTORY COULD BE OBTAINED **ONLY** VIA **PINFALL**, AND HOLDS WERE ADMINISTERED IN ORDER TO **MANEUVER** AN OPPONENT'S **SHOULDERS** TO THE MAT...

...HIS STRANGLEHOLD--IN THE HANDS OF SUCH A TALENTED **HOOKER**-- WAS A **MATCH-ENDER**.

IN 1914, AT ONLY **TWENTY-TWO YEARS OLD,** LEWIS JOINED FORCES WITH **BILLY SANDOW.**

**SEVEN YEARS** LEWIS'S SENIOR, SANDOW WAS A FORMER **WRESTLER** HIMSELF, HAVING TAKEN HIS **RING NAME** FROM PIONEERING BODYBUILDER **EUGEN SANDOW.**

SANDOW WAS **TALENTED,** WORKING THROUGHOUT THE **SOUTHERN** CARNIVAL CIRCUIT, BUT HE WASN'T **CHAMPIONSHIP** MATERIAL.

DURING HIS CARNIVAL DAYS, HOWEVER, HE DISCOVERED **ANOTHER** ROLE, ONE AT WHICH HE **EXCELLED...**

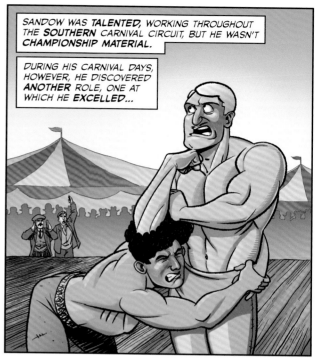

...MANAGER.

PROFESSIONAL WRESTLING HAD BEEN LARGELY **FIXED** FOR **THIRTY YEARS,** SO IT WAS CRUCIAL FOR WRESTLERS TO HAVE SOMEONE **ADVOCATING** FOR THEM. TALENT **WASN'T** ENOUGH.

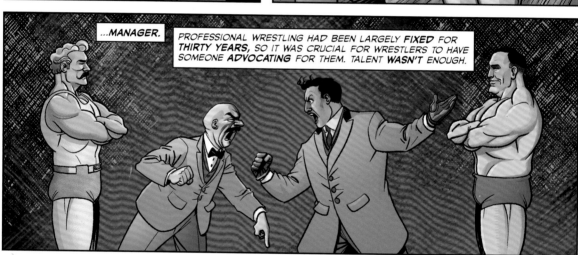

LESS LIKE **CONTEMPORARY** WRESTLING AND MORE LIKE A **BOXING** MANAGER, SANDOW WAS RESPONSIBLE FOR **NEGOTIATING** CUTS OF THE **HOUSE** AS WELL AS WHO **ACTUALLY** WON EACH MATCH.

AND IF A WRESTLER DIDN'T GO **ALONG?** CHANCES ARE THEY COULDN'T BEAT THE **PRETERNATURALLY** TALENTED LEWIS **ANYWAY.**

AS LEWIS RACKED UP **WINS**, SANDOW KEPT HIS EYE ON WRESTLING'S **GREATEST** PRIZE: THE **WORLD HEAVYWEIGHT CHAMPIONSHIP.**

JOE STECHER--WITH HIS **BODY SCISSORS PIN**--WAS ONCE AGAIN CHAMPION AFTER HAVING DEFEATED **EARL CADDOCK**, A **FARMER BURNS** STUDENT.

LEWIS HAD FACED STECHER BEFORE, IN **1915**, WHEN HE WAS **COUNTED OUT** AFTER FALLING OUT OF THE RING AND HITTING HIS HEAD ON A **CHAIR**.

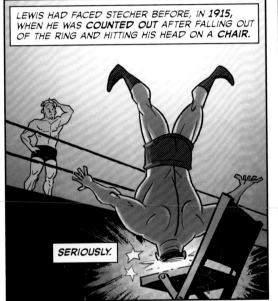

SERIOUSLY.

AND IN **1916**, THE PAIR WRESTLED A **PAINFULLY** DULL MATCH THAT LASTED MORE THAN **FOUR HOURS...**

...NECESSITATING THAT **CARS** BE BROUGHT IN TO SHINE THEIR **LIGHTS** ON THE RING--AFTER LEWIS AND SANDOW **REFUSED** TO **RESTART** THE MATCH THE NEXT MORNING.

SANDOW BECAME KNOWN FOR RUNNING HIS MOUTH AS A **BRASH**, VILLAINOUS MANAGER, WHILE **LEWIS** WRESTLED AN EVASIVE, ALMOST **COWARDLY** STYLE.

IT WAS AN **EARLY** VERSION OF A **HEEL** MANAGER/WRESTLER DYNAMIC THAT WOULD BE USED **AGAIN** AND **AGAIN**.

ON **DECEMBER 13, 1920**, LEWIS FINALLY **BEAT** JOE STECHER IN A MATCH THAT SAW HIM UTILIZE HIS SIGNATURE MOVE **SEVEN TIMES**.

**REPORTS** OF THE MATCH'S FINAL MOMENTS SOUND AS **DRAMATIC** AS TODAY'S **BEST** MATCHES, **SUGGESTING** THAT IT WAS, IN ALL LIKELIHOOD...FIXED.

AS **EFFECTIVE** AS THE LEWIS–SANDOW TANDEM WAS, THEY WERE STILL **MISSING** SOMETHING: AN **INNOVATOR.**

THEY HADN'T YET MET **JAMES ERVIN MONDT,** WHO FIRST CAME TO WRESTLING THROUGH FARMER BURNS'S **CORRESPONDENCE COURSE.**

MONDT, CALLED **"TOOTS"** ON ACCOUNT OF HIS **BOYISH** FACE, EVENTUALLY CAME TO THE ATTENTION OF **BURNS** HIMSELF.

IN THE EARLY 1920S, LEWIS AND SANDOW WERE LOOKING FOR A NEW **TRAINING PARTNER,** AND BURNS MADE A **FORTUITOUS** INTRODUCTION.

MONDT, WHO **CLAIMED** HE WAS A **BETTER** WRESTLER THAN LEWIS, SERVED **ABLY** AS HIS TRAINING PARTNER.

BUT HIS **CONTRIBUTIONS** WENT FAR **BEYOND** JUST KEEPING LEWIS (WHO WAS PRONE TO WEIGHT GAIN) IN **SHAPE.**

IN **SUBSEQUENT** DECADES, THE THREE MEN-- LEWIS, SANDOW, AND MONDT-- WOULD COME TO BE KNOWN AS THE **GOLD DUST TRIO.**

IT WAS A NOD TO NOT ONLY HOW MUCH **MONEY** THEY MADE TOGETHER, BUT THEIR MASSIVE **CONTRIBUTIONS** TO PROFESSIONAL WRESTLING.

IN THE WAKE OF **GOTCH'S** RETIREMENT, INTEREST IN WRESTLING HAD **WANED.**

BUT **MONDT** WAS READY TO **CHANGE** THAT WITH SOMETHING HE CALLED...

**SLAM BANG WESTERN-STYLE WRESTLING!**

SINCE **HACKENSCHMIDT** AND **GOTCH,** WRESTLING HAD BEEN A BLEND OF **GRECO-ROMAN** AND **CATCH-AS-CATCH-CAN** STYLES.

BUT MONDT LOOKED TO BRING IN **OTHER** INFLUENCES.

HE PULLED FROM **EVERYWHERE,** INCLUDING **CARNIVAL** WRESTLING, **CROWD-PLEASING** THEATER...

...AND THE EXPLOSIVE, **CHAOTIC** ACTION **UNIQUE** TO **ROUGH-AND-TUMBLE** FIGHTS.

HE INTRODUCED A **SLEW** OF NEW MOVES, ONES THAT, WHILE LESS **REALISTIC** THAN A TRADITIONAL GRAPPLE, WERE **FAR** MORE EXCITING TO BEHOLD.

THESE INCLUDED **ARM DRAGS, SLAMS,** AND EVEN **SUPLEXES,** MANY OF WHICH ARE **NOW** CONSIDERED **TRADITIONAL** MANEUVERS.

THIS NEW STYLE WAS **ALSO** INFLUENCED BY **BOXING,** UTILIZING CLOSED-FIST **STRIKES.**

(THOUGH DEPENDING ON THE **MATCH,** THEY COULD BE OF **QUESTIONABLE** LEGALITY.)

IT'S NO EXAGGERATION TO SAY THAT MONDT WAS A **CREATIVE VISIONARY.** HE **ORIGINATED** MUCH OF WHAT WRESTLING IS **TODAY.**

HE COMPLETED WRESTLING'S TRANSFORMATION FROM A **SPORT** THAT ACTED LIKE A **SHOW** TO A **SHOW** THAT ACTED LIKE A **SPORT.**

WHO WON **LEWIS'S** MATCHES WAS LARGELY **PREDETERMINED.** BUT THAT WAS NOTHING **NEW.**

AFTER ALL, WRESTLING IN AMERICA HAD BEEN MOSTLY **FIXED** GOING BACK TO **AT LEAST** THE 1880S.

WHAT MAKES MONDT **SIGNIFICANT** ISN'T THAT HE DECIDED WHO **WON** LEWIS'S MATCHES.

IT'S THAT HE UNDERSTOOD THAT THE MOST **IMPORTANT** THING **WASN'T** WHO **WON** A MATCH...

...BUT RATHER **HOW** THEY WON IT AND WHAT THE MANNER OF THEIR VICTORY **SAID** ABOUT THE COMPETITORS.

**FIXED** MATCHES AND **FINISHING MOVES** ALREADY EXISTED, BUT MONDT CREATED THE IDEA OF A **FINISH.**

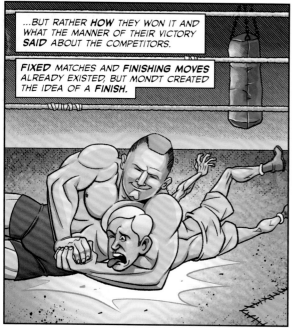

BY DICTATING THE **WAY** IN WHICH MATCHES ENDED, THE **GOLD DUST TRIO** COULD OPTIMIZE THEM FOR **MAXIMUM** DRAMA.

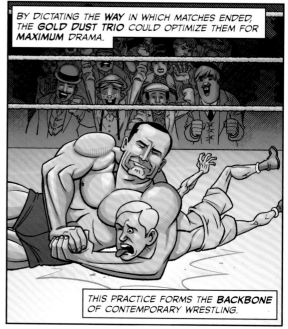

THIS PRACTICE FORMS THE **BACKBONE** OF CONTEMPORARY WRESTLING.

LIKE **CARNIVAL OWNERS** BEFORE THEM, THE GOLD DUST TRIO RAMPED UP THE **DRAMA** BY MAKING THEIR CONTESTS **LESS** LEGITIMATE.

THAT MEANT MAKING SURE THAT THE AUDIENCE **BELIEVED** THERE WAS A **CHANCE** A CHALLENGER COULD **DEFEAT** LEWIS.

BUT IN ORDER FOR **THAT** TO HAPPEN, A **CHALLENGER** HAD TO GET IN SOME **OFFENSE**, WHICH PRESENTED A **SIGNIFICANT** RISK...

...AS IT GAVE THE CHALLENGER AN OPPORTUNITY TO GO INTO **BUSINESS** FOR **HIMSELF**, POTENTIALLY WINNING THE MATCH OR EVEN THE **TITLE**.

EVEN THOUGH WRESTLING WASN'T **LEGIT**, IT WAS **CRUCIAL** TO HAVE THE TITLE ON A **TALENTED** GRAPPLER LIKE **LEWIS**.

THAT WAY, IF THINGS WENT **SOUTH**, HE COULD STEP IN AND TURN THE MATCH INTO A **LEGITIMATE** CONTEST--A **SHOOT**.

AND ON THE OFF CHANCE THAT LEWIS **COULDN'T** GET CONTROL OF THE MATCH?

**MONDT** WAS ALWAYS AT **RINGSIDE**, READY TO PUT PEOPLE IN THEIR **PLACE**.

THE GOLD DUST TRIO ALSO BROUGHT ABOUT ANOTHER MASSIVE CHANGE TO PROFESSIONAL WRESTLING.

THE INTRODUCTION OF TIME LIMITS.

THE MOST OBVIOUS THING THIS CHANGE ACCOMPLISHED WAS THE END OF INTERMINABLE MATCHES.

IF A CONTEST IS, AT MOST, ONLY TWENTY OR THIRTY MINUTES LONG, THERE'S LESS TIME TO GET BORED.

TIME LIMITS ALSO MEANT THAT WRESTLERS HAD TO MOVE FASTER.

IT SPED UP THE PACE AND AVOIDED THE DRAWN-OUT CONTESTS THAT HAD DEFINED WRESTLING PREVIOUSLY.

AND THE CROWD? THEY LOVED IT, OF COURSE.

ESPECIALLY AS IT ADDED ANOTHER LAYER OF DRAMA. WRESTLERS COULD NO LONGER WAIT ONE ANOTHER OUT INDEFINITELY.

HURRY UP AND PIN HIM!

BUT **TIME LIMITS** ALSO SERVED **ANOTHER**, EXTREMELY IMPORTANT ROLE, AS THEY INTRODUCED **ANOTHER** WAY FOR MATCHES TO END...

...THE **TIME LIMIT DRAW**.

*DING! DING! DING!*

**TIME!**

...7...8... 9...!

A DRAW WAS AN OUTCOME THAT COULD MAKE A **YOUNG GRAPPLER** LOOK LIKE A STAR, WHILE KEEPING THE TITLE ON **LEWIS**.

AND SINCE **TIME** WAS THE DECIDING FACTOR, NOT **SKILL**, IT CREATED **ANTICIPATION** FOR A **REMATCH**.

ANOTHER **SIMILAR** INNOVATION WAS THE **DOUBLE COUNT OUT**, WHEREIN THE ENTIRE MATCH IS RULED A **NO CONTEST**.

**DOUBLE COUNT OUTS** HAVE THE ADDED BONUS OF MAKING A **RIVALRY** SEEM PARTICULARLY **HEATED**, ONCE AGAIN SETTING UP A **REMATCH**.

WITH **FIXED** MATCHES, **PLANNED** FINISHES, **EXCITING** MOVES, AND **INNOVATIVE** MATCH OUTCOMES, THE GOLD DUST TRIO BEGAN TO BUILD **NEW STARS**.

BUT WHAT WAS THE POINT OF **NEW** STARS IF LEWIS WAS **THE GUY**?

IN GOTCH'S DAY, PROMOTERS COULD PACK OUT A VENUE, A CONCERT HALL, OR EVEN A BASEBALL STADIUM...

...WITH A SINGLE, HEAVILY PROMOTED MATCH.

BUT BY THE 1920S, WITH LESS INTEREST IN WRESTLING AS A WHOLE...

...A SINGLE MATCH WASN'T ENOUGH, EVEN IF THE WORLD TITLE WAS ON THE LINE.

SO, IN A FIRST, THE GOLD DUST TRIO BEGAN TO PROMOTE NOT JUST MATCHES, BUT ENTIRE CARDS.

EVENTS WERE ANCHORED BY A TITLE DEFENSE, BUT ALSO BOASTED A SERIES OF FIXED MATCHES FEATURING...

...THE VERY WRESTLERS THAT LEWIS LEGITIMIZED THROUGH MONDT'S FINISHES.

WITH BIGGER SHOWS, WITH MORE VARIETY AND WITH MORE WRESTLERS...

...THE GOLD DUST TRIO COULD BOOK BIGGER VENUES AND MAKE MORE MONEY.

WITH **LEGITIMATE** WRESTLING BACKGROUNDS AND **COMPETITIVE** NATURES...

...IT MIGHT BE **DIFFICULT** TO UNDERSTAND WHY WRESTLERS WOULD **THROW IN** WITH A GROUP THAT WOULD ONLY EVER SEE THEM AS A **SIDESHOW** TO LEWIS.

BUT THAT **UNDERESTIMATES** THE VALUE OF COLD, HARD **CASH.**

AND JUST HOW **MUCH** OF IT THE GOLD DUST TRIO HAD **COMING IN.**

SANDOW, A FORMER **WRESTLER** HIMSELF, WOULD **TEST** PROSPECTIVE GRAPPLERS.

AND IF THEY **PASSED,** HE'D SIGN THEM TO AN **EXCLUSIVE CONTRACT**--ANOTHER FIRST FOR WRESTLING.

THEN THEY'D GO TO **MONDT** TO LEARN EFFECTIVE HOLDS, HOOKS, AND OTHER **FINISHES.**

THE TRAINING PROCESS PROBABLY **ALSO** INCLUDED A FAIR BIT OF **STRETCHING**--LOCKING A WRESTLER IN A **HOLD** AND PUSHING THEM TO THEIR **LIMITS.**

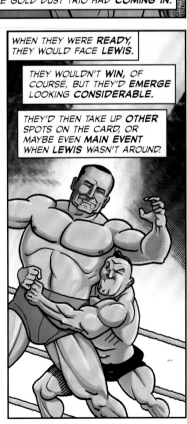

WHEN THEY WERE **READY,** THEY WOULD FACE **LEWIS.**

THEY WOULDN'T **WIN,** OF COURSE, BUT THEY'D **EMERGE** LOOKING **CONSIDERABLE.**

THEY'D THEN TAKE UP **OTHER** SPOTS ON THE CARD, OR MAYBE EVEN **MAIN EVENT** WHEN **LEWIS** WASN'T AROUND.

TO MAKE IT TO THE **TOP** OF THE GOLD DUST TRIO'S PROMOTION, YOU HAD TO BE A **LEGIT** GRAPPLER.

AFTER ALL, THEY NEEDED TO BE ABLE TO **TRUST** WRESTLERS TO TAKE **CARE** OF **THEMSELVES** AS WELL AS THE TRIO'S **INVESTMENTS**.

BUT THEY WOULD ALSO TAKE ON **LESS TALENTED** GRAPPLERS, IF THEY WERE **CHARISMATIC**...

...AND OF A **MARKETABLE** ETHNIC BACKGROUND.

THE GOLD DUST TRIO FEATURED WRESTLERS OF **NUMEROUS**, THOUGH STILL **EUROPEAN**, ETHNICITIES: IRISH, ITALIAN, POLISH...

...ANYTHING THAT MIGHT ENTICE **IMMIGRANT** COMMUNITIES TO BUY A **TICKET**.

BUT DON'T BE **MISTAKEN**--THIS WASN'T A TACTIC TO **DIVERSIFY** WRESTLING OR TO INCREASE ETHNIC REPRESENTATION...

...IT WAS A WAY TO MAKE **MONEY**, ONE THAT IS STILL **REGULARLY** UTILIZED BY WRESTLING PROMOTIONS **TODAY**.

ONE SUCH WRESTLER WAS LEGENDARY POLISH STRONGMAN **STANISLAUS ZBYSZKO**, WHO TRADED THE WORLD TITLE WITH **LEWIS**.

BUT ZBYSZKO WAS A **LEGITIMATE** GRAPPLER, AND TURNED A 1925 CHAMPIONSHIP MATCH AGAINST FOOTBALL PLAYER **WAYNE MUNN**...

...INTO A **SHOOT**, DOUBLE-CROSSING THE GOLD DUST TRIO AND WINNING MUNN'S CHAMPIONSHIP IN WHAT WAS THE LAST **LEGIT** WORLD TITLE MATCH IN WRESTLING HISTORY.

MUNN'S INABILITY TO **PROTECT** HIMSELF WAS **EXACTLY** WHY IT WAS SO IMPORTANT TO HIRE **LEGITIMATE** WRESTLERS.

ZYBYSKO'S **BETRAYAL** WAS DONE IN ORDER FOR HIM TO DROP THE TITLE TO **JOE STECHER**, WHO HAD EARLIER **SPLIT** FROM THE GOLD DUST TRIO.

HOWEVER, AFTER A **THREE-YEAR** REIGN, STECHER ONCE AGAIN LOST THE TITLE TO LEWIS IN **1928**, JUST AS HE HAD EIGHT YEARS PRIOR.

WHILE TITLES COULD **ALWAYS** BE WON BACK, THERE WERE OTHER **RIFTS** WIDENING IN THE **GOLD DUST TRIO**...

...NOTABLY SURROUNDING BILLY SANDOW'S BROTHER **MAX**, WHO USED THE TWO'S LEGAL LAST NAME, **BAUMANN**.

A **POWER STRUGGLE** WITH MONDT ENSUED IN 1928, AND AS SO OFTEN **HAPPENS**...

...**BLOOD** WAS THICKER THAN **WATER**. THE **CREATIVE VISIONARY** OF THE GOLD DUST TRIO WAS OUT.

AND SHORTLY **AFTERWARD**? THE BAUMANN BOYS SPLIT FROM **LEWIS** AS WELL.

THE WRESTLER'S **WEIGHT** HAD **ALWAYS** BEEN AN ISSUE, BUT THE TWO DECIDED LEWIS AND HIS **POOR** CONDITIONING WERE NO LONGER ESSENTIAL TO THE OPERATION.

SANDOW AND BAUMANN FOUND **NEW** TALENT TO DEVELOP AND **PROMOTE**, INCLUDING **ROY DUNN** AND **EVERETT MARSHALL**.

BUT WITHOUT THE **DOMINANT** GOLD DUST TRIO, THE WRESTLING WORLD SPLINTERED **FURTHER** INTO NUMEROUS **REGIONAL** FIEFDOMS.

MONDT CHOSE ONE OF THESE, **PHILADELPHIA**, AS THE SITE OF HIS NEW VENTURE, JOINING UP WITH PROMOTER **RAY FABIANI**.

PHILADELPHIA WAS A **BIG CITY** IN ITS OWN RIGHT, BUT **JUST** AS IMPORTANTLY, IT WAS CLOSE ENOUGH FOR MONDT TO BEGIN MAKING **INROADS** INTO NEW YORK.

THERE, HE THREW HIS **CONSIDERABLE** CREATIVE PROWESS BEHIND **DICK SHIKAT**, AND MORE **NOTABLY**, "THE GOLDEN GREEK" **JIM LONDOS**.

THOUGH NOT AS **SKILLED** AS LEWIS, LONDOS MADE UP FOR IT WITH HIS **GOOD LOOKS** AND INCREDIBLE **PHYSIQUE**.

UNDER MONDT'S **GUIDANCE**, LONDOS LEANED INTO THESE **ASSETS**, PRIMARILY FACING THE MOST **HIDEOUS** AND UNAPPEALING WRESTLERS AVAILABLE.

AS A RESULT, HE BECAME ONE OF THE MOST **POPULAR** WRESTLERS IN THE COUNTRY, EVENTUALLY WINNING THE **WORLD TITLE** IN 1938.

HOWEVER, BREAKING INTO **NEW YORK** WASN'T EASY, AS THE CITY WAS CONTROLLED BY PROMOTER **JACK CURLEY**.

MONDT WAS **WELL-ACQUAINTED** WITH CURLEY, AS HIS WRESTLING "TRUST" HAD ORCHESTRATED **ZBYSZKO'S** DEFEAT OF **MUNN** IN 1925.

EVENTUALLY, RECOGNIZING HOW **PROFITABLE** LONDOS WAS, CURLEY JOINED FORCES WITH HIS **OLD RIVAL**.

AS WELL AS **ANOTHER** NEW YORK PROMOTER BY THE NAME OF **JACK PFEFER**.

CURLEY HAD PROMOTED THE SECOND *GOTCH/HACKENSCHMIDT* MATCH, AND WITH MONDT AND PFEFER'S HELP...

...HE DREW TENS OF THOUSANDS OF FANS TO CATCH A GLIMPSE OF *JIM LONDOS*, DESPITE THE ONSET OF THE *GREAT DEPRESSION*.

BUT IN 1932, A CONTRACTUAL *DISPUTE* SAW LONDOS LEAVE FOR A *RIVAL GROUP*, WITH *PFEFER* FOLLOWING HIM SOON AFTER.

WHEN THINGS GOT *SMOOTHED OVER*, AND NEW *ALLIANCES* WERE ESTABLISHED, PFEFER FOUND HIMSELF *LOCKED OUT*.

HE WAS *FURIOUS*. SO, TO GET EVEN, HE GAVE AN *EXPLOSIVE* INTERVIEW TO THE *NEW YORK DAILY MIRROR*.

IN IT, PFEFER *EXPOSED* WRESTLING, READILY ADMITTING WHAT HAD BEEN TRUE SINCE THE 1880S: IT *WASN'T A LEGITIMATE* SPORT.

*OTHER* PAPERS PICKED UP ON THE STORY AND BEGAN FREELY POINTING OUT THE *ARTIFICE OF PROFESSIONAL WRESTLING*.

THIS *REVELATION* CAUSED WRESTLING'S FAN BASE TO *CONTRACT*, JUST AS IT HAD DECADES *PRIOR*.

IT ALSO *GIVES LIE* TO THE *COMMONLY* HELD NOTION THAT UNTIL RELATIVELY *RECENTLY*, WRESTLING FANS WERE IN THE *DARK* ABOUT THE *TRUE* NATURE OF THE ONE TRUE SPORT.

JACK CURLEY **PASSED AWAY** IN 1937, EFFECTIVELY DEMOLISHING HIS DELICATE, MULTI-CITY **TRUST**...

...WHILE OPENING THE DOOR FOR **TOOTS** MONDT TO TAKE OVER **NEW YORK**.

MONDT SET ABOUT **SOLIDIFYING** HIS RELATIONSHIPS WITH NEW YORK MANAGERS AND PROMOTERS, INCLUDING **FABIANI**, FELLOW BURNS TRAINEE **RUDY DUSEK**, AND EVEN **JACK PFEFER**.

AS ALWAYS, MONDT CARED LESS ABOUT KEEPING WRESTLING **LEGITIMATE** THAN KEEPING IT **PROFITABLE**, SOMETHING PFEFER **EXCELLED** AT.

MONDT ALSO TRAINED **FUTURE** STARS, LIKE THE ARGENTINIAN **ANTONINO ROCCA**, WHO WAS BELOVED BY **HISPANIC** AND **ITALIAN** IMMIGRANTS...

...AS WELL AS THE LEGENDARY **CANADIAN** GRAPPLER, **STU HART**.

HART BECAME A **RENOWNED** TRAINER, AS WELL AS THE **PATRIARCH** OF ONE OF WRESTLING'S **GREATEST** FAMILIES.

BRET HART

OWEN HART

JIM NEIDHART

THE BRITISH BULLDOG

DYNAMITE KID

TYSON KIDD

NATALYA NEIDHART

DAVEY BOY SMITH, JR.

TEDDY HART

BUT MONDT'S MOST **IMPORTANT** ALLIANCE WAS WITH A PROMOTER WHOSE FAMILY WOULD HAVE MORE INFLUENCE ON **PROFESSIONAL WRESTLING** THAN ANY OTHER IN HISTORY...

...JESS MCMAHON.

# WRESTLING SLANG

PROFESSIONAL WRESTLING IN THE UNITED STATES GREW **DIRECTLY** OUT OF THE **CARNIVALS** AND **FAIRS** OF THE NINETEENTH CENTURY, SO PERHAPS NOT SURPRISINGLY, MUCH OF THE MEDIUM'S **SLANG** AND **JARGON** ALSO HAS ITS **ROOTS** IN THAT WORLD.

WHILE MANY OF THESE TERMS USED TO BE PROTECTED, A WAY OF DISCUSSING THE **INTRICACIES** OF PROFESSIONAL WRESTLING WITHOUT REVEALING ANY **SECRETS** TO THE FANS, THAT HASN'T BEEN THE CASE FOR **MANY** YEARS. THERE ARE **DIFFERING** PERSPECTIVES ON WHETHER NON-WRESTLERS SHOULD USE THESE TERMS, BUT WITH THE RISE OF THE **INTERNET**, THEY'VE BECOME **COMMONPLACE** WITHIN WRESTLING FAN COMMUNITIES AND ARE OFTEN USED PUBLICLY BY WRESTLERS **THEMSELVES**. IN ADDITION, USING THESE TERMS IS GENERALLY **QUICKER** AND MORE **EXPEDIENT** THAN TALKING AROUND THEM WITH **IMPERFECT** SYNONYMS.

THE FOLLOWING IS NOT MEANT TO BE A **COMPLETE** LIST, BUT RATHER A COLLECTION OF THE MOST COMMON, MOST INDISPENSABLE TERMS, **MANY** OF WHICH YOU'LL SEE USED IN SUBSEQUENT CHAPTERS OF THIS BOOK!

**FACE:** SHORT FOR "BABYFACE," THE HERO OF A MATCH. A REFERENCE TO HOW MANY EARLY HEROES WERE GOOD-LOOKING.

**HEEL:** A VILLAIN, CARRYING THE SAME CONNOTATIONS AS WHEN USED FOR A SYNONYM FOR "JERK."

**WORK:** FROM THE WAY A CARNIVAL PERFORMER WOULD "WORK THE CROWD," A WORK IS ANYTHING PLANNED. CAN ALSO BE USED AS A VERB FOR THE ACT OF PARTICIPATING IN A PLANNED EVENT.

**SHOOT:** THE OPPOSITE OF A WORK, SOMETHING LEGITIMATE AND REAL, OFTEN UNPLANNED. CAN REFER TO UNSCRIPTED EVENTS OR DIALOGUE OR EVEN A REAL FIGHT.

**GIMMICK:** MOST OFTEN USED TO REFER TO A WRESTLER'S CHARACTER. CAN ALSO BE USED FOR A PROP, FOREIGN OBJECT, OR, MORE RECENTLY, AN ALL-PURPOSE STAND-IN FOR "THING."

**KAYFABE:** OF UNKNOWN ORIGINS, "KAYFABE" REFERS TO THE OVERALL CONCEIT OF WRESTLING. WRESTLERS ARE SAID TO "KEEP KAYFABE" IF THEY REFUSE TO ACKNOWLEDGE WRESTLING'S ARTIFICE.

**MARK:** A MARK WAS ORIGINALLY SOMEONE WHO COULD BE TAKEN ADVANTAGE OF, SIMILAR TO HOW THE WORD IS STILL USED IN CONFIDENCE GAMES. THESE DAYS, IT TENDS TO BE USED AS A SYNONYM FOR "WRESTLING FAN," WITH VARYING DEGREES OF PEJORATIVE UNDERTONES.

**POP:** AN EXPLOSIVE REACTION FROM THE CROWD, TYPICALLY IMPLYING A POSITIVE RECEPTION, THOUGH NOT EXCLUSIVELY.

**OVER:** ACCEPTED BY THE FANS. LIKE "POP," IT TYPICALLY CARRIES A POSITIVE CONNOTATION, BUT NOT ALWAYS. WRESTLERS TRY TO "GET OVER" AND WILL "GO OVER ON" SOMEONE BY DEFEATING THEM.

**HEAT:** WHAT A VILLAINOUS WRESTLER WANTS TO GET FROM THE CROWD. CAN BE BOOS, JEERS, CHANTS, INSULTS, OR EVEN SILENCE.

**BOOKING:** THE ACT OF PLOTTING OUT AND PLANNING A WRESTLING STORYLINE OR PROMOTION. DIFFERENT PROMOTIONS IN DIFFERENT ERAS MAY HAVE A SINGLE BOOKER, A BOOKING COMMITTEE, OR AN ENTIRE CREATIVE TEAM.

**ANGLE:** A STORYLINE, WHICH CAN LAST FOR A SINGLE MATCH UP TO A NUMBER OF YEARS. PROBABLY A REFERENCE TO CARNIVAL WORKERS AND CONMEN "WORKING AN ANGLE."

**BUMP:** THE ACT OF FALLING--FLAT BACKED, CHIN TUCKED IN--ONTO THE MAT. AN ESSENTIAL PART OF MOST WRESTLING MATCHES, BUMPING WORKS TO PROTECT THE WRESTLER WHILE MAKING THE LOUDEST NOISE POSSIBLE.

**SELL:** TO ACT AS IF SOMETHING HURTS-- TYPICALLY AN EXAGGERATION OF THE ACTUAL PAIN FELT. WRESTLERS CAN SELL PHYSICALLY AS WELL AS DIALOGUE, ESPECIALLY INSULTS.

**SPOT:** A MOVE OR SEQUENCE THAT HAS BEEN PLANNED, AS OPPOSED TO IMPROVISED IN THE RING. OFTEN REFERS TO COMPLEX, COMPLICATED, OR RISKY MOMENTS. A "HIGH SPOT" IS ONE THAT TAKES PLACE OFF OF AN ELEVATED SURFACE.

**BLADING:** THE ACT OF USING A SHARP OBJECT, TYPICALLY A SMALL RAZOR BLADE, TO CUT OPEN ONE'S FOREHEAD DURING A WRESTLING MATCH. SYNONYMS INCLUDE "JUICING" AND "GETTING COLOR."

**PROMO:** ORIGINALLY SHORT FOR "PROMOTIONAL INTERVIEW," IN WHICH WRESTLERS WOULD HYPE UP MATCHES OR EVENTS. NOW MORE GENERALLY REFERS TO ANY KIND OF NON-WRESTLING SPEAKING SEGMENT, INCLUDING INTERVIEWS AND MONOLOGUES.

**JOBBER:** A WRESTLER WHOSE PRIMARY FUNCTION IS TO LOSE, MAKING OTHER WRESTLERS LOOK IMPRESSIVE. TO "DO THE JOB" IS TO LOSE FOR ANOTHER WRESTLER.

**FACTION:** ANY GROUP OF MORE THAN TWO WRESTLERS WHO TYPICALLY ACCOMPANY ONE ANOTHER TO THE RING, COMPETE IN MULTI-PERSON MATCHES, OR EVEN HELP ONE ANOTHER OUT DURING A MATCH.

**STABLE:** A GROUP OF MORE THAN TWO WRESTLERS WHO ARE ALL CONTROLLED AND LED BY A SINGLE PERSON, TYPICALLY A MANAGER.

BY THE 1940S, PROMOTERS ACROSS THE **COUNTRY** HAD FOLLOWED THE EXAMPLE SET BY THE **GOLD DUST TRIO** AND CURLEY'S **TRUST.**

THEY SET UP THEIR OWN **PROMOTIONS** AND, IN THE WAKE OF **WORLD WAR II,** BUSINESS BEGAN TO PICK **UP.**

MEANWHILE, IN **NEW YORK,** MONDT AND HIS ASSOCIATES CONTINUED TO **PROFIT** FROM THEIR POSITION IN THE COUNTRY'S MOST **POPULOUS** CITY.

MADISON SQ. GARDEN

MADISON SQ GARDEN
GORGEOUS GEORGE
vs
ERNIE DUSEK
TONIGHT!

AND IN **1948,** THEY BROUGHT WRESTLING BACK TO **MADISON SQUARE GARDEN** FOR THE FIRST TIME IN **TWELVE YEARS.**

*Gorgeous George*

IT'S DIFFICULT TO **OVERSTATE** HOW BIG OF A DEAL THIS WAS. **MSG** WAS NEW YORK'S **PREMIERE** SPORTING VENUE.

AND **GORGEOUS GEORGE** WAS ONE OF THE BIGGEST NAMES IN WRESTLING, A **PIONEER** THAT CREATED THE **PREENING,** ARROGANT WRESTLING **HEEL.**

GEORGE WAS A **PROUD,** DEFIANT VILLAIN. AND, AS YOU CAN IMAGINE, HE DREW **MASSIVE** CROWDS HOPING TO SEE HIM **HUMBLED.**

**WIN** IF YOU CAN, **LOSE** IF YOU MUST, BUT **ALWAYS** CHEAT!

**MUHAMMAD ALI** EVEN CREDITED GEORGE AS THE INSPIRATION BEHIND HIS **COMBATIVE** PUBLIC PERSONA.

BUT 1948 ALSO SAW AN EVEN MORE **EARTH-SHATTERING** EVENT IN THE WORLD OF **PROFESSIONAL WRESTLING...**

NWA
NATIONAL WRESTLING ALLIANCE

...THE FOUNDING OF THE **NWA.**

WRESTLING WAS **GROWING**, WITH AN INCREASING NUMBER OF **REGIONAL** PROMOTIONS, BUT THERE WAS A **PROBLEM:**

EACH PROMOTION CLAIMED TO HAVE THEIR OWN **WORLD CHAMPION.**

IN 1930, THE NATIONAL BOXING ASSOCIATION CREATED THE **NATIONAL WRESTLING ASSOCIATION** WITH AN EYE TOWARD **REGULATING** PROFESSIONAL WRESTLING.

HOWEVER, THE TITLE THEY **RECOGNIZED** AND AWARDED TO **JIM LONDOS** WASN'T EVEN THE SAME TITLE THAT **LEWIS** AND OTHER **LUMINARIES** HAD HELD BEFORE.

THERE WAS NO **LEGITIMACY** TO THE TITLE, SO THERE WAS NO REASON FOR **SMALLER** PROMOTIONS TO **RECOGNIZE** IT.

WORLD TITLE ★ MATCH ★

WORLD TITLE MATCH

AND SINCE THOSE PROMOTIONS HAD NO **SAY** IN WHO HELD IT AND NO HOPE OF **BOOKING** LONDOS, THEY TYPICALLY JUST CREATED THEIR **OWN** TITLES.

THE **PLETHORA** OF WORLD TITLES WAS **DAMAGING** WRESTLING. THE TITLES' **PREPONDERANCE** MEANT THAT NONE OF THEM SEEMED **LEGITIMATE.**

SOMETHING **NEEDED** TO BE DONE IF WRESTLING WAS GOING TO CONTINUE TO **THRIVE.**

IN **1948,** PAUL "PINKIE" **GEORGE,** SAM **MUCHNICK,** ORVILLE **BROWN,** AND A GROUP OF OTHER, MOSTLY **MIDWESTERN,** PROMOTERS SETTLED ON THE SOLUTION:

MULTIPLE, **PROTECTED,** INDEPENDENT **TERRITORIES** THAT VOTED ON AND **SHARED** A SINGLE **WORLD CHAMPION.**

TOGETHER, THEY FORMED THE **NATIONAL WRESTLING ALLIANCE.**

AT ITS **HEIGHT**, THE NATIONAL WRESTLING ALLIANCE HAD TERRITORIES SPREAD OUT ACROSS THE UNITED STATES, CANADA, MEXICO, AND **JAPAN**.

**GENE KINISKI**
ALL STAR WRESTLING
VANCOUVER, BC

**STU HART**
STAMPEDE WRESTLING
CALGARY, AB

**"PLAYBOY" BUDDY ROSE**
PACIFIC NORTHWEST WRESTLING
PORTLAND, OR

**VERNE GAGNE**
AMERICAN WRESTLING ASSOCIATION
MINNEAPOLIS, MN

**PEPPER GOMEZ**
AMERICAN WRESTLING ALLIANCE/
NWA SAN FRANCISCO
SAN FRANCISCO, CA

**DORY FUNK, JR. & TERRY FUNK**
WESTERN STATES SPORTS
AMARILLO, TX

**FREDDIE BLASSIE**
WORLD WRESTLING ASSOCIATION/
NWA HOLLYWOOD WRESTLING
LOS ANGELES, CA

**"HIGH CHIEF" PETER MAIVIA**
50TH STATE BIG TIME WRESTLING/
POLYNESIAN PACIFIC WRESTLING
HONOLULU, HI

**CARLOS COLÓN**
WORLD WRESTLING COUNCIL
SAN JUAN, PR

(NOTE: THE PROMOTIONS AND WRESTLERS HERE WEREN'T NECESSARILY ACTIVE SIMULTANEOUSLY.)

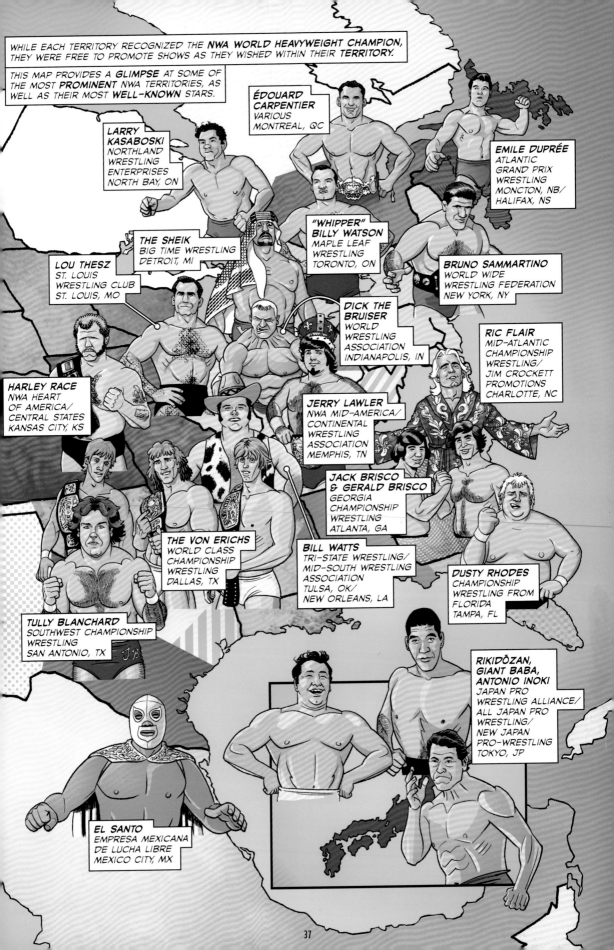

WHILE EACH TERRITORY RECOGNIZED THE **NWA WORLD HEAVYWEIGHT CHAMPION,** THEY WERE FREE TO PROMOTE SHOWS AS THEY WISHED WITHIN THEIR **TERRITORY.**

THIS MAP PROVIDES A **GLIMPSE** AT SOME OF THE MOST **PROMINENT** NWA TERRITORIES, AS WELL AS THEIR MOST **WELL-KNOWN** STARS.

ÉDOUARD CARPENTIER
VARIOUS
MONTREAL, QC

LARRY KASABOSKI
NORTHLAND WRESTLING ENTERPRISES
NORTH BAY, ON

EMILE DUPRÉE
ATLANTIC GRAND PRIX WRESTLING
MONCTON, NB/ HALIFAX, NS

THE SHEIK
BIG TIME WRESTLING
DETROIT, MI

"WHIPPER" BILLY WATSON
MAPLE LEAF WRESTLING
TORONTO, ON

LOU THESZ
ST. LOUIS WRESTLING CLUB
ST. LOUIS, MO

BRUNO SAMMARTINO
WORLD WIDE WRESTLING FEDERATION
NEW YORK, NY

DICK THE BRUISER
WORLD WRESTLING ASSOCIATION
INDIANAPOLIS, IN

RIC FLAIR
MID-ATLANTIC CHAMPIONSHIP WRESTLING/ JIM CROCKETT PROMOTIONS
CHARLOTTE, NC

HARLEY RACE
NWA HEART OF AMERICA/ CENTRAL STATES
KANSAS CITY, KS

JERRY LAWLER
NWA MID-AMERICA/ CONTINENTAL WRESTLING ASSOCIATION
MEMPHIS, TN

JACK BRISCO & GERALD BRISCO
GEORGIA CHAMPIONSHIP WRESTLING
ATLANTA, GA

THE VON ERICHS
WORLD CLASS CHAMPIONSHIP WRESTLING
DALLAS, TX

BILL WATTS
TRI-STATE WRESTLING/ MID-SOUTH WRESTLING ASSOCIATION
TULSA, OK/ NEW ORLEANS, LA

DUSTY RHODES
CHAMPIONSHIP WRESTLING FROM FLORIDA
TAMPA, FL

TULLY BLANCHARD
SOUTHWEST CHAMPIONSHIP WRESTLING
SAN ANTONIO, TX

RIKIDŌZAN, GIANT BABA, ANTONIO INOKI
JAPAN PRO WRESTLING ALLIANCE/ ALL JAPAN PRO WRESTLING/ NEW JAPAN PRO-WRESTLING
TOKYO, JP

EL SANTO
EMPRESA MEXICANA DE LUCHA LIBRE
MEXICO CITY, MX

AS FOR **WHO** WOULD BE THEIR **FIRST** CHAMPION? THE FOUNDING PROMOTERS CHOSE ONE OF THEIR OWN: **ORVILLE BROWN**.

BROWN RAN THE **MIDWEST WRESTLING ASSOCIATION** IN KANSAS CITY, MO, WHERE HE ALSO HELD THE PROMOTION'S VERSION OF THE **WORLD CHAMPIONSHIP**.

THE WRESTLER/PROMOTER DEFEATED **SONNY MYERS** ON JULY 14, 1948, AND WAS RECOGNIZED AS THE FIRST-EVER **NWA WORLD HEAVYWEIGHT CHAMPION**.

BROWN **IMMEDIATELY** SET ABOUT DEFEATING WORLD CHAMPIONS FROM **OTHER** PROMOTIONS AS A WAY OF **UNIFYING** THEIR TITLES.

BUT ON NOVEMBER 1, 1949, BROWN WAS INVOLVED IN A **CAR ACCIDENT** THAT FORCED HIM INTO **EARLY RETIREMENT**.

IN EXISTENCE FOR LITTLE MORE THAN A **YEAR**, THE FLEDGLING ORGANIZATION NEEDED A **CHAMPION**, SO THEY SETTLED UPON BROWN'S **NEXT** CHALLENGER.

LOU THESZ WASN'T JUST A **PROMOTER** AND THE HOLDER OF THE NATIONAL WRESTLING **ASSOCIATION** CHAMPIONSHIP...

...HE WAS ALSO A RENOWNED **HOOKER** AND PROTÉGÉ OF **ED "STRANGLER" LEWIS**. THAT MEANT THAT HE COULD BE TRUSTED TO **PROTECT** THE TITLE.

WITH THE BOOKING AND GUIDANCE OF **SAM MUCHNICK**, WHO WAS ELECTED NWA PRESIDENT IN 1950, THESZ CONTINUED **UNIFYING** WORLD TITLES.

IN THE PROCESS OF HIS **2,300-DAY** FIRST REIGN, THESZ BECAME **INEXTRICABLY** LINKED WITH THE **NWA WORLD HEAVYWEIGHT CHAMPIONSHIP**.

THESZ POSITIONED HIMSELF AS A **THROWBACK.** WHILE HE DIDN'T WORK THE **CARNIVAL** CIRCUIT, HE CERTAINLY HAD HIS **BONA FIDES.**

HE LEARNED **GRECO-ROMAN** FROM HIS FATHER...

...BEFORE TRAINING IN **CATCH WRESTLING** WITH **AD SANTEL**...

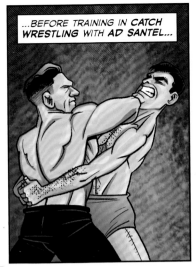

...AND, FINALLY, **HOOKING** WITH **ED LEWIS.**

THESZ HAD **NO LOVE** FOR MORE GIMMICKY WRESTLERS LIKE GORGEOUS GEORGE, ANTONINO ROCCA, AND ESPECIALLY THE ORIGINAL "NATURE BOY," **BUDDY ROGERS.**

INSTEAD, HE **INSISTED** ON TAKING WRESTLING **SERIOUSLY.**

MY "GIMMICK" IS **WRESTLING.**

WITH HIS **SIMPLE** ROBE, UTILITARIAN TOWEL, AND **NO-NONSENSE** DEMEANOR, THESZ WAS A **BELIEVABLE** CHAMPION.

BUT IF FANS THOUGHT THESZ WOULD BE **BORING** OR DRY, LIKE THE OLD WRESTLERS HE COMMONLY **EVOKED**...

...THEY WERE **MISTAKEN,** AS THESZ'S MATCHES WERE HIGH-OCTANE, **EXHILARATING** AFFAIRS THAT SAW HIM USE NEWER, MORE **UNREALISTIC** MOVES...

...INCLUDING THE **DROPKICK,** WHAT WOULD **LATER** BE KNOWN AS THE **GERMAN SUPLEX,** THE **THESZ PRESS,** AND, OF COURSE, THE **POWERBOMB.**

DESPITE THIS, THESZ STILL CLAIMED **KINSHIP** WITH **CARNIVAL HOOKERS** AND **EARLY** PROFESSIONAL **WRESTLERS.**

THIS CONNECTION WAS **REINFORCED** BY HIS RELATIONSHIP WITH **LEWIS,** WHO TRAVELED WITH HIM AS HIS **MANAGER.**

THESZ ENGAGED IN THE SAME **SLEIGHT-OF-HAND** THAT WRESTLING **ALWAYS** DOES, SUBTLY IMPLYING THAT IT **ISN'T** REAL, BUT THAT IT **USED** TO BE.

(EVEN THOUGH IT **DIDN'T.**)

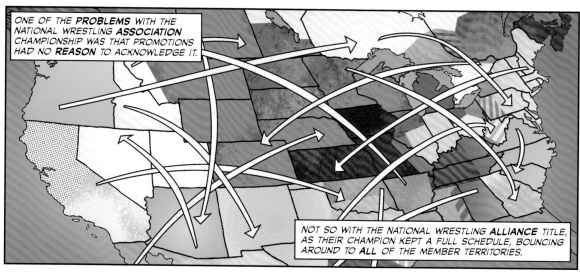

ONE OF THE **PROBLEMS** WITH THE NATIONAL WRESTLING **ASSOCIATION** CHAMPIONSHIP WAS THAT PROMOTIONS HAD NO **REASON** TO ACKNOWLEDGE IT.

NOT SO WITH THE NATIONAL WRESTLING **ALLIANCE** TITLE, AS THEIR CHAMPION KEPT A FULL SCHEDULE, BOUNCING AROUND TO **ALL** OF THE MEMBER TERRITORIES.

THIS **SCHEDULE**, AND THE **BOOKING** OF THE CHAMPION, WAS ONE OF THE MOST **IMPORTANT** DUTIES OF THE **NWA PRESIDENT**.

PRESIDENT SAM MUCHNICK SHOULD **ABSOLUTELY** SHARE CREDIT WITH THESZ FOR THE PRESTIGE THAT THE **STILL-NEW** TITLE ACQUIRED DURING THE 1950s.

IT WAS A **DIFFICULT**, EXTREMELY **POLITICAL** JOB. **EVERY** PROMOTION WANTED THE **NWA CHAMPION** PRETTY MUCH **ALL** OF THE TIME.

WHILE THE PROMOTERS WERE **OSTENSIBLY** IN LEAGUE WITH ONE ANOTHER, POLITICAL JOCKEYING WAS **CONSTANT**, ESPECIALLY WHEN IT CAME TIME TO VOTE ON A **NEW** CHAMPION.

IT WAS THE JOB OF THE **CHAMPION** TO HAVE BELIEVABLE, **IMPRESSIVE** MATCHES EVERY SINGLE NIGHT.

AND JUST AS **IMPORTANTLY**, TO MAKE SURE THAT THE WRESTLER HE WAS **FACING** LOOKED LIKE HE MIGHT **JUST WIN**...

...UP UNTIL THE POINT WHEN THE CHAMPION **FINISHED** THINGS, AS THESZ MIGHT WITH HIS **STEPOVER TOEHOLD FACELOCK**.

THAT WAY, THE CHAMPION MADE THE **LOCAL TALENT** LOOK GOOD, BUT COULD STILL DEFEND HIS TITLE IN THE **NEXT** TOWN.

OTHER TALENT WOULD *INTERMITTENTLY* PERFORM THIS ROLE THROUGH THE 1950s AND EARLY 1960s, WITH THE TITLE TYPICALLY FINDING ITS WAY BACK TO *THESZ*.

IN 1966, THESZ ENDED HIS FINAL REIGN AT THE AGE OF *FORTY-NINE* BY DROPPING THE TITLE TO FORMER FOOTBALL PLAYER *GENE KINISKI*.

IT WAS A *CONTROVERSIAL* DECISION, AS MEMORIES OF STANISLAUS ZBYSZKO'S 1925 SHOOT ON *WAYNE MUNN* STILL *LINGERED*.

BUT KINISKI CARRIED THE CHAMPIONSHIP WELL, BEFORE HANDING IT OFF TO *DORY FUNK, JR.*

THE LIST OF MEN WHO HELD THE TITLE DURING THE *1970S* READS LIKE A *HALL OF FAME* ROSTER.

THESE MEN *HONED* AND *REFINED* THE PATTERN LAID OUT BY THESZ, DISCOVERING THROUGH *TRIAL AND ERROR* THE BEST WAY TO *PROTECT* THE TITLE...

DORY FUNK, JR.

HARLEY RACE

JACK BRISCO

GIANT BABA

...WHILE STILL *ELEVATING* OTHER WRESTLERS. THESE *TECHNIQUES* FOUND THEIR FINEST PRACTITIONER IN THE MAN WHO FIRST WON THE CHAMPIONSHIP IN *1981*...

TERRY FUNK

DUSTY RHODES

TOMMY RICH

RIC FLAIR

FLAIR WAS AN **ARROGANT**, COWARDLY, UNSCRUPULOUS **VILLAIN**, WHICH ALLOWED HIM TO MAKE **BABYFACES** LOOK EVEN **MORE** HEROIC.

HE WAS **CONFIDENT** ENOUGH IN HIS OWN ABILITIES TO BE INCREDIBLY **GIVING** IN THE RING--HE COULD HAVE A **TOP-NOTCH** MATCH WITH **ANYONE.**

SO WHEN FLAIR **MOVED ON**, HE INEVITABLY LEFT NEW **STARS** IN HIS **WAKE.**

STARS THAT WOULD CONTINUE TO **MAIN EVENT** SHOWS, DEFENDING THEIR **REGIONAL** CHAMPIONSHIPS.

AND IF THE CROWD GOT **BORED** OF THEM?

THEY COULD ALWAYS GO TO **ANOTHER** MEMBER TERRITORY, FRESHEN UP ANOTHER ROSTER, AND POSSIBLY EVEN CHANGE THEIR **NAME** AND GIMMICK.

THE **TERRITORY SYSTEM** WAS BENEFICIAL TO MOST **EVERYONE** INVOLVED, ESPECIALLY WRESTLERS THAT EMBODIED THE **SPECTACLE** OF **THE ONE TRUE SPORT.**

GRAPPLERS LIKE THE VILLAINOUS **KILLER KOWALSKI** WOULD KEEP INTENSE SCHEDULES, MOVING FROM **PROMOTION** TO PROMOTION...

...ENSURING THAT THE CROWDS NEVER GREW **ACCUSTOMED** TO THEM, NEVER TOOK THEM FOR **GRANTED**, AND WERE ALWAYS **WOWED.**

THE NWA WAS **BENEFICIAL** AND **PROFITABLE** FOR EVERYONE WHO HAD A **SEAT** AT THE TABLE.

BUT IF YOU WERE PART OF AN **UNAFFILIATED** GROUP, A SO-CALLED **OUTLAW PROMOTION**...

...YOU COULD FIND YOURSELF FIGHTING FOR **SCRAPS**. SOME PROMOTIONS SIMPLY WEREN'T **INVITED** TO JOIN, SO AS TO MAKE MEMBER TERRITORIES **LARGER**...

...WHILE OTHERS WERE **NEWER** COMPANIES THAT HOPED TO **CARVE OUT** A PLACE FOR THEMSELVES WITHIN **PREEXISTING** TERRITORIES.

ONE OF THESE PROMOTIONS WAS **INTERNATIONAL CHAMPIONSHIP WRESTLING**, RUN BY **ANGELO POFFO** OUT OF LEXINGTON, KY, FROM 1978 TO 1984.

ICW WAS IN DIRECT CONFLICT WITH **JERRY LAWLER** AND **JERRY JARRETT'S** CWA, WHICH LED TO PHYSICAL ALTERCATIONS INVOLVING POFFO'S SON, A YOUNG **RANDY SAVAGE**.

ANOTHER PROMOTER THAT FOUND SUCCESS ON THE **MARGINS** WAS **JACK PFEFER**, WHO BEGAN FEATURING THE MORE **OUTRÉ** ELEMENTS OF PROFESSIONAL WRESTLING.

HE EMPLOYED **SOUND-ALIKE** VERSIONS OF POPULAR WRESTLERS, ACROMEGALY SUFFERERS LIKE THE **FRENCH ANGEL** AND **SWEDISH ANGEL**...

...AND COLORFUL CHARACTERS LIKE THE **ELEPHANT BOY** AND HIS VALET, **MOOLAH**.

**MOOLAH** WAS A WRESTLER **HERSELF**, BUT THE NWA STIPULATED THAT WOMEN WERE **PROHIBITED** FROM COMPETING ON A CARD WHERE THE **WORLD TITLE** WAS DEFENDED...

...EVEN THOUGH MOOLAH, **MILDRED BURKE**, AND OTHERS WERE **TOP DRAWS**.

THIS SEPARATION WAS IN ORDER TO **PROTECT** THE TITLE, AND IT ALSO APPLIED TO ANOTHER **FAN-FAVORITE** FORM OF GRAPPLING, WHAT WAS FORMERLY KNOWN AS *"MIDGET WRESTLING."*

IN ADDITION TO DECIDING WHO HELD THE **WORLD HEAVYWEIGHT** AND **JUNIOR HEAVYWEIGHT** TITLES, THE NWA WORKED TO MAINTAIN THEIR **EXCLUSIVITY** AND **DOMINANCE.**

THEY ACHIEVED THIS GOAL BY **BLOCKING** AND **EXTORTING** PROMOTERS OF **OUTLAW** PROMOTIONS, AND EVEN **BLACKLISTING** THE WRESTLERS WHO WORKED FOR THEM.

BUT WHILE **EFFECTIVE,** THESE ACTIONS WERE IN DIRECT **VIOLATION** OF **ANTITRUST** LAWS MEANT TO PREVENT **MONOPOLIES.**

FOLLOWING **YEARS** OF COMPLAINTS FROM PROMOTERS, **REFEREES,** AND FORMER **WORLD CHAMPIONS** LIKE **STANISLAUS ZBYSZKO** AND **MILDRED BURKE...**

...THE DEPARTMENT OF JUSTICE LAUNCHED AN **INVESTIGATION** IN 1955.

THE DOJ FILED A CIVIL SUIT ON OCTOBER 15, 1956, ACCUSING THE NWA OF ATTEMPTS TO "**RESTRICT AND MONOPOLIZE**" THE WRESTLING INDUSTRY.

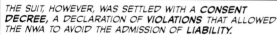

THE SUIT, HOWEVER, WAS SETTLED WITH A **CONSENT DECREE,** A DECLARATION OF **VIOLATIONS** THAT ALLOWED THE NWA TO AVOID THE ADMISSION OF **LIABILITY.**

THE CONSENT DECREE WAS BARELY A **SLAP** ON THE **WRIST.** THERE WERE **NO** FINES AND THE NWA WAS ALLOWED TO **CONTINUE** WITH CHANGES TO ITS **BYLAWS.**

THIS OUTCOME WAS LIKELY MADE POSSIBLE THROUGH THE RELATIONSHIPS THAT NWA PROMOTERS HAD FORGED WITH **POLITICIANS** THROUGH DONATIONS, **FUNDRAISERS,** AND GOOD OLD-FASHIONED **BRIBERY.**

THE NWA WAS FORCED TO PURSUE THEIR **RESTRICTION** AND **MONOPOLIZATION** IN A MORE **SUBTLE** FASHION, WHICH CAUSED THEIR DOMINANCE TO **WANE.**

THOUGH STILL **PROMINENT,** THE ORGANIZATION WAS **DRAMATICALLY** WEAKENED IN THE WAKE OF THE CONSENT DECREE, DROPPING FROM **THIRTY-EIGHT** MEMBERS TO **LESS THAN TWENTY** BY THE END OF THE DECADE.

THE NWA DIDN'T JUST HAVE TO DEAL WITH ATTACKS FROM **NON-MEMBERS** AND THE **FEDERAL GOVERNMENT,** THEY ALSO HAD ONGOING **INTERNECINE** CONFLICTS.

WHO WAS NAMED CHAMPION, **WHERE** TERRITORY LINES WERE DRAWN, **WHO** WAS ADMITTED INTO THE ORGANIZATION...THESE WERE ALL POINTS OF **CONTENTION.**

THAT ANIMOSITY ONLY **INCREASED** WITH THE GROWING POPULARITY OF **WRESTLING** ON TELEVISION AND THE **POWER** IT GAVE PROMOTERS.

**FEW** UNDERSTOOD THAT POWER BETTER THAN CHICAGO'S **FRED KOHLER,** WHO BEGAN BROADCASTING WRESTLING ON THE **DUMONT TELEVISION NETWORK** IN THE 1940s.

INITIALLY, PROMOTERS WORRIED THAT TELEVISED WRESTLING WOULD **UNDERCUT** THEIR BOX OFFICE **RECEIPTS.**

BUT THE **OPPOSITE** PROVED TRUE, AS TELEVISION WAS **REMARKABLY** EFFECTIVE AT ENTICING FANS TO COME OUT AND SEE THE EVENTS THEY **THRILLED** TO AT HOME.

BEFORE TELEVISION, VILLAINS WERE MOSTLY OF THE **FOREIGN MENACE** VARIETY, BUT THE SCREEN GAVE RISE TO **NEW** TYPES OF HEELS, LIKE **GORGEOUS GEORGE.**

AS MUCH AS TELEVISION HELPED **PROFESSIONAL WRESTLING** EVOLVE AND GAIN A **FOOTHOLD** IN THE PUBLIC CONSCIOUSNESS...

...TELEVISION DEALS CREATED EVEN **MORE** CONFLICTS SINCE THEY COULD LEAD TO **ONE** MEMBER'S MATCHES BEING BROADCASTED INTO **ANOTHER** MEMBER'S TERRITORY.

**TELEVISED** WRESTLING ALSO PRESENTED ANOTHER WAY FOR **UNAFFILIATED** PROMOTERS TO **INFILTRATE** MEMBER TERRITORIES.

BUT THE **BIGGEST** PROBLEMS WITHIN THE NWA REVOLVED AROUND THE **WORLD HEAVYWEIGHT CHAMPIONSHIP.**

ON JUNE 14, 1957, LOU THESZ DEFENDED THE TITLE AGAINST CANADA'S **ÉDOUARD CARPENTIER.** AS WAS STILL **STANDARD** FOR TITLE MATCHES AT THE TIME, IT WAS **TWO OUT OF THREE FALLS.**

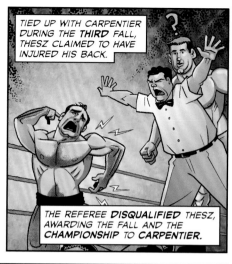

TIED UP WITH CARPENTIER DURING THE **THIRD** FALL, THESZ CLAIMED TO HAVE INJURED HIS BACK.

THE REFEREE **DISQUALIFIED** THESZ, AWARDING THE FALL AND THE **CHAMPIONSHIP** TO CARPENTIER.

BUT SINCE TITLES COULDN'T BE **LOST** VIA **DISQUALIFICATION,** THESZ STILL **CLAIMED** TO BE CHAMPION, DEFENDING HIS **DISPUTED** TITLE **INTERNATIONALLY** WHILE CARPENTIER DEFENDED **HIS** IN **NORTH AMERICA.**

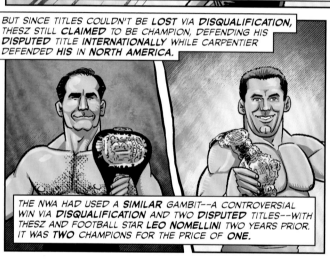

THE NWA HAD USED A **SIMILAR** GAMBIT--A CONTROVERSIAL WIN VIA **DISQUALIFICATION** AND TWO **DISPUTED** TITLES--WITH THESZ AND FOOTBALL STAR **LEO NOMELLINI** TWO YEARS PRIOR. IT WAS **TWO** CHAMPIONS FOR THE PRICE OF **ONE.**

THESZ WON THE TITLE BACK--VIA **DISQUALIFICATION**--FORTY DAYS LATER, BUT SOME TERRITORIES STILL RECOGNIZED **CARPENTIER** AS THEIR CHAMPION.

THIS PROBLEM WAS **EXACERBATED** IN 1958, WHEN **MONTREAL** PROMOTER **EDDIE QUINN** LEFT THE NWA, TAKING **CARPENTIER** WITH HIM.

UNDER QUINN'S MANAGEMENT, **CARPENTIER** LOST MATCHES TO KILLER KOWALSKI, FREDDIE BLASSIE, VERNE GAGNE, AND **OTHERS,** GIVING THEM **EACH** A CLAIM ON THE **WORLD TITLE.**

IT WAS **EXACTLY** WHAT THE NWA HAD BEEN **CREATED** TO **PREVENT:** MULTIPLE WORLD TITLE CLAIMS THAT ALL WORKED TO **DEVALUE** ONE ANOTHER.

OF THESE **RIVAL** CLAIMANTS, **VERNE GAGNE** IS THE MOST **SIGNIFICANT**.

A **STANDOUT** COLLEGIATE WRESTLER, GAGNE COULD HAVE GONE TO THE **OLYMPICS** IF HE HADN'T BEEN **PAID** TO WRESTLE IN CARNIVALS, COMPROMISING HIS **AMATEUR** STATUS.

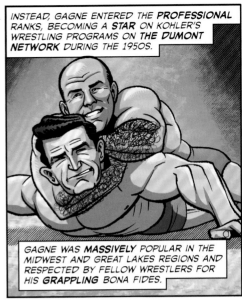

INSTEAD, GAGNE ENTERED THE **PROFESSIONAL** RANKS, BECOMING A **STAR** ON KOHLER'S WRESTLING PROGRAMS ON **THE DUMONT NETWORK** DURING THE 1950S.

GAGNE WAS **MASSIVELY** POPULAR IN THE MIDWEST AND GREAT LAKES REGIONS AND RESPECTED BY FELLOW WRESTLERS FOR HIS **GRAPPLING** BONA FIDES.

HAVING ALREADY HELD THE **WORLD JUNIOR HEAVYWEIGHT TITLE** AND **CARPENTIER'S** VERSION OF THE **MAIN** CHAMPIONSHIP, GAGNE MADE HIS CASE TO THE **NWA**.

BUT DUE TO **POLITICAL** MACHINATIONS, THEY **REFUSED** TO PUT THE WORLD HEAVYWEIGHT TITLE ON HIM.

SO, IN **1960**, GAGNE TOOK MATTERS INTO HIS **OWN** HANDS, LEADING A **GROUP** OF TERRITORIES OUT OF THE NWA TO FORM THE **AMERICAN WRESTLING ASSOCIATION**.

THEY **INITIALLY** ACKNOWLEDGED NWA CHAMPION **PAT O'CONNOR** AS THEIR TOP TITLEHOLDER, GIVING HIM THREE MONTHS TO DEFEND THE **AWA** TITLE AGAINST GAGNE.

THE NWA IGNORED THE CHALLENGE, AS IT WOULD HAVE ONLY **LEGITIMIZED** THE NEW PROMOTION. GAGNE THEN PLACED THE **NEW** TITLE ON **HIMSELF**, WHICH HAD BEEN THE **ENDGAME** ALL ALONG.

GAGNE'S AWA WAS ONE OF THE **BIGGEST** DEFECTIONS FROM THE NWA, AS HE USED HIS **CONSIDERABLE** STAR POWER TO CREATE A WRESTLING **EMPIRE**.

WHILE RUNNING HIS PROMOTION, HE ALSO TRAINED **DOZENS** OF FUTURE STARS.

RIC FLAIR

DICK THE BRUISER

RICKY STEAMBOAT

CURT HENNIG

BOB BACKLUND

THE IRON SHEIK

HULK HOGAN

THE **CONFLICT** BETWEEN THOSE IN THE NWA WHO ADHERED TO ITS **OLD WAYS** AND ITS MORE INNOVATIVE PROMOTERS IS BEST EXEMPLIFIED BY THE **RIVALRY** BETWEEN LOU THESZ AND BUDDY ROGERS.

ROGERS WASN'T THE **WRESTLER** THAT THESZ WAS, BUT HE HAD SOMETHING ELSE IN **SPADES**, SOMETHING THAT WAS BECOMING MORE AND MORE IMPORTANT: **CHARISMA**.

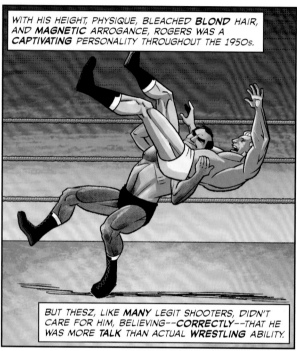

WITH HIS HEIGHT, PHYSIQUE, BLEACHED **BLOND** HAIR, AND **MAGNETIC** ARROGANCE, ROGERS WAS A **CAPTIVATING** PERSONALITY THROUGHOUT THE 1950s.

BUT THESZ, LIKE **MANY** LEGIT SHOOTERS, DIDN'T CARE FOR HIM, BELIEVING--**CORRECTLY**--THAT HE WAS MORE **TALK** THAN ACTUAL **WRESTLING** ABILITY.

IN 1963, ROGERS WAS **RELUCTANT** TO DROP THE NWA WORLD HEAVYWEIGHT TITLE BACK TO **THESZ**, SO THE NWA TOOK ACTIONS TO ENSURE HIS **COMPLIANCE**.

ONE OF THESE WAS A **THREAT** TO GIVE ROGERS'S $25,000 DEPOSIT ON THE BELT (REQUIRED OF ALL NWA CHAMPIONS) TO **CHARITY**. A SECOND WAS THE FACT THAT THESZ COULD **SHOOT** ON HIM IF **NECESSARY**.

AND FINALLY, THE NWA DECREED THAT THE TITLE WOULD BE DEFENDED IN A **SINGLE** FALL AS OPPOSED TO THE STANDARD **TWO OUT OF THREE** FALLS FOR CHAMPIONSHIP MATCHES.

THE **THINKING** WAS THAT A SINGLE FALL WOULD MAKE IT EVEN HARDER TO **DOUBLE-CROSS** THESZ OR FURTHER MUDDY THE WATERS OF THE TITLE'S **LEGITIMACY**.

THESZ WON THE TITLE **WITHOUT** ISSUE, BUT HIS SINGLE FALL VICTORY CREATED **OTHER** PROBLEMS.

THE SAFEGUARD TO PROTECT THE TITLE **BACKFIRED**, CREATING AN **OPPORTUNITY** IN THE NORTHEAST.

AND POISED TO TAKE ADVANTAGE OF THE SITUATION? THE CREATIVE VISIONARY OF THE GOLD DUST TRIO, **TOOTS MONDT**...

...AND **VINCENT JAMES MCMAHON**, THE SON OF MONDT'S OLD BUSINESS PARTNER, **JESS MCMAHON**.

WITH THE BENEFIT OF NEW YORK CITY'S MASSIVE POPULATION, MONDT AND MCMAHON'S **CAPITOL WRESTLING CORPORATION** HAD BECOME **EXTREMELY** SUCCESSFUL.

AND WITH THAT **SUCCESS** CAME **POWER**, AS THROUGH MONDT'S MASSIVE **ROSTER** OF TALENT, THEY COULD CONTROL THE **BOOKING** FOR MOST OF THE NWA'S MEMBER TERRITORIES.

THEY HAD ONE OF THE MOST **PROFITABLE** TERRITORIES, A MURDERER'S ROW OF **TALENT**, AND A MAIN EVENT **STAR**.

**THE WORLD WIDE WRESTLING FEDERATION W.W.W.F.**

SO, IN 1963, JUST **MONTHS** AFTER ROGERS LOST TO THESZ, THEY LEFT THE NWA AND FORMED THE **WORLD WIDE WRESTLING FEDERATION**.

AND **NATURALLY**, AS THEIR INAUGURAL **WWWF WORLD HEAVYWEIGHT CHAMPION**, THEY CHOSE "NATURE BOY" BUDDY ROGERS...

...REASONING THAT SINCE **THESZ** HADN'T WON THE WORLD TITLE IN A **TWO OUT OF THREE FALLS** MATCH, ROGERS HAD **NEVER** LOST IT.

ROGERS WAS A **HUGE** DRAW IN THE NORTHEAST DUE TO HIS **SHOWMANSHIP**, AS WELL AS HOW **OFTEN** MONDT HAD BOOKED HIM IN THE TERRITORY DURING HIS TITLE REIGN.

THE NWA HAD LOST SOME OF ITS MOST **POWERFUL** MEMBERS FROM ITS MOST **PROFITABLE** TERRITORIES.

AND WHILE THE NEW PROMOTIONS AND THEIR REGIONAL TITLES **WEAKENED** THE GROUP'S LEGITIMACY, THE NWA DIDN'T HAVE THE **FUNDS**, THE **NUMBERS**, OR THE **POWER** TO FIGHT THEM.

NOT SURPRISINGLY, ROGERS **RELIABLY** DREW AUDIENCES HOPING TO SEE HIM GET **BEAT,** BUT MONDT AND MCMAHON WANTED A CHAMPION TO **BUILD** THEIR **PROMOTION** AROUND.

SO, THE DECISION WAS MADE TO BRING IN A **NEW** CHAMPION, A YOUNG HERO WHO COULD **EXCITE** THEIR **ENTIRE** TERRITORY.

ROGERS HELD THE TITLE FOR LESS THAN A **MONTH** BEFORE **BRUNO SAMMARTINO** BEAT HIM IN UNDER **ONE MINUTE.**

IN TRUE **HEEL** FASHION, ROGERS MADE THE **SPURIOUS** CLAIM THAT THE LOSS ONLY CAME BECAUSE OF A **HEART ATTACK** HE HAD **ALLEGEDLY** SUFFERED A WEEK PRIOR.

BUT IF THE VICTORY WAS **TAINTED** BY ROGERS'S CLAIMS, SAMMARTINO'S **FANS** DIDN'T NOTICE.

THE BODYBUILDER AND WEIGHTLIFTER WAS **OUTRAGEOUSLY** POPULAR THROUGHOUT THE NORTHEAST AND COMMANDED **LEGIONS** OF FANS.

WHILE A **VILLAIN** LIKE ROGERS WAS USEFUL AS A **TRAVELING** CHAMPION, THE WWWF NEEDED SOMEONE WHO COULD **CONSISTENTLY** PULL IN AUDIENCES OVER THE **LONG TERM.**

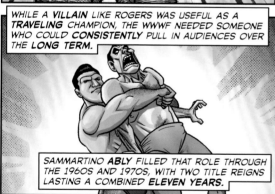

SAMMARTINO **ABLY** FILLED THAT ROLE THROUGH THE 1960S AND 1970S, WITH TWO TITLE REIGNS LASTING A COMBINED **ELEVEN YEARS.**

ANOTHER **KEY** COMPONENT OF WWWF WAS THE USE OF **ETHNIC** TARGETING, AS WITH **ITALIAN** IMMIGRANT SAMMARTINO.

THIS WAS A PAGE OUT OF MONDT'S **PLAYBOOK** GOING BACK TO THE **GOLD DUST TRIO** DAYS, AND WOULD **CONTINUE** TO BE A USEFUL TACTIC FOR WWWF AND ITS **DESCENDANTS.**

ANDRE THE GIANT

IVAN KOLOFF

PEDRO MORALES

IVAN PUTSKI

SAMMARTINO WAS A **BRAWLER,** AND HE **SLUGGED IT OUT** WITH A STEADY PROCESSION OF VILLAINS INCLUDING KILLER KOWALSKI, STAN HANSEN, GIANT BABA, GENE KINISKI, AND **MORE.**

THE TOP **BABYFACE** THAT HEELS WOULD ATTEMPT TO UNSEAT BECAME A **HALLMARK** OF WWWF AND, GENERALLY SPEAKING, **NORTHEASTERN** WRESTLING.

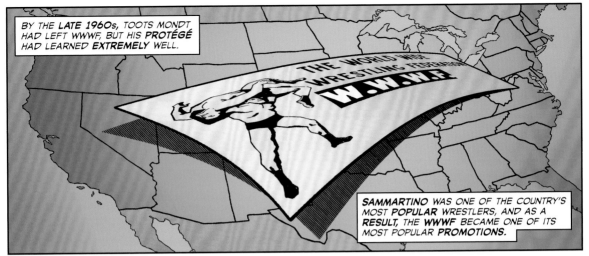

BY THE **LATE 1960s**, TOOTS MONDT HAD LEFT WWWF, BUT HIS **PROTÉGÉ** HAD LEARNED **EXTREMELY** WELL.

**SAMMARTINO** WAS ONE OF THE COUNTRY'S MOST **POPULAR** WRESTLERS, AND AS A **RESULT**, THE **WWWF** BECAME ONE OF ITS MOST POPULAR **PROMOTIONS**.

IN 1971, VINCENT JAMES MCMAHON LED THE WWWF **BACK** INTO THE NWA'S **EMBRACE**; UNSURPRISING, AS THE GROUP STILL HELD SWAY **THROUGHOUT** THE COUNTRY.

BUT THE **ONCE-DOMINANT** SYNDICATE STILL FACED A **HOST** OF PROBLEMS.

AS **ALWAYS**, DECISIONS INVOLVING THE NWA CHAMPION WERE **CONTENTIOUS** AND HIGHLY **POLITICIZED**.

AND THINGS WERE ONLY GETTING **MORE** COMPLICATED WITH THE CONTINUED **PROLIFERATION** OF TELEVISION AND **SYNDICATED** WRESTLING SHOWS THAT INFRINGED ON THE OLD TERRITORIAL BOUNDARIES.

OF PARTICULAR INTEREST WAS **GEORGIA CHAMPIONSHIP WRESTLING**, WHICH AIRED ON TBS AND WENT **NATIONWIDE** IN 1979.

THE MOVE WAS SEEN BY **MANY** NWA MEMBERS AS THE BREAKING OF A **TABOO**, AN EFFORT TO CREATE A TRULY **NATIONAL** PROMOTION.

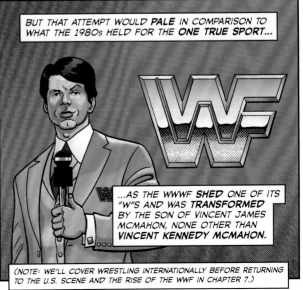

BUT THAT ATTEMPT WOULD **PALE** IN COMPARISON TO WHAT THE 1980s HELD FOR THE **ONE TRUE SPORT**...

...AS THE WWWF **SHED** ONE OF ITS "W"S AND WAS **TRANSFORMED** BY THE SON OF VINCENT JAMES MCMAHON, NONE OTHER THAN **VINCENT KENNEDY MCMAHON**.

(NOTE: WE'LL COVER WRESTLING INTERNATIONALLY BEFORE RETURNING TO THE U.S. SCENE AND THE RISE OF THE WWF IN CHAPTER 7.)

THE HISTORY OF **PROFESSIONAL WRESTLING** CAN BE SEEN AS THE PURSUIT OF A **SINGULAR** GOAL:

FIGURING OUT HOW TO CONVINCE AS **MANY** PEOPLE AS POSSIBLE TO SPEND AS **MUCH** MONEY AS POSSIBLE TO WATCH TWO PEOPLE **FIGHT**.

AND ONE OF THE **BEST** WAYS TO DO THAT? MAKE ONE WRESTLER, LIKE **VERNE GAGNE**, A **HERO**.

GIVE FANS A **REASON** TO CHEER THEM, WHETHER IT'S THEIR **TALENT**, THEIR **FIGHTING SPIRIT**, OR EVEN JUST HOW THEY **LOOK**.

AND THE **OTHER** WRESTLER? THEY NEED TO BE A **VILLAIN**. LIKE **OX BAKER**.

THIS CAN BE ACHIEVED THROUGH **CHEATING**, A SENSE OF **ARROGANCE** OR **VICIOUSNESS**, OR AGAIN, HOW THEY **LOOK**.

THE **BEST** WRESTLING **MATCHES** MAKE AUDIENCES **YEARN** TO SEE ONE WRESTLER WIN...

...AND THE BEST **PROMOTIONS** KNOW HOW TO **DELAY** THE WIN UNTIL THAT YEARNING REACHES A **FEVER PITCH**.

WITHOUT THE **MORALITY PLAY** ASPECT OF WRESTLING, THE **ONE TRUE SPORT** IS JUST A REGULAR OLD **SPORT**, WHERE DRAMA HAPPENS BY **ACCIDENT**, NOT **DESIGN**.

AND WHO WANTS **THAT**?

GENERALLY SPEAKING, IT'S **AMERICAN** WRESTLING THAT'S HAD THE LARGEST INFLUENCE ON THE **ONE TRUE SPORT.**

BUT IT'S **FAR** FROM THE **ONLY** NOTABLE WRESTLING TRADITION IN EXISTENCE. AND ONE OF THE MOST **VIBRANT** AND **UNIQUE?**

**LUCHA LIBRE,** A SPANISH PHRASE MEANING **"FREE FIGHT."** (AS CONTRASTED WITH THE MORE **STRINGENT** RULES OF **GRECO-ROMAN** WRESTLING.)

THOUGH IT IS USED **THROUGHOUT** THE SPANISH-SPEAKING WORLD, IN **PRACTICE,** "LUCHA LIBRE" MOST OFTEN REFERS TO **MEXICAN** WRESTLING.

WHILE THERE HAS ALWAYS BEEN **CROSSOVER,** ESPECIALLY ALONG THE **BORDER...**

...LUCHA LIBRE EVOLVED LARGELY **INDEPENDENTLY** FROM AMERICAN WRESTLING AND, AS A RESULT, IS **DISTINCTLY** AND **PROUDLY** MEXICAN.

THAT **TANGIBLE** IDENTITY IS A **HUGE** PART OF WHAT HAS MADE LUCHA LIBRE SUCH A **DOMINANT** AND **POPULAR** STYLE.

NACHOS

CON QUESO

THESE DAYS, THE LUCHA LIBRE **AESTHETIC** CAN BE SEEN EVERYWHERE, FROM **CARTOONS** AND **MOVIES** TO FASHION AND CORPORATE **MASCOTS,** EVEN MEXICAN **RESTAURANTS.**

AND WHILE **MUCH** OF THE INTEREST IN LUCHA LIBRE CENTERS AROUND THE FORM'S UBIQUITOUS **MASKS,** THERE'S MUCH MORE THAT SETS IT **APART.**

THIS PART OF OUR STORY BEGINS WITH THE MAN COMMONLY ACKNOWLEDGED AS THE **FATHER** OF LUCHA LIBRE, **SALVADOR LUTTEROTH.**

BORN IN 1897, LUTTEROTH FOUGHT UNDER **GENERAL OBREGON** IN THE **MEXICAN REVOLUTION** BEFORE BECOMING A **PROPERTY INSPECTOR** FOR THE TAX DEPARTMENT.

IN 1929, THAT JOB BROUGHT HIM TO **CIUDAD JUÁREZ,** WHERE HE FELL IN **LOVE** WITH AMERICAN PROFESSIONAL WRESTLING.

AT THE TIME, WRESTLING **MOSTLY** OCCURRED WHEN **FOREIGN** PROMOTERS CAME TO TOWN, AND THUS WAS MOST POPULAR IN **BORDER TOWNS** LIKE **JUÁREZ.**

BUT IN 1933, LUTTEROTH TOOK PROFESSIONAL WRESTLING FROM **REGIONAL** TO **NATIONAL,** FOUNDING **EMPRESA MEXICANA DE LUCHA LIBRE** IN **MEXICO CITY.**

NOW KNOWN AS **CONSEJO MUNDIAL DE LUCHA LIBRE,** IT IS THE **OLDEST** STILL–ACTIVE WRESTLING PROMOTION IN THE **WORLD.**

CONSEJO MUNDIAL
**CMLL**
DE LUCHA LIBRE

LUTTEROTH ESTABLISHED **ARENA MODELO** AS HIS PROMOTION'S HOME BASE AND EVENTUALLY BUILT THE LARGER **ARENA MÉXICO** ON THE SAME SITE IN 1956.

THE VENUE STILL HOLDS **TWO** WEEKLY WRESTLING SHOWS, AS WELL AS CMLL **PAY–PER–VIEWS,** EARNING IT THE TITLE "THE **CATHEDRAL** OF LUCHA LIBRE."

AFTER ONLY A **YEAR** IN OPERATION, LUTTEROTH INTRODUCED A TALENT THAT WOULD CHANGE LUCHA LIBRE **FOREVER...**

...**LA MARAVILLA ENMASCARADA,** OR **THE MASKED MARVEL.**

SOMEWHAT **IRONICALLY**, LUCHA LIBRE'S FIRST **MASKED** WRESTLER WAS ACTUALLY AN **AMERICAN**.

DEPENDING ON THE **YEAR** AND PROMOTION, LA MARAVILLA ENMASCARADA WRESTLED AS **CYCLONE MACKEY** OR UNDER A **VARIETY** OF MASKED GIMMICKS.

MASKED WRESTLERS WERE NOTHING **NEW** AT THE TIME. MORT HENDERSON-- WHO TRAINED **AD SANTEL**--PORTRAYED A **DIFFERENT** MASKED MARVEL IN NYC IN 1915.

AND IN PARIS **THIEBAUD BAUER** BECAME ONE OF THE **FIRST** WRESTLERS TO COMPETE IN A MASK, POSSIBLY AS **EARLY** AS 1867!

BUT WHILE MASKED WRESTLERS WERE **POPULAR** IN AMERICA, THEY WERE TYPICALLY SEEN AS **ODDITIES** AND **MIDCARDERS** RATHER THAN MAJOR STARS.

NOT SO IN **MEXICO**, WHERE FANS LATCHED ONTO THE **MYSTERY** OF THE MEN BEHIND THOSE **SIMPLE**, OFTEN **MONOCHROMATIC** MASKS.

LUTTEROTH SAW THE **RESPONSE** LA MARAVILLA ENMASCARADA RECEIVED AND **POUNCED** ON IT...

...INTRODUCING A **SERIES** OF MASKED LUCHADORES.

THOUGH NOT A **MEXICAN** INVENTION, LUCHA LIBRE **APPROPRIATED** THE MASK, MAKING IT A **DEFINING** ASPECT OF THE FORM.

AS A **RESULT**, THE MASK WAS SOON IMBUED WITH NEW LAYERS OF **MEANING** AND **SIGNIFICANCE**.

MASKS WERE AN IMPORTANT PART OF **AZTEC** AND **MAYAN** TRADITIONS, AND LUCHA LIBRE MASKS, AS THEY BECAME MORE **ORNATE**...

...PROVIDED A **LINK** TO THE HISTORY OF MEXICO'S **INDIGENOUS** PEOPLES, ALBEIT A SOMEWHAT **MANUFACTURED** ONE.

THE MASK IS SO **IMPORTANT** THAT IT IS REGULARLY USED IN **LUCHAS DE APUESTAS**, OR "MATCHES WITH WAGERS."

THIS TRADITION **BEGAN** IN 1940 WITH A FEUD BETWEEN "THE MASKED BAT" **EL MURCIÉLAGO ENMASCARADO** AND OCTAVIO GAONA.

THE **HEROIC** GAONA CHALLENGED THE **VILLAINOUS** MURCIÉLAGO TO A MATCH WITH HIS **MASK** ON THE LINE.

MURCIÉLAGO **ACCEPTED**, BUT STIPULATED THAT GAONA'S HAIR WOULD **ALSO** HAVE TO BE AT STAKE.

IN **LUCHA LIBRE**, MASKS AND HAIR ARE TANGIBLE SYMBOLS OF A WRESTLER'S **PRIDE** AND **HONOR**, SO LOSING EITHER IS **SERIOUS** BUSINESS.

LUCHAS DE APUESTAS DRASTICALLY INCREASE THE **STAKES** AND **DRAMA** AND HAVE BECOME AN **INTEGRAL** PART OF LUCHA LIBRE AS WELL AS **OTHER** FORMS OF THE **ONE TRUE SPORT**.

THE MEXICAN **FASCINATION** WITH MASKED LUCHADORES MIRRORED THE GROWING **AMERICAN** INFATUATION WITH MASKED **PULP CHARACTERS** AND **SUPERHEROES**.

AND IN 1942, THE TWO TRADITIONS **COLLIDED**, WITH THE COMING OF ONE OF THE **GREATEST** MASKED WRESTLERS AND **LUCHADORES** OF ALL TIME...

...EL SANTO!

# EL SANTO

THOUGH HE **DEBUTED** AS A VILLAIN, AND FEUDED WITH THE **BELOVED** TARZAN LOPEZ, SANTO'S STAR POWER WAS **UNDENIABLE**.

AND IN **NO** TIME...

...LUTTEROTH **TRANSFORMED** SANTO INTO A HERO.

JUST AS **FRANK GOTCH** HAD DONE IN THE UNITED STATES, **SANTO** PROPELLED WRESTLING INTO MEXICO'S **NATIONAL CONSCIOUSNESS**.

SANTO BECAME A **MULTIMEDIA** SUPERSTAR, WITH A COMIC THAT RAN FOR **DECADES**, TOYS, AND MORE.

PERHAPS MOST **NOTABLE**, HOWEVER, WERE HIS APPEARANCES IN MORE THAN **FIFTY** FILMS, IN WHICH HE FOUGHT ZOMBIES, VAMPIRES, AND OTHER **MONSTROUS** THREATS.

SANTO WAS **SO** POPULAR, AND **SO** CLOSELY IDENTIFIED WITH HIS ICONIC **SILVER MASK**, THAT LUTTEROTH TOLD HIM TO **NEVER** REMOVE IT.

THIS BECAME A **TRADITION** FOR MASKED WRESTLERS AROUND THE **WORLD**, WHO GUARD THEIR **IDENTITY** AS CLOSELY AS ANY COMIC BOOK **SUPERHERO**.

SANTO DIDN'T REMOVE HIS MASK **PUBLICLY** UNTIL 1984 AND EVEN THEN, ONLY FOR AN **INSTANT** ON THE TELEVISION SHOW **CONTRAPUNTO**.

ONE WEEK LATER, HE PASSED AWAY FROM A **HEART ATTACK**, AND WAS **BURIED** IN HIS MASK.

SANTO WASN'T JUST A FAMOUS **WRESTLER**, HE WAS A MEXICAN **FOLK HERO**.

IT'S **IMPOSSIBLE** TO OVERSTATE HIS INFLUENCE AND POPULARITY, NOT JUST ON **WRESTLING** AND **CMLL**, BUT ON MEXICAN CULTURE AS A **WHOLE**.

BUT HIS **BIGGEST** INFLUENCE ON PROFESSIONAL WRESTLING WAS SEEN IN THE **EXPLOSION** OF MASKED LUCHADORES THAT CAME IN HIS **WAKE**.

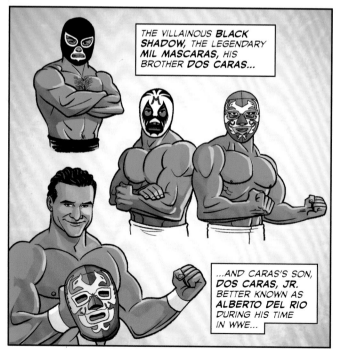

THE VILLAINOUS **BLACK SHADOW**, THE LEGENDARY **MIL MASCARAS**, HIS BROTHER **DOS CARAS**...

...AND CARAS'S SON, **DOS CARAS, JR.** BETTER KNOWN AS **ALBERTO DEL RIO** DURING HIS TIME IN WWE...

...AND OF COURSE, **BLUE DEMON**, WHO WAS ONCE SANTO'S **RIVAL**...

...BUT ULTIMATELY WENT ON TO COSTAR WITH HIM IN A **SERIES** OF FILMS AFTER BECOMING A **HERO**, OR IN LUCHA LIBRE PARLANCE, A **TÉCNICO**.

"TÉCNICO" LITERALLY MEANS "TECHNICIAN" AND IS THE NAME GIVEN TO LUCHA LIBRE **HEROES** DUE TO THEIR TENDENCY TO USE ACTUAL **WRESTLING** MOVES AND HOLDS.

THIS STANDS IN STARK CONTRAST TO LUCHA LIBRE **VILLAINS**...

...WHO ARE KNOWN AS **RUDOS**, WHICH LITERALLY MEANS "ROUGH GUYS," REFERENCING THEIR **PROPENSITY** FOR BRAWLING AND BREAKING THE **RULES**.

THOUGH HARDLY **UNIVERSAL**, THESE GENERALIZATIONS TEND TO BE **STRICTER** THAN IN AMERICAN WRESTLING, WHERE BRAWLERS ARE OFTEN **HEROES** AND TECHNICAL WRESTLERS ARE **VILLAINS**.

THIS **TENDENCY** AIDES IN ANOTHER **DIFFERENCE** FROM AMERICAN WRESTLING.

WHILE AMERICAN WRESTLING GENERALLY USES SOME KIND OF **STORY** TO GET THE AUDIENCE TO **CHEER** THE HEROES AND **BOO** THE VILLAINS...

...LUCHA LIBRE INSTEAD RELIES ON THE **SPECTACLE** OF ITS TÉCNICOS AND THE **BRUTALITY** OF ITS RUDOS TO ACHIEVE THE SAME **GOAL**.

TO THE **UNINITIATED**, THIS APPROACH CAN SOMETIMES READ AS BEING MORE **SIMPLISTIC**, BUT THAT ITSELF IS A GROSS **OVERSIMPLIFICATION**.

OUTSIDE OF THE TÉCNICO/RUDO DIVIDE ARE **EXÓTICOS** LIKE **CASSANDRO**, MALE WRESTLERS THAT TAKE ON AN OVERTLY **FEMININE**, ANDROGYNOUS, OR OTHERWISE **FLAMBOYANT** APPEARANCE.

THOUGH INITIALLY MERELY A **GIMMICK**, IN RECENT YEARS, MORE EXÓTICOS HAVE BEEN OPENLY **HOMOSEXUAL**, INCORPORATING THEIR REAL-LIFE **SEXUAL ORIENTATION** INTO THEIR CHARACTER.

ANOTHER **BIG** DIFFERENCE BETWEEN LUCHA LIBRE AND AMERICAN WRESTLING IS **SIZE.**

AMERICAN WRESTLING **TYPICALLY** FOCUSES ON **BIG MEN.** EVEN THE NWA WORLD JUNIOR HEAVYWEIGHT TITLE'S UPPER LIMIT WAS **220 POUNDS!**

WHILE NOT A **UNIVERSAL** CHARACTERIZATION, LUCHADORES TEND TO BE **SMALLER,** LIGHTER, FASTER, AND MORE **ACROBATIC** THAN THEIR COUNTERPARTS TO THE **NORTH.**

EVEN **EL SANTO** WAS ONLY BILLED AT 5' 10" AND 210 POUNDS, WHICH, LIKE **MOST** HEIGHTS AND WEIGHTS IN WRESTLING, WAS LIKELY **EXAGGERATED.**

THE **REASON** BEHIND THIS DIFFERENCE IS LUCHA LIBRE'S ADHERENCE TO **BOXING-STYLE** WEIGHT DIVISIONS.

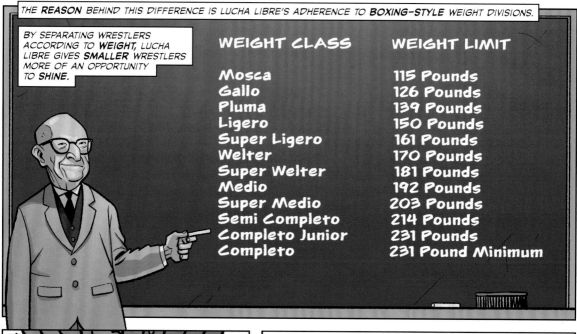

BY SEPARATING WRESTLERS ACCORDING TO **WEIGHT,** LUCHA LIBRE GIVES **SMALLER** WRESTLERS MORE OF AN OPPORTUNITY TO **SHINE.**

| WEIGHT CLASS | WEIGHT LIMIT |
| --- | --- |
| Mosca | 115 Pounds |
| Gallo | 126 Pounds |
| Pluma | 139 Pounds |
| Ligero | 150 Pounds |
| Super Ligero | 161 Pounds |
| Welter | 170 Pounds |
| Super Welter | 181 Pounds |
| Medio | 192 Pounds |
| Super Medio | 203 Pounds |
| Semi Completo | 214 Pounds |
| Completo Junior | 231 Pounds |
| Completo | 231 Pound Minimum |

BECAUSE OF THIS, AFTER LUTTEROTH'S EMLL JOINED THE NWA IN **1953,** THE PROMOTION WAS GIVEN CONTROL OF THE **WORLD LIGHT HEAVYWEIGHT** TITLE.

THOUGH WEIGHT DIVISIONS WEREN'T **UNIVERSALLY** ENFORCED, THE TITLE WAS WON AND DEFENDED BY **SEMI COMPLETO** LUCHADORES.

THE TITLE WAS ONE OF THE MOST **SIGNIFICANT** IN EMLL, WHICH HELD ON TO IT EVEN AFTER **LEAVING** THE NWA AND CHANGING ITS NAME TO **CONSEJO MUNDIAL DE LUCHA LIBRE.**

NWA **WORLD LIGHT HEAVYWEIGHT CHAMPIONS** INCLUDE RAY MENDOZA, DR. WAGNER, EL DANDY, VAMPIRO, AND **MORE,** BUT THE **GREATEST** AMONG THESE...

...WAS **GORY GUERRERO**, WHO EARNED HIS MONIKER FROM A TENDENCY TO HAVE PARTICULARLY **BLOODY** MATCHES.

THOUGH BORN IN **ARIZONA**, STARTING IN THE MID-1940s, GUERRERO BECAME A **PROFOUNDLY** INFLUENTIAL FIGURE IN MEXICO.

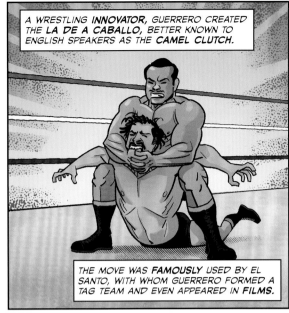

A WRESTLING **INNOVATOR**, GUERRERO CREATED THE **LA DE A CABALLO**, BETTER KNOWN TO ENGLISH SPEAKERS AS THE **CAMEL CLUTCH**.

THE MOVE WAS **FAMOUSLY** USED BY EL SANTO, WITH WHOM GUERRERO FORMED A TAG TEAM AND EVEN APPEARED IN **FILMS**.

HE ALSO INVENTED THE **GORY SPECIAL**, A BACKBREAKER SUBMISSION THAT TODAY IS COMMONLY USED TO SET UP A **NECKBREAKER** OR **FACEBUSTER**.

BUT GUERRERO'S **GREATEST** CONTRIBUTION TO WRESTLING...

...WAS HIS **FAMILY**. GORY AND HIS WIFE, HERLINDA, HAD **SIX** CHILDREN, AND ALL **FOUR** OF THE BOYS BECAME SUCCESSFUL **LUCHADORES**.

THE OLDEST SON, **CHAVO**, COMPETED IN **JAPAN** AND **CALIFORNIA**, BEFORE EVENTUALLY ENDING UP IN **WWE** ALONGSIDE HIS SON, ALSO NAMED **CHAVO**.

NEXT UP WAS MANDO, WHO WORKED IN **CALIFORNIA** AND THE **AWA**, AS WELL AS TRAINING THE WOMEN OF THE **GORGEOUS LADIES OF WRESTLING** FEDERATION IN THE 1980s...

...AND **HECTOR**, WHO WAS THE INFAMOUS **GOBBLEDY GOOKER** TURKEY AT WWE'S INAUGURAL **SURVIVOR SERIES**, AND LATER BECAME THE SPANISH ANNOUNCER FOR **TNA**.

THE **GREATEST** OF THE GUERREROS, HOWEVER, **SURPASSING** EVEN GORY...

...WAS **EDDIE**. FIRST BROADLY INTRODUCED TO **AMERICAN** AUDIENCES THROUGH WCW'S **CRUISERWEIGHT DIVISION** IN THE 1990s (COVERED IN CHAPTER 8), HE HAD **EVERYTHING**.

HE WAS **MUSCULAR** AND **STRONG** FOR A CRUISERWEIGHT, AS **QUICK** AS ANYONE, AND HAD THE **TECHNICAL** ABILITY BEFITTING HIS **LINEAGE**.

TOGETHER WITH MANY OTHERS, INCLUDING **REY MYSTERIO**, WHOM HE FACED IN A LEGENDARY **CRUISERWEIGHT TITLE VS. MASK MATCH** AT WCW HALLOWEEN HAVOC 1997...

...GUERRERO BROUGHT **LUCHA LIBRE** TO THE **MASSES** IN AMERICA AND **BEYOND**.

THE **FAST-PACED**, HIGH-FLYING ACTION THAT THE **CRUISERWEIGHTS** DISPLAYED IN WCW WAS A **WELCOME** CONTRAST TO THE PROMOTION'S LARGER, SOMETIMES **PLODDING** TOP STARS.

THOUGH THE CRUISERWEIGHTS WERE BROUGHT IN ALMOST AS A **SIDESHOW**, THEIR **KINETIC** MATCHES SOON BECAME A **MAJOR** DRAW.

AND IN THE **PROCESS**, THEY INFLUENCED **GENERATIONS** OF WRESTLERS, **CROSS-POLLINATING** LUCHA LIBRE WITH STYLES SEEN AS MORE **TRADITIONAL** IN THE **UNITED STATES**.

THEY EXPOSED AMERICAN AUDIENCES TO THE **HALLMARKS** OF LUCHA LIBRE: **SMALLER** WRESTLERS, **SPECTACULAR** MOVES, COLORFUL **MASKS**, AND **FAMILY**.

IN **LUCHA LIBRE**, YOUNG WRESTLERS DON'T JUST FOLLOW FAMILY MEMBERS INTO THE BUSINESS, THEY OFTEN ADOPT AND ADAPT THEIR **GIMMICK**, AS **REY MYSTERIO** DID.

REY MISTERIO, SR. WAS A TALENTED WRESTLER, BUT HIS MOST SIGNIFICANT CONTRIBUTIONS TO WRESTLING WERE HIS **TRAINEES**...

...INCLUDING KONNAN, PSICOSIS, CASSANDRO, AND MISTERIO'S **NEPHEW**, WHO WOULD DON THE MASK TO BECOME **REY MYSTERIO**.

MYSTERIO, GOING BY THE NAME **REY MISTERIO, JR.**, FIRST ROSE TO PROMINENCE IN **ASISTENCIA ASESORÍA Y ADMINISTRACIÓN**.

AAA WAS FORMED IN 1992 BY **ANTONIO PEÑA**, WHO HAD BEEN INVOLVED WITH **EMLL'S** REBRANDING INTO **CMLL** FOLLOWING ITS DEPARTURE FROM THE **NWA**.

AT THE TIME, **CMLL**--WHICH HAS ALWAYS POSITIONED ITSELF AS A **TRADITIONAL** PROMOTION--WAS **PRIMARILY** FOCUSED ON LARGER, **VETERAN** COMPETITORS.

BUT PEÑA WANTED TO SHOWCASE **SMALLER** GRAPPLERS, EVEN CREATING THE **MINI-ESTRELLA** DIVISION, WHICH FEATURED DWARVES AND DIMINUTIVE TALENT AS TINY VERSIONS OF ESTABLISHED WRESTLERS.

WHEN PEÑA LEFT, HE TOOK MUCH OF CMLL'S **YOUNGER** TALENT, CREATING A COLORFUL, **FAST-PACED** PRODUCT, **CO-PROMOTING** WHEN WORLDS COLLIDE WITH WCW IN 1994.

AAA'S **STYLE** AND **TALENT**--INCLUDING NAMES LIKE MYSTERIO, JUVENTUD GUERRERA, PSICOSIS, AND LA PARKA-- WAS A **PRECURSOR** TO WCW'S LUCHA LIBRE **EXPLOSION**.

THOUGH **CMLL** AND **AAA** REMAIN MEXICO'S LARGEST, MOST **POPULAR** PROMOTIONS, THERE HAVE BEEN MANY MORE PURVEYORS OF LUCHA LIBRE.

AMONG THEM ARE THE **UNIVERSAL WRESTLING ASSOCIATION**, COFOUNDED BY RAY MENDOZA IN 1975, KONNAN'S **PROMO AZTECA**, AND LATER **THE CRASH**...

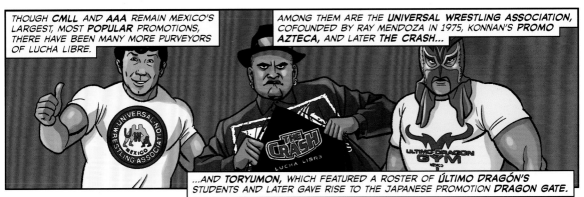

...AND **TORYUMON**, WHICH FEATURED A ROSTER OF **ÚLTIMO DRAGÓN'S** STUDENTS AND LATER GAVE RISE TO THE JAPANESE PROMOTION **DRAGON GATE**.

WHILE PEOPLE **TYPICALLY** THINK ABOUT MEXICAN WRESTLING WHEN THEY HEAR "LUCHA LIBRE," THE TERM IS USED THROUGHOUT THE SPANISH-SPEAKING WORLD, INCLUDING IN **PUERTO RICO.**

THERE, **LUCHA LIBRE** IS EXPRESSED AS A BLEND OF **DIVERSE** WRESTLING TRADITIONS, INCLUDING MEXICAN, AMERICAN, AND CANADIAN.

PUERTO RICO WAS EXPOSED TO **PROFESSIONAL WRESTLING** AS EARLY AS THE **1950s,** BUT ONLY THROUGH BROADCASTS OF **FOREIGN** PROMOTIONS.

**DOMESTIC** PROMOTIONS BEGAN CROPPING UP IN 1960, BUT THEY SHOWCASED TOO MUCH **FOREIGN** TALENT FOR THE PUERTO RICAN FANS, WHO WANTED HEROES OF THEIR **OWN.**

IN 1973, **CARLOS COLÓN** AND HIS BUSINESS PARTNERS FORMED THE **WORLD WRESTLING COUNCIL** AND SET OUT TO GIVE PUERTO RICANS **EXACTLY** WHAT THEY WANTED.

WITH A MIX OF **MEXICAN** ATHLETICISM, **AMERICAN** BRAWLING, AND NO FRILLS **CANADIAN** GRAPPLING, COLÓN WAS A **SENSATION.** BUT JUST AS IMPORTANT WAS WHO HE **FACED:**

A STEADY PROCESSION OF **FOREIGN** VILLAINS. COLÓN WAS **INVARIABLY** POSITIONED AS A PUERTO RICAN ICON, DEFENDING THE ISLAND FROM VICIOUS, UNSCRUPULOUS **INVADERS.**

AND ONCE WWC JOINED THE **NWA** IN THE EARLY 1980s, THE PROMOTION GAINED ACCESS TO EVEN MORE **AMERICAN** TALENT, INCLUDING, NOTABLY, **RIC FLAIR.**

THE FORMULA WAS A **PROFITABLE** ONE THAT CARLOS LATER USED WITH HIS SONS **CARLY** AND **EDDIE,** AND NEPHEW **ORLANDO** (KNOWN IN WWE AS CARLITO, PRIMO, AND EPICO, RESPECTIVELY).

BUT EARLY ON, WITH **HEATED** COMPETITION FROM **FOREIGN** PROMOTIONS STILL INTENT ON **RUNNING** PUERTO RICO, THE WWC NEEDED SOMETHING **ELSE** TO PULL AHEAD...

...*VIOLENCE.* IN ORDER TO DRAW AN AUDIENCE, WWC WENT TO VIOLENT, BRUTAL, **BLOODY** EXTREMES.

AND PERHAPS **NO ONE** WAS MORE BRUTAL THAN **ABDULLAH THE BUTCHER**, A CANADIAN WRESTLER BILLED FROM **SUDAN.**

OFTEN UNABLE TO COMPETE WITH THE **TALENT** IN FOREIGN PROMOTIONS, COLÓN, ABDULLAH, AND OTHERS CUT A **BLOODY** SWATH ACROSS THE ISLAND.

THEY USED **FOREIGN OBJECTS** LIKE ABDULLAH'S FORK, WILD **BRAWLS**, AND BUCKETS OF BLOOD BROUGHT FORTH BY HIDDEN **RAZOR BLADES**, ALL TO DRAW **RIOTOUS** CROWDS.

PUERTO RICO WAS ALSO WHERE **FIRE** WAS FIRST INTRODUCED TO WRESTLING, LATER GIVING BIRTH TO **DEATH MATCHES**...

...AN EXCESSIVELY VIOLENT FORM OF WRESTLING THAT FEATURES **FLAMES**, WEAPONS, **BARBED WIRE**, TACKS, AND EVEN (LATER) **EXPLOSIONS.**

AND THE **FANS** RESPONDED IN KIND, PELTING MAINLAND HEEL WRESTLERS LIKE **DIRTY DUTCH MANTEL** WITH ANYTHING THEY COULD PUT THEIR **HANDS** ON...

...INCLUDING ROCKS, BATTERIES, AND EVEN **BEER CANS** THAT HAD BEEN FILLED WITH **SAND** AND STOMPED DOWN INTO **DISKS.**

WWC WELCOMED **MANY** INDEPENDENT WRESTLERS TO THE TERRITORY, INCLUDING **BRUISER BRODY**, A HULKING, YET AGILE, **BRUTE** WHO CODIFIED THE **"BIG MAN"** STYLE OF WRESTLING.

TRAGICALLY, THE **VIOLENCE** OF PUERTO RICAN WRESTLING EXTENDED INTO **REAL LIFE**, AS BRODY WAS **STABBED** TO DEATH BY WWC'S BOOKER, **JOSÉ GONZÁLEZ** IN 1988.

THE KILLING WAS RULED AN ACT OF **SELF-DEFENSE**, BUT DUE TO AMERICAN WITNESSES NOT RECEIVING THEIR **SUBPOENAS**, ACCUSATIONS OF A **COVER-UP** AND **BRIBERY** AROSE...

...WHILE NUMEROUS WITNESSES THAT **DID** RECEIVE SUBPOENAS REFUSED TO TESTIFY FOR FEAR OF **REPRISALS** FROM THE INFLUENTIAL **COLÓN.**

MANY AMERICAN WRESTLERS **REFUSED** TO GO BACK IN THE **WAKE** OF THE VERDICT, AND AS A RESULT, WRESTLING IN PUERTO RICO **SUFFERED.**

LUCHADORES HAVE LONG HAD A PRESENCE IN AMERICAN WRESTLING, FROM **GORY GUERRERO** IN TEXAS BORDER TOWNS...

...TO **PEDRO MORALES**, WHO THRILLED THE NEW YORK **PUERTO RICAN** COMMUNITY BY WINNING THE **WWWF HEAVYWEIGHT TITLE** FROM IVAN KOLOFF IN 1971.

AND STARTING IN THE 1990S, WITH THE POPULARITY OF MEXICAN **CRUISERWEIGHTS** LIKE **JUVENTUD GUERRERA** IN WCW...

...LUCHA LIBRE BECAME **ENORMOUSLY** INFLUENTIAL.

TODAY, WITH SO MANY MATCHES AVAILABLE ON THE INTERNET, AND WITH AN **INCREASING** AMOUNT OF PROMOTIONS THAT **STREAM** THEIR EVENTS...

...IT'S EASIER THAN **EVER** FOR WRESTLING FANS INTERESTED IN **LUCHA LIBRE** TO GET ACCESS TO A COMPLETELY **DIFFERENT** FLAVOR OF THE ONE TRUE SPORT.

AS A **RESULT**, IT'S NOW **COMMON** TO SEE MOVES **PREVIOUSLY** ASSOCIATED WITH LUCHA LIBRE PERFORMED BY **EVERYONE**...

...FROM WRESTLERS IN SMALL, LOCAL **INDEPENDENT** PROMOTIONS...

...TO THOSE IN THE **LARGEST** WRESTLING PROMOTION IN THE WORLD, **WWE**.

BUT THE **CLEAREST** EXAMPLE OF LUCHA LIBRE'S ASCENDANCY IN MAINSTREAM AMERICAN WRESTLING IS **LUCHA UNDERGROUND**...

...A **BILINGUAL** WRESTLING PROMOTION FILMED IN THE TRADITIONALLY **MEXICAN** LOS ANGELES NEIGHBORHOOD OF **BOYLE HEIGHTS**.

THE SHOW USES A BLEND OF **LEGACY** MEXICAN TALENT, NEW-TO-AMERICA GRAPPLERS FROM **AAA**, **ESTABLISHED** INDEPENDENT PERFORMERS, AND EVEN FORMER **WWE** STARS.

BLUE DEMON, JR.

CHAVO GUERRERO

PENTAGÓN, JR.

PRINCE PUMA, AKA RICOCHET

FENIX

JOEY RYAN

THEY CREATE A SENSE OF **PLACE** THAT IS UNLIKE ANY OTHER WRESTLING PROMOTION, DUE TO ITS **INSTANTLY** IDENTIFIABLE, **PROUDLY** MEXICAN AESTHETIC...

...INCLUDING **VIGNETTES** THAT OWE MORE THAN A LITTLE BIT TO MEXICAN **TELENOVELAS**.

THE SHOW HAS ALSO BEEN **INSTRUMENTAL** IN THE POPULARIZATION OF WRESTLING **TROPES** THAT WERE PREVIOUSLY **LARGELY** CONFINED TO **LUCHA LIBRE**...

SON OF HAVOC

ANGÉLICO

IVELISSE

...INCLUDING **INTERGENDER** CONTESTS AND **TRIOS** MATCHES--TAG TEAMS WITH **THREE** COMPETITORS INSTEAD OF **TWO**.

THOUGH ORIGINALLY A WHOLLY **SEPARATE** FORM OF WRESTLING, ASPECTS OF LUCHA LIBRE CONTINUE TO BE ADOPTED AND **EMBRACED** BY AUDIENCES **WORLDWIDE**...

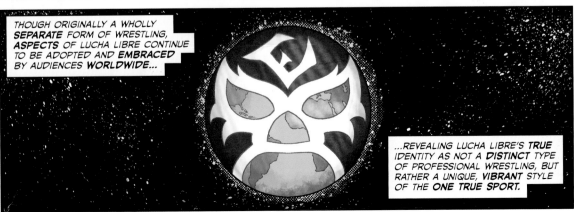

...REVEALING LUCHA LIBRE'S **TRUE** IDENTITY AS NOT A **DISTINCT** TYPE OF PROFESSIONAL WRESTLING, BUT RATHER A UNIQUE, **VIBRANT** STYLE OF THE **ONE TRUE SPORT**.

IT'S **IMPOSSIBLE** TO OVERSTATE THE IMPORTANCE OF **MENACE** TO PROFESSIONAL WRESTLING.

THE ENTIRE **ART FORM** IS BASED UPON THE AUDIENCE CHOOSING TO BELIEVE THAT WRESTLERS **CAN AND WILL** HURT ONE ANOTHER.

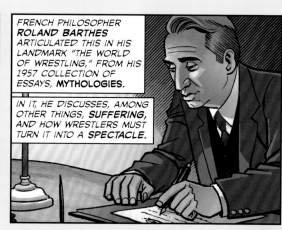

FRENCH PHILOSOPHER **ROLAND BARTHES** ARTICULATED THIS IN HIS LANDMARK "THE WORLD OF WRESTLING," FROM HIS 1957 COLLECTION OF ESSAYS, **MYTHOLOGIES.**

IN IT, HE DISCUSSES, AMONG OTHER THINGS, **SUFFERING,** AND HOW WRESTLERS MUST TURN IT INTO A **SPECTACLE.**

THIS IS AS TRUE FOR **HEELS,** WHO ELICIT **BOOS** FOR THE SUFFERING THEY INFLICT...

RIC FLAIR AND HIS FIGURE-FOUR LEGLOCK.

...AS IT IS FOR **FACES,** WHO FANS CHEER FOR THE **WELL-DESERVED VIOLENCE** THEY DISH OUT TO THEIR **RIVALS.**

DUSTY RHODES AND HIS BIONIC ELBOW.

GIANT BABA

THE ROAD WARRIORS

THE UNDERTAKER

BIG SHOW

MARK HENRY

THE MOST **EXPEDIENT** WAY TO ESTABLISH THIS MENACE IS THROUGH **APPEARANCE,** BE IT A **MONSTROUS** GIMMICK, INCREDIBLE **MUSCLES,** OR JUST SHEER **SIZE.**

BUT MENACE CAN **ALSO** BE CREATED THROUGH **OTHER** MEANS, INCLUDING SPEED, TECHNIQUE OR MICROPHONE SKILLS.

JUSHIN THUNDER LIGER

REY MYSTERIO

DANIEL BRYAN

RODDY PIPER

MICK FOLEY

MENACE, THE **PERCEIVED** ABILITY TO INFLICT **SUFFERING,** IS AN **INDISPENSABLE** PART OF PROFESSIONAL WRESTLING...

...BUT HOW IT'S **PERFORMED** IS WHAT GIVES THE **ONE TRUE SPORT** ITS CONSTANTLY EVOLVING VARIETY.

FROM ITS BEGINNINGS IN THE AMERICAN **MIDWEST**, THE NWA, AT ITS **HEIGHT**, GREW TO TOUCH WRESTLING IN THE UNITED STATES, MEXICO, CANADA, AND EVEN **JAPAN**...

...BUT NOT THE **UNITED KINGDOM**, DESPITE THE FACT THAT THE COUNTRY'S **INFLUENCE** IS ALL OVER **PROFESSIONAL WRESTLING**.

THE **CATCH-AS-CATCH-CAN** STYLE WAS INVENTED IN **LONDON** BY J. G. CHAMBERS AROUND **1870**.

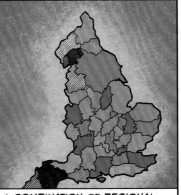

A **COMBINATION** OF REGIONAL BRITISH STYLES, **CATCH WRESTLING** FORMS THE **FOUNDATION** OF ALL PROFESSIONAL WRESTLING.

AND IT WAS IN **ENGLAND** THAT FUTURE WORLD CHAMPION GEORGE HACKENSCHMIDT LEARNED **SHOWMANSHIP**.

MELDING IT WITH HIS NATURAL **DOMINANCE** FOR INCREASED **DRAMA** AND **PROFIT**.

BUT DESPITE ALL THAT, THERE WASN'T AN NWA AFFILIATE **ANYWHERE** IN EUROPE UNTIL **NWA UK HAMMERLOCK** IN THE 1990s, WELL AFTER THE SYNDICATE'S **HEYDAY**.

LIKE **LUCHA LIBRE**, WRESTLING IN THE U.K. DEVELOPED ALONG A **SEPARATE** EVOLUTIONARY PATH. AND THE POINT OF **DIVERGENCE**?

IT CAME IN **1930**, WHEN WRESTLER AND SEVENTH BARONET OF SHREWSBURY, **SIR EDWARD ATHOLL OAKELEY**, FORMED A PROMOTION WITH AUSTRIAN-BORN GRAPPLER **HENRY IRSLINGER**.

TOGETHER, THEY INTRODUCED WHAT THEY CALLED **AMERICAN CATCH-AS-CATCH-CAN**, BUT WHAT WOULD LATER COME TO BE KNOWN AS **ALL-IN WRESTLING**.

IN THE WAKE OF **GOTCH'S** WIN OVER **HACKENSCHMIDT,** BRITISH WRESTLERS IN THE 1910s MIGRATED TO THE **UNITED STATES,** DEPLETING THE COUNTRY'S RANKS.

THEN, AS IN AMERICA, THE ONE-TWO PUNCH OF GOTCH'S **RETIREMENT** AND THE OUTBREAK OF **WORLD WAR I** TORPEDOED BRITISH INTEREST IN **PROFESSIONAL WRESTLING.**

IN 1930, OAKELEY AND IRSLINGER SET OUT TO **REVIVE** THAT INTEREST WITH A STYLE THAT COMBINED **CATCH WRESTLING** AND AMERICAN **SHOWMANSHIP.**

AND OF COURSE, THE MATCHES WERE **FIXED,** WITH OAKELEY HIMSELF BECOMING THE FIRST **BRITISH HEAVYWEIGHT CHAMPION.**

**ALL-IN**--NAMED FOR ITS **AGGREGATION** OF STYLES--**EXPLODED** IN POPULARITY, BUT THERE WEREN'T ENOUGH **EXPERIENCED WRESTLERS** TO FILL THE DEMAND.

AS A RESULT, ENTERPRISING ENGLISH PROMOTERS FOUND OTHER, MORE **VIOLENT** WAYS TO GRAB AUDIENCES, JUST AS **CARLOS COLÓN** WOULD IN **PUERTO RICO** DECADES LATER (SEE PAGE 65).

AND AS HAS HAPPENED MANY TIMES SINCE, IN THEIR PURSUIT OF **SPECTACLE,** PROMOTERS TURNED TO **TITILLATION...**

...SHOWCASING **WOMEN'S** WRESTLING, WHICH WAS STILL **FROWNED-UPON,** ESPECIALLY WHEN CONTESTED IN RINGS FULL OF **MUD.**

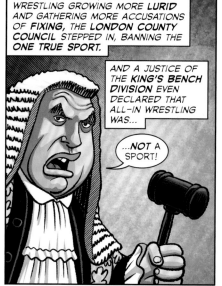

IN THE LATE 1930s, WITH ALL-IN WRESTLING GROWING MORE **LURID** AND GATHERING MORE ACCUSATIONS OF **FIXING,** THE **LONDON COUNTY COUNCIL** STEPPED IN, BANNING THE **ONE TRUE SPORT.**

AND A JUSTICE OF THE **KING'S BENCH DIVISION** EVEN DECLARED THAT ALL-IN WRESTLING WAS...

...NOT A SPORT!

BETWEEN THE **LONDON BAN**, FAN **SKEPTICISM**, AND THE DEVASTATION OF **WORLD WAR II**, INTEREST IN WRESTLING **LANGUISHED** UNTIL 1947.

IT WAS IN THAT YEAR THAT **ADMIRAL EDWARD EVANS**, FIRST BARON MOUNTEVANS, SET OUT TO **BURNISH** THE ONE TRUE SPORT'S IMAGE.

AFTER HAVING AN EVENT HE PROMOTED DECLARED **FAKE** BY THE PRESS, **ADMIRAL-LORD MOUNTEVANS** FORMED A **COMMITTEE** TO CREATE STANDARDIZED **RULES** FOR WRESTLING.

THAT COMMITTEE INCLUDED RADIO STAR **COMMANDER A. B. CAMPBELL**, PARLIAMENT MEMBER **MAURICE WEBB**, AND OLYMPIC WRESTLER/PROMOTER **NORMAN MORRELL**.

THE RULES STIPULATED THAT MATCHES WOULD BE BEST OF **THREE** FALLS, AND THAT THEY COULD BE SCORED BY **PINFALL, SUBMISSION, KNOCKOUT, TECHNICAL KNOCKOUT,** OR **DISQUALIFICATION...**

...AND AS IN **LUCHA LIBRE**, THEY SET UP **WEIGHT DIVISIONS** THAT, WHILE NOT **DRACONICALLY** ENFORCED, WERE CERTAINLY MUCH MORE HEEDED THAN IN **AMERICA**.

| WEIGHT CLASS | WEIGHT LIMIT |
|---|---|
| Lightweight | 154 pounds |
| Welterweight | 165 pounds |
| Middleweight | 176 pounds |
| Heavy Middleweight | 187 pounds |
| Light Heavyweight | 198 pounds |
| Mid-Heavyweight | 209 pounds |
| Heavyweight | 210 pound minimum |

ALONG WITH **PROHIBITIONS** ON MOVES DELIVERED TO **DOWNED** OPPONENTS, AS WELL AS **PUBLIC WARNINGS** FOR RULE BREAKING...

...THE MOST **NOTABLE** DIVERGENCE FROM AMERICAN WRESTLING WAS THE INTRODUCTION OF BOXING-STYLE **ROUNDS** IN AN EFFORT TO MAKE WRESTLING APPEAR MORE **LEGITIMATE**.

THE RAUCOUS **ANARCHY** OF ALL-IN WRESTLING HAD BEEN SUCCESSFULLY **TRANSFORMED** INTO...

MODERN FREESTYLE

THESE EFFORTS AT **REBRANDING** WRESTLING WERE **EXTREMELY** SUCCESSFUL AND WERE EVENTUALLY **ADOPTED** BY THE **VAST MAJORITY** OF BRITISH PROMOTERS.

WHILE **PROFESSIONAL** WRESTLING HAD SUFFERED IN BRITAIN IN THE WAKE OF THE ALL-IN **CRACKDOWN** AND **WORLD WAR II...**

...**CATCH-AS-CATCH-CAN** CONTINUED TO BE TAUGHT, NOTABLY IN **WIGAN**, THE ORIGIN OF **LANCASHIRE WRESTLING.**

AND THE MOST **IMPORTANT** FIGURE IN THAT PARTICULAR SCENE? **BILLY RILEY.**

BORN IN 1889, RILEY LEARNED **LANCASHIRE** WRESTLING FROM WIGAN MINERS AND BECAME A HOOKER WHO WAS **INFAMOUS** FOR SNAPPING THE ARMS OF HIS RIVALS...

...THOUGH AS WE'VE **MENTIONED**, PROFESSIONAL WRESTLING WAS MOSTLY **FIXED** BY THE TIME RILEY WAS EVEN **BORN.**

IN THE 1950s, RILEY OPENED UP A CATCH WRESTLING **GYM** THAT WOULD BECOME **LEGENDARY:** THE **SNAKE PIT.**

THERE, HE TRAINED **KARL GOTCH,** THE WRESTLER **JACK DEMPSEY,** BILLY ROBINSON, AND MANY MORE, WHO WOULD LATER **SPREAD** CATCH WRESTLING AS **TRAINERS** IN THEIR OWN RIGHT.

THE **ORIGINAL** SNAKE PIT CLOSED, ITS **OWNERSHIP** CHANGING HANDS. BUT WIGAN'S WRESTLING **TRADITION** WAS KEPT ALIVE...

...ESPECIALLY VIA THE **GLOBAL** SUCCESS OF HOMETOWN HEROES DAVEY BOY SMITH AND **DYNAMITE KID** TOM BILLINGTON, BETTER KNOWN AS THE **BRITISH BULLDOGS.**

WITH SUCH STRONG **REGIONAL** WRESTLING TRADITIONS STILL **INTACT,** MODERN FREESTYLE WAS ABLE TO QUICKLY **REPLENISH** ITS RANKS.

AND IT WAS A **GOOD THING,** AS A NEW BRITISH **ORGANIZATION** WAS POISED TO MAKE THE ONE TRUE SPORT **EXPLODE** IN POPULARITY.

DESPITE THE FACT THAT THE NWA WAS FORMED THE YEAR AFTER **MOUNTEVANS'S** COMMITTEE, THE ORGANIZATION WAS A **BAD** FIT FOR BRITISH PROMOTERS...

...DUE TO THE **RULES** THAT THE COMMITTEE ESTABLISHED, AS WELL AS THE FACT THAT BRITISH PROMOTERS AIMED TO CREATE THEIR **OWN** SYNDICATE: **JOINT PROMOTIONS.**

BEGINNING IN 1952, THE PROMOTERS PURPORTED TO USE THE GROUP TO ENFORCE THE **ADMIRAL-LORD MOUNTEVANS** RULES, BUT IN **REALITY**...

...THEY BEHAVED LIKE THE **NWA**, CARVING OUT **TERRITORIES**, SHARING **TALENT**, AND LOCKING OUT **RIVAL** PROMOTERS IN A SUCCESSFUL BID TO **DOMINATE** BRITISH WRESTLING.

**ALSO**, LIKE THE NWA, JOINT PROMOTIONS AIMED TO CONTROL THE **CHAMPIONSHIPS** CONTESTED IN THEIR COUNTRY.

BUT BETWEEN **WORLD**, BRITISH, AND INDIVIDUAL **REGION** AND **WEIGHT CLASS** TITLES, THE TOTAL COUNT **BALLOONED** TO MORE THAN **SEVENTY** CHAMPIONSHIPS.

BY THE MID-1970s, JOINT PROMOTIONS HAD SHIFTED FROM A **CARTEL** TO A **SINGLE ENTITY** AND CHANGED HANDS **SEVERAL** TIMES.

WITH AN EYE TOWARD **REVIVING** THE FLAGGING ORGANIZATION, THE COMPANY TURNED TO A FORMER WRESTLER AND BOOKER BY THE NAME OF **MAX CRABTREE.**

HOWEVER, IT WAS HIS BROTHER **SHIRLEY** THAT WOULD HAVE THE **LARGEST** IMPACT ON BRITISH WRESTLING.

A FORMER CHAMPION WITH A **RIVAL** ORGANIZATION, SHIRLEY CRABTREE'S **POST-RETIREMENT** RETURN WOULD PLAY OUT ON A MONUMENTALLY **IMPORTANT** PLATFORM FOR PROFESSIONAL WRESTLING...

...TELEVISION! FIRST BROADCAST IN ENGLAND IN 1955, WRESTLING WAS A NATURAL FIT FOR THE **STILL-NEW** MEDIUM...

IN 1965, AFTER YEARS AS A **SEASONAL** PROGRAM, WRESTLING BECAME A REGULAR FIXTURE ON THE U.K. TELEVISION SHOW **WORLD OF SPORT.**

WORLD OF SPORT WAS A WEEKLY SHOWCASE FOR **MULTIPLE** SPORTS: **SOCCER** AND **HORSE RACING** WERE THE PRIMARY FOCUS, BUT IT ALSO INCLUDED **OTHERS,** LIKE **SNOOKER.**

ALL THE SPORTS FEATURED WERE **LEGITIMATE** COMPETITIONS EXCEPT FOR ONE: **THE ONE TRUE SPORT.**

DUE TO THE **INFLUENCE OF THE ADMIRAL-LORD MOUNTEVANS RULES,** EARLY TELEVISED BRITISH WRESTLING HAD CONTINUED THE FORM'S EMPHASIS ON **SPORTSMANSHIP.**

AND WITH WRESTLING'S **INCLUSION** ON **WORLD OF SPORT,** A **LEGITIMATE** SPORTS SHOW, THAT EMPHASIS **CONTINUED.**

MOST OF THE WRESTLERS WERE **BLUE-EYES** (THE BRITISH TERM FOR **BABYFACE**), AND THEY HAD LARGELY **STRAIGHTFORWARD** MATCHES.

THERE WERE NO OUTLANDISH **GIMMICKS,** WOMEN'S WRESTLING REMAINED **BANNED** THROUGH MOST OF THE 1970s, AND TAG TEAM MATCHES WERE A **RARITY** IN THE EARLY YEARS.

LEANING INTO **REALISM,** BUOYED BY **WORLD OF SPORT,** BRITISH WRESTLING NOT ONLY **SURVIVED** A LACK OF THE FEATURES THAT MADE PROFESSIONAL WRESTLING POPULAR ELSEWHERE...

...BUT IT **THRIVED.** EVEN NOW IT REMAINS **UNCLEAR** HOW MUCH OF THE CROWD WAS IN ON THE SHOW'S FIXED NATURE, BUT **REGARDLESS:** THEY **LOVED** IT.

BLOND ADONIS SHIRLEY CRABTREE AND HIS 64-INCH CHEST WALKED AWAY FROM WRESTLING IN 1966, A RESULT OF UNSCRIPTED, PUBLIC CHALLENGES FROM BERT ASSIRATI.

ASSIRATI WAS A FAR MORE TALENTED WRESTLER AND AIMED TO FINAGLE HIMSELF A MATCH FOR CRABTREE'S BRITISH HEAVYWEIGHT TITLE.

AFTER SIX YEARS AWAY, CRABTREE RETURNED TO WRESTLING, THROWING IN WITH JOINT PROMOTIONS A FEW YEARS PRIOR TO HIS BROTHER JOINING.

NOTABLY OLDER AND HEAVIER, CRABTREE'S FIRST GIMMICK BACK WAS AS A GUARDSMAN, A NOD TO HIS BACKGROUND WITH THE BRITISH ARMY.

BUT WHEN MAX CAME ON BOARD, HE HAD A DIFFERENT VISION FOR HIS BROTHER: BIG DADDY, A REFERENCE TO TENNESSEE WILLIAMS'S CAT ON A HOT TIN ROOF.

BIG DADDY WAS PLACED IN A TANDEM WITH AN EVEN LARGER WRESTLER, GIANT HAYSTACKS, WHO IS BEST KNOWN IN AMERICA FOR HIS RUN AS WCW'S LOCH NESS MONSTER.

BUT THOUGH THE TWO WERE POSITIONED AS VILLAINS, THE CROWD BEGAN TO GROW FOND OF BIG DADDY.

DESPITE BEING IN HIS LATE FORTIES, DECIDEDLY OVERWEIGHT, AND LIMITED IN HIS MOBILITY EVEN IN HIS YOUNGER DAYS, THE CROWD STARTED TO GET BEHIND THE WORKING-CLASS BRAWLER.

WITH INCREASING FAN SUPPORT, BIG DADDY TURNED ON THE VILLAINOUS HAYSTACKS, COMPLETING HIS TRANSITION TO A BLUE-EYE.

THE PAIR REVISITED THEIR FEUD FOR FIFTEEN YEARS, AND IN THE PROCESS, BECAME TWO OF THE BIGGEST STARS IN BRITISH WRESTLING HISTORY.

BUT AFTER A LONG HISTORY OF **SERIOUS**, SPORTSMANLY **CATCH** WRESTLING, FOLLOWING THE INTRODUCTION OF THE **ADMIRAL-LORD MOUNTEVANS** RULES...

...HOW DID TWO **HUMONGOUS**, NOT VERY **AGILE**, DECIDEDLY **UNTECHNICAL** WRESTLERS BECOME SO VERY **POPULAR**?

IN THE WAKE OF **ALL-IN** WRESTLING, BRITISH PROMOTERS HAD TRIED TO **PREVENT** PROFESSIONAL WRESTLING'S **NATURAL** INCLINATION TOWARD **ARTIFICE**.

BUT YOU CAN'T HALT THE **INEVITABLE**, AND **SPECTACLE** CAME ROARING BACK IN THE FORM OF A **POORLY CONDITIONED**, MIDDLE-AGED GRAPPLER AND HIS **MONSTROUS** RIVAL.

BIG DADDY AND GIANT HAYSTACKS WERE **FAR** FROM THE ONLY **GIMMICKY** WRESTLERS TO APPEAR ON THE SCENE, **HOWEVER**.

ONE OF THE MOST **SIGNIFICANT** WAS GRAPPLER **PETER THORNLEY**, BETTER KNOWN AS HIS MYSTICAL SAMURAI CHARACTER, **KENDO NAGASAKI**.

NAGASAKI HAD FACED BIG DADDY **BEFORE**, WHEN THEY WERE BOTH **VILLAINS**, WITH BIG DADDY EVENTUALLY **UNMASKING** HIS OPPONENT.

THOUGH **PROBLEMATIC** BY TODAY'S STANDARDS, NAGASAKI BECAME **EXCEPTIONALLY** POPULAR AND WAS A **HUGE** PART OF **WORLD OF SPORT'S** SUCCESS.

WITH A **REGULAR** WEEKEND **TIME SLOT** THAT COULD BE VIEWED BY **EVERYONE**, BRITISH WRESTLING FANDOM **EXPLODED**.

AND DUE TO WRESTLING'S INCREASINGLY **SPECTACULAR** NATURE, THERE WAS A **DRAMATIC** UPTICK IN **YOUNGER** FANS.

BIG DADDY CONTINUED TO BE A **TOP DRAW** INTO THE **1990s**, NOT JUST FOR **WRESTLING**, BUT FOR **WORLD OF SPORT** AS A WHOLE.

HE WAS A **CROSSOVER** STAR, APPEARING IN POPULAR **COMICS**, **ADVERTISEMENTS**, AND MORE.

BUT THERE WAS A **PROBLEM** WITH BUILDING AN ENTIRE **PROMOTION** AROUND ONE **DRAMATICALLY OVERWEIGHT, AGING STAR:**

HIS **CONDITIONING** AND **ABILITY** TO PERFORM IN THE RING WERE SEVERELY **LACKING**.

THE **SOLUTION?** PAIR BIG DADDY UP WITH MORE **MOBILE** TALENT, LIKE A YOUNG **DYNAMITE KID.**

THIS STRATEGY SERVED A **DUAL** PURPOSE, AS IT ALSO ALLOWED NEWER WRESTLERS TO **SIPHON OFF** SOME OF BIG DADDY'S **POPULARITY**...

...WHILE DOING ALL OF THE **HEAVY LIFTING** AND **RUNNING** AND **THROWING** IN A MATCH...

...SO THAT **BIG DADDY** COULD GET **TAGGED** IN AND BRING IT ON **HOME**.

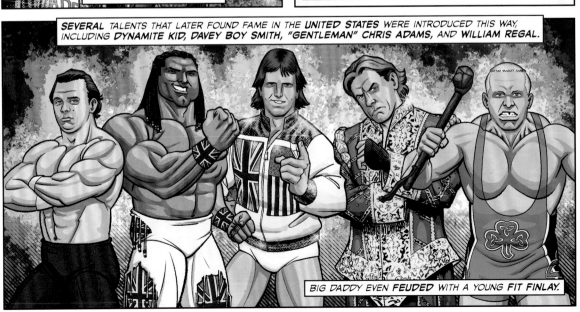

SEVERAL TALENTS THAT LATER FOUND FAME IN THE **UNITED STATES** WERE INTRODUCED THIS WAY, INCLUDING **DYNAMITE KID, DAVEY BOY SMITH, "GENTLEMAN" CHRIS ADAMS,** AND **WILLIAM REGAL**.

BIG DADDY EVEN **FEUDED** WITH A YOUNG **FIT FINLAY**.

BIG DADDY WAS HULK HOGAN-LEVEL **FAMOUS** IN ENGLAND, SO HIS HEAVYWEIGHT MATCHES ALWAYS TOOK **PRIORITY.**

BUT LIKE **LUCHA LIBRE,** BRITISH WRESTLING FEATURED MORE **RIGOROUS** WEIGHT DIVISIONS...

...WHICH ALLOWED **SMALLER** COMPETITORS LIKE **DYNAMITE KID** TO BECOME **BREAKOUT** STARS.

BUT **MANY** OF THE JUNIOR HEAVYWEIGHTS WEREN'T **CONTENT** TO JUST PERFORM IN BIG DADDY'S **CONSIDERABLE** SHADOW.

SO THEY WENT **ELSEWHERE,** SPREADING THE **STYLE** AND **INFLUENCE** OF CATCH WRESTLING **ACROSS** THE GLOBE.

IN **CALGARY,** DYNAMITE KID AND DAVEY BOY SMITH WERE WELCOMED INTO **STU HART'S** STAMPEDE WRESTLING.

DAVEY BOY EVEN **MARRIED** ONE OF HART'S **DAUGHTERS!**

BRET HART

JIM NEIDHART

OWEN HART

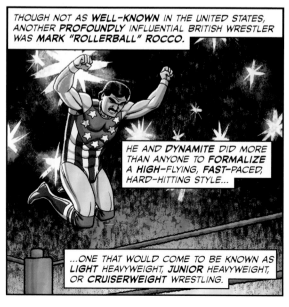

THOUGH NOT AS **WELL-KNOWN** IN THE UNITED STATES, ANOTHER **PROFOUNDLY** INFLUENTIAL BRITISH WRESTLER WAS **MARK "ROLLERBALL" ROCCO.**

HE AND **DYNAMITE** DID MORE THAN ANYONE TO **FORMALIZE** A **HIGH**-FLYING, **FAST**-PACED, HARD-HITTING STYLE...

...ONE THAT WOULD COME TO BE KNOWN AS **LIGHT** HEAVYWEIGHT, **JUNIOR** HEAVYWEIGHT, OR **CRUISERWEIGHT** WRESTLING.

LIKE **DYNAMITE** AND **DAVEY BOY,** ROCCO ALSO MADE HIS WAY TO **JAPAN,** WHERE HE BECAME THE FIRST WRESTLER TO TAKE UP THE MASK OF THE **BLACK TIGER** (SEE PAGE 93).

THIS MOVE LED TO **GROUNDBREAKING** FEUDS WITH DYNAMITE AND, MOST NOTABLY, THE **ORIGINAL** TIGER MASK, **SATORU SAYAMA.**

JOINT PROMOTIONS HAD ITS SPOT ON **WORLD OF SPORT**, WHICH ENSURED THAT THEY MAINTAINED A REGULAR PRESENCE IN HOMES **ACROSS** THE COUNTRY.

BUT WITH SO MUCH **YOUNGER** TALENT GOING ELSEWHERE, AND THE SHOW BUILT ALMOST **ENTIRELY** AROUND **BIG DADDY**...

...**TALENT** AND **ATTENDANCE** BOTH BEGAN TO **SUFFER** AT THE HOUSE SHOWS THEY PROMOTED THROUGHOUT THE COUNTRY.

THIS TURN WAS **DISASTROUS**, AS LIVE EVENTS ARE **CRITICALLY** IMPORTANT NOT JUST FOR THE MONEY THEY BRING IN, BUT ALSO FOR THE **CULTIVATION** OF A **FAN BASE**.

BUT THE **BIGGEST** BLOW TO JOINT PROMOTIONS (AND WRESTLING IN THE U.K. AS A **WHOLE**) CAME IN 1985, WHEN **WORLD OF SPORT** WAS TAKEN OFF THE AIR.

WRESTLING WAS GIVEN ITS **OWN** SHOW, BUT AT A **DIFFERENT** TIME EVERY WEEK, MAKING IT **DIFFICULT** FOR FANS TO FIND IN THE DAYS BEFORE **DVR**.

PLUS, JOINT PROMOTIONS HAD TO **SHARE** ITS TELEVISION TIME WITH ITS **RIVALS**, LIKE **ALL STAR WRESTLING**...

...WHICH CARVED OUT A **NICHE** FOR ITSELF WITH NAMES LIKE **KENDO NAGASAKI, ROLLERBALL ROCCO, ROBBIE BROOKSIDE, GIANT HAYSTACKS**, AND **FIT FINLAY**.

BUT THE **BIGGEST** THREAT THAT JOINT PROMOTIONS WOULD HAVE TO **SHARE TIME** WITH WAS THE **WORLD WRESTLING FEDERATION**.

UNDER THE GUIDANCE OF **VINCENT KENNEDY MCMAHON**, THE PROMOTION, HAVING LARGELY **CONQUERED** THE UNITED STATES, SET ITS EYES ON **EUROPE**.

AS INTEREST IN AMERICAN PROMOTIONS **WWF** AND **WCW** INCREASED, THE POPULARITY OF BRITISH WRESTLING **FLAGGED**...

...ESPECIALLY WITH THE 1993 RETIREMENT OF BOTH **BIG DADDY** AND **KENDO NAGASAKI**.

BOTH BRITISH AND AMERICAN GRAPPLING GREW OUT OF **CATCH WRESTLING**, BUT FOR **DECADES** WRESTLING IN THE U.K. FOLLOWED A PATH OF ITS **OWN**.

CATCH WRESTLING

THE ONE TRUE SPORT

IN THE 1990S, THOSE PATHS **CONVERGED**, WITH MANY BRITISH WRESTLING **IDIOSYNCRASIES**--LIKE MATCHES WITH **ROUNDS**--BECOMING **LOST** IN THE PROCESS.

THAT'S NOT TO SAY THAT BRITISH WRESTLING WAS **FORGOTTEN**, HOWEVER--FAR FROM IT.

THE STARS SPAWNED BY THE **WORLD OF SPORT** DAYS CONTINUED TO THRIVE, WITH **DAVEY BOY SMITH** MAIN-EVENTING WWF'S **SUMMERSLAM** IN **WEMBLEY STADIUM** AGAINST BRET HART IN 1992.

AND ALL THE **WHILE**, WHILE NOT THE **MAINSTREAM** ATTRACTION IT ONCE WAS, WRESTLING WAS KEPT **ALIVE** VIA SMALLER PROMOTIONS IN THE BRITISH ISLES...

...WHICH WENT ON TO PRODUCE TALENTS IN THE **NEW MILLENNIUM**, LIKE **NIGEL McGUINNESS, SHEAMUS,** AND **PAIGE**.

PRESENTLY, BRITISH WRESTLING IS UNDERGOING A **RENAISSANCE**, WITH NAMES LIKE **NEVILLE, ZACK SABRE, JR., WILL OSPREAY,** AND **MARTY SCURLL** LEADING THE WAY.

BY **RECONTEXTUALIZING** THE WORLD OF SPORT-ERA APPROACH FOR **MODERN** AUDIENCES, THIS **CURRENT** GENERATION IS ENSURING THAT THE TRADITION OF BRITISH WRESTLING WILL **CONTINUE** TO LIVE ON.

# SUBMISSIONS

SINCE **HOOKERS** FIRST BEGAN TRAVELING WITH **CARNIVALS**, HOLDS HAVE BEEN AN **IMPORTANT** PART OF PROFESSIONAL WRESTLING...

...THOUGH **ORIGINALLY** THEY WERE USED NOT TO FORCE AN OPPONENT TO **SUBMIT**, BUT TO POSITION THEM FOR A **PIN**.

THESE DAYS, SUBMISSIONS AREN'T JUST A WAY TO **END** A MATCH, BUT A WAY FOR A WRESTLER TO INFLICT **SUFFERING** AND CREATE **MENACE**.

AND THE **FINEST** OF THESE SUBMISSIONS? IT'S THE ONE MADE **FAMOUS** BY TWO OF WRESTLING'S **GREATEST** VILLAINS, **BUDDY ROGERS** AND **RIC FLAIR**...

...THE **FIGURE-FOUR LEGLOCK**.

WHAT MAKES THE FIGURE-FOUR SO **GREAT?** FOR STARTERS, YOU CAN SEE **BOTH** WRESTLER'S FACES DURING IT...

...SO THERE'S **NO** QUESTION HOW MUCH **AGONY** THE RECIPIENT IS IN.

AND JUST AS **IMPORTANTLY:** THERE'S A WAY **OUT.** WITH THEIR ARMS STILL **FREE**, A WRESTLER CAN REACH OUT FOR A **ROPE BREAK**.

THE POTENTIAL FOR **ESCAPE** IS **CRUCIAL** FOR CREATING **DRAMA** (AS WITHOUT IT, THE MATCH MAY AS WELL BE CONSIDERED **OVER**).

THERE'S EVEN AN **ESTABLISHED** WAY TO **REVERSE** THE MOVE, BY ROLLING OVER ONTO ONE'S **STOMACH**.

IT'S A **BEAUTIFUL**, STRANGE BIT OF WRESTLING LOGIC THAT ENSURES THAT A VILLAIN CAN GET THEIR **COMEUPPANCE**, AND MOST IMPORTANTLY...

...THAT THE FANS GET TO SEE IT **HAPPEN**.

JAPAN HAS A **LONG** HISTORY WITH PROFESSIONAL WRESTLING, STRETCHING BACK TO ITS **ORIGINS** IN THE CARNIVAL CIRCUITS...

...AND FORMER SUMO WRESTLER **SORAKICHI MATSUDA**, WHO ARRIVED IN NEW YORK CITY IN **1883.**

MATSUDA PLAYED THE *"INVADING FOREIGNER,"* A DYNAMIC THAT WOULD LATER COME TO **DEFINE** JAPANESE WRESTLING.

THROUGHOUT THE **NORTHEAST** AND INTO THE **MIDWEST,** MATSUDA FACED CATCH CHAMPION **EDWIN BIBBY,** GRECO-ROMAN CHAMPION **WILLIAM MULDOON,** A YOUNG **FARMER BURNS,** AND OTHERS.

AS HE WRESTLED IN THE **1880s,** AND WAS **UNDOUBTEDLY** TALENTED, THERE'S A **POSSIBILITY** THAT **SOME** OF HIS MATCHES WERE **LEGIT.**

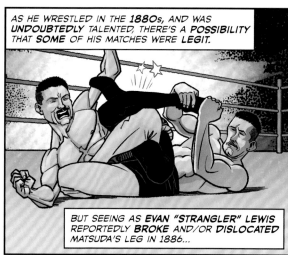

BUT SEEING AS **EVAN "STRANGLER" LEWIS** REPORTEDLY **BROKE** AND/OR **DISLOCATED** MATSUDA'S LEG IN 1886...

...ONLY FOR MATSUDA TO **RETURN** TO THE RING A **MONTH** LATER...IT SEEMS **UNLIKELY** THAT **ALL** HIS MATCHES WERE ON THE **UP-AND-UP.**

AFTER WITNESSING THE **GROWING** POPULARITY OF PROFESSIONAL WRESTLING IN **AMERICA,** MATSUDA ATTEMPTED TO BRING THE ONE TRUE SPORT **HOME** TO JAPAN.

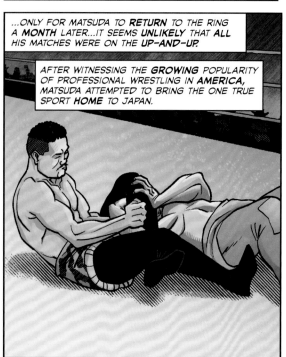

HIS EFFORTS AT PREACHING THE **GOOD WORD** OF PROFESSIONAL WRESTLING, HOWEVER, WERE **UNSUCCESSFUL.**

プロレス

TO POPULARIZE **PURORESU**--A PORTMANTEAU OF **"PROFESSIONAL WRESTLING"** FILTERED THROUGH **JAPANESE**--IT WOULD TAKE THE EFFORTS OF **ANOTHER** FORMER SUMO WRESTLER:

MITSUHIRO MOMOTA, BETTER KNOWN AS RIKIDŌZAN.

WHILE *MATSUDA* WAS A *FOREIGNER* IN THE *UNITED STATES*, MOMOTA WAS A FOREIGNER IN HIS OWN *COUNTRY*...

...BECAUSE WHEN MOMOTA WAS BORN IN 1924, IT WAS AS *KIM SIN-RAK,* IN WHAT IS NOW *NORTH KOREA.*

AT THAT TIME, THE KOREAN PENINSULA HAD BEEN UNDER *JAPANESE RULE* FOR *FOURTEEN* YEARS.

SO, WHILE MOMOTA WAS *TECHNICALLY* JAPANESE, HE WAS *CULTURALLY* KOREAN, CAUSING *PROBLEMS* IN THE *PROUDLY* JAPANESE, *TRADITIONALIST* SPORT OF *SUMO.*

THOUGH HE FOUND *SUCCESS,* REACHING THE RANK OF *SEKIWAKI,* SUMO'S *THIRD* HIGHEST...

...HE WAS *SUBJECTED* TO ANTI-KOREAN *RACISM,* TO WHICH SOME SOURCES ATTRIBUTE HIS 1950 *RETIREMENT* FROM SUMO.

THOUGH RIKIDŌZAN *HIMSELF* CLAIMED THE RETIREMENT WAS DUE TO *FINANCIAL* CONCERNS...

...IT'S *IMPORTANT* TO NOTE THAT HIS SUMO CAREER TOOK PLACE BETWEEN 1940 AND 1950, A DECADE THAT ALSO INCLUDED *WORLD WAR II.*

IT WAS A TIME OF *INTENSE* NATIONAL PRIDE AND *JINGOISM* FOR *JAPAN,* WHICH IS WHY HE TOOK THE *JAPANESE* NAME *RIKIDŌZAN.*

AND IT WAS WHY, WHEN HE MADE HIS **PROFESSIONAL WRESTLING** DEBUT IN 1951, RIKIDŌZAN POSITIONED HIMSELF AS **JAPANESE.**

FOLLOWING THEIR **DEFEAT** IN WORLD WAR II, THE JAPANESE PEOPLE WERE READY FOR A **HERO**, AND RIKIDŌZAN **PROUDLY** FILLED THAT ROLE.

HOW DID HE **DO** IT? IN MUCH THE SAME WAY THAT **CARLOS COLÓN** LATER DID IN PUERTO RICO:

BY BEATING UP A **PROCESSION** OF VILLAINOUS AMERICAN **GAIJIN**, WHICH IS JAPANESE FOR **FOREIGNERS.** MEN LIKE **THE DESTROYER.**

AND JUST AS RIKIDŌZAN CATERED TO HIS COUNTRY'S **NATIONALISM,** SO TOO DID **AMERICAN** PROMOTIONS CATER TO **THEIRS,** POSITIONING THE VISITING RIKIDŌZAN AS A **VILLAIN.**

ON **BOTH** SIDES OF THE PACIFIC, THE ONE TRUE SPORT **COOPTED** AND **MONETIZED** ITS AUDIENCES' MORE **XENOPHOBIC** TENDENCIES.

BUT THOUGH AMERICAN CROWDS **HATED** RIKIDŌZAN, LOU THESZ RESPECTED HIM ENOUGH TO WRESTLE TO DRAWS IN JAPAN WITH THE **NWA HEAVYWEIGHT TITLE** ON THE LINE.

THEIR MATCHES **POPULARIZED** WRESTLING IN JAPAN, WITH ONE GARNERING A **87.0** TELEVISION RATING-- THAT'S **87 PERCENT** OF TELEVISIONS IN THE COUNTRY!

AND IN 1958, RIKIDŌZAN **DEFEATED** THESZ FOR THE **NWA INTERNATIONAL HEAVYWEIGHT CHAMPIONSHIP.**

IT WAS A **NEW** TITLE, AND A **CRUCIAL** PART OF THE **BURGEONING** JAPANESE WRESTLING SCENE.

THE NWA INTERNATIONAL HEAVYWEIGHT CHAMPIONSHIP BECAME THE TOP TITLE IN RIKIDŌZAN'S PROMOTION, *NIHON PURORESU KYŌKAI...*

...WHICH IS TRANSLATED AS *JAPAN PRO WRESTLING ALLIANCE*, BUT TYPICALLY ABBREVIATED AS *JWA*.

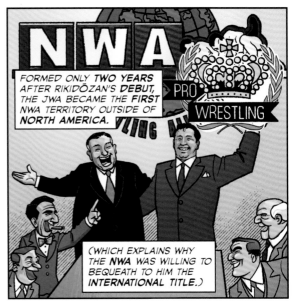

**NWA PRO WRESTLING**

FORMED ONLY *TWO YEARS* AFTER RIKIDŌZAN'S *DEBUT*, THE JWA BECAME THE *FIRST* NWA TERRITORY OUTSIDE OF *NORTH AMERICA.*

(WHICH EXPLAINS WHY THE *NWA* WAS WILLING TO BEQUEATH TO HIM THE *INTERNATIONAL TITLE.*)

THE ONE TRUE SPORT *EXPLODED* IN POPULARITY, DUE TO THE *INCREASING* AMOUNT OF TELEVISION OWNERS IN JAPAN...

...AS WELL AS RIKIDŌZAN BECOMING A *NATIONAL HERO* THROUGH HIS USE OF *VILLAINOUS GAIJIN...*

...AND STARS FROM THE WORLDS OF *SUMO* AND *JUDO*, LIKE *MASAHIKO KIMURA*, FOR WHOM THE *EPONYMOUS* ARM SUBMISSION IS NAMED.

THEIR FEUD WAS *PARTICULARLY* SIGNIFICANT, AS THE JUDOKA CLAIMED RIKIDŌZAN ATTACKED HIM *LEGITIMATELY.*

LATER, KIMURA *IMPLIED* THAT *RETRIBUTION* CAME IN 1963...

...WHEN A *YAKUZA* GANGSTER *STABBED* RIKIDŌZAN WITH A *KNIFE* SOAKED IN *URINE.* HE *DIED* ONE WEEK LATER.

THE *MURDER* HAS ALSO BEEN *ATTRIBUTED* TO RIKIDŌZAN'S OWN CONNECTIONS TO THE *YAKUZA*, WHO *INVESTED* IN PURORESU FOR *YEARS* TO COME.

DESPITE HIS EARLY, *TRAGIC* DEATH, RIKIDŌZAN'S *LEGACY* LIVED ON THROUGH TWO *LEGENDARY* STUDENTS...

# GIANT BABA

# ANTONIO INOKI

A FORMER **PITCHER** FOR THE **YOMIURI GIANTS**, THE **MASSIVE** SHOHEI BABA IS TYPICALLY VIEWED AS RIKIDŌZAN'S **PRIMARY** PROTÉGÉ...

...BUT HE WASN'T RIKIDŌZAN'S **ONLY** STUDENT, AS HE **ALSO** TRAINED PIONEERING MIXED MARTIAL ARTIST **KANJI INOKI**, WHO TOOK HIS RING NAME FROM **ANTONINO ROCCA**.

TOGETHER, BOTH MEN WOULD HAVE AN **ENORMOUS**, LASTING IMPACT ON TWO STRAINS OF **PURORESU**, WHICH WERE BUILT **LARGELY** AROUND THE **WRESTLERS'** DIFFERENCES.

BILLED AT 6' 10" AND 298 LBS.*

PLAYED **BASEBALL** FOR FIVE YEARS, MOSTLY IN THE **MINOR LEAGUES**.

FOUNDED **ALL JAPAN PRO WRESTLING**.

PROMOTED "KING'S ROAD" WRESTLING, TAKING CUES FROM **AMERICAN-STYLE** STORYTELLING OF THE PERIOD.

BILLED AT 6' 3" AND 224 LBS.

TRAINED IN **CATCH WRESTLING** WITH A STUDENT OF WIGAN'S **SNAKE PIT**.

FOUNDED **NEW JAPAN PRO-WRESTLING**.

PROMOTED "STRONG STYLE" WRESTLING, FOCUSING ON **REALISM**.

* REPORTEDLY DUE TO **ACROMEGALY**, THE SAME CONDITION THAT AFFECTED **ANDRE THE GIANT**, THE **SWEDISH ANGEL**, AND THE **BIG SHOW**.

IN THE WAKE OF **RIKIDŌZAN'S** DEATH, BABA AND INOKI BOTH **STEPPED UP**, BUT INOKI SOON FOUND THAT HE COULD NOT ESCAPE BABA'S **HUMONGOUS** SHADOW.

SO IN 1966, HE LEFT **JWA** FOR AN **AMERICAN** EXCURSION AND THEN JOINED THE RIVAL **TOKYO PRO WRESTLING**, BEFORE **RETURNING** TO JWA THE FOLLOWING YEAR.

UPON INOKI'S **RETURN**, HE WAS PLACED IN A **TAG TEAM** WITH BABA, WHICH BECAME THE **FOCAL POINT** OF THE JWA.

SOON AFTER, THE TEAM DEFEATED **BILL WATTS & TARZAN TYLER** TO WIN THE **NWA INTERNATIONAL TAG TEAM TITLES**, WHICH THEN BECAME JAPAN-EXCLUSIVE.

BUT INOKI WANTED **MORE**. HE WANTED TO **CONTROL** THE ENTIRE JWA.

IN 1971, HIS TAKEOVER PLANS WERE **DISCOVERED** AND HE WAS **FIRED** FROM THE PROMOTION.

THE FOLLOWING YEAR, INOKI STARTED HIS **OWN** PROMOTION, **NEW JAPAN PRO-WRESTLING**...

...WHERE HE WOULD **CULTIVATE** AND **POPULARIZE** HIS OWN UNIQUE VISION FOR **PURORESU** UNDER THE NAME OF "**STRONG STYLE**" WRESTLING.

MEANWHILE, JWA WAS **CRUMBLING**. IN 1972, BABA FOLLOWED INOKI'S LEAD, LEAVING TO CREATE **ALL JAPAN PRO WRESTLING**.

BABA TOOK WITH HIM RIKIDŌZAN'S SONS, **MITSUO** AND **YOSHIHIRO**, THE **TAG TITLES**, AND, MOST **IMPORTANTLY**...

...JWA'S MEMBERSHIP IN THE **NATIONAL WRESTLING ALLIANCE.**

THE NWA WAS THRILLED TO MAINTAIN A PRESENCE IN **JAPAN,** AND BABA WAS EAGER FOR WHAT THE GROUP COULD OFFER HIS **ALL JAPAN PRO WRESTLING.**

THOUGH AJPW EMPLOYED **NUMEROUS** JAPANESE WRESTLERS, IT WAS RIKIDŌZAN'S **"FOREIGN INVADER"** STRATEGY THAT STILL DREW MOST **RELIABLY.**

AND THE NWA OFFERED BABA A STEADY STREAM OF **VILLAINOUS GAIJIN** TO DEFEAT, EVEN SENDING OVER **NWA CHAMPIONS** LIKE **JACK BRISCO, RIC FLAIR,** AND **HARLEY RACE.**

THE **STRATEGY** WORKED AS WELL AS IT HAD FOR **RIKIDŌZAN,** ESPECIALLY WHEN THE WORLD'S MOST **COVETED** WRESTLING TITLE WAS ON THE LINE.

BABA EVEN BECAME THE FIRST **JAPANESE** WRESTLER TO WIN THE **NWA WORLD HEAVYWEIGHT TITLE,** AND LATER WON IT **TWICE** MORE, BOTH TIMES FROM **HARLEY RACE.**

WHILE ALL JAPAN **BEGAN** BY USING RIKIDŌZAN'S **FOREIGN INVADER** BOOKING, THEY SLOWLY BUT STEADILY **CHANGED** COURSE...

...AS GAIJIN TALENT SUCH AS AMERICA'S **DORY FUNK, JR.,** AND **TERRY FUNK,** AND MEXICO'S **MIL MASCARAS** WON OVER THE AUDIENCE, BECOMING **HUGE** STARS IN JAPAN.

IT WAS FROM THESE **WESTERN** WRESTLERS THAT BABA'S **"KING'S ROAD"** STYLE EVOLVED WITH A FOCUS ON **AMERICAN-STYLE** GRAPPLING AND STORYTELLING.

THE APPROACH PLACED MORE **EMPHASIS** ON THE **NARRATIVE** OF INDIVIDUAL MATCHES, AS WELL AS OVERARCHING **STORIES** THAT COULD LAST **MONTHS,** AS BABA AND RACE'S DID.

WHILE BABA'S ALL JAPAN FOCUSED ON **NARRATIVE DRAMA**, INOKI'S **NEW JAPAN** FOCUSED ON **SOMETHING ELSE...**

...REALISM.

EAGER TO **DIFFERENTIATE** HIMSELF FROM BABA, INOKI LEANED INTO WHAT MADE HIM **SPECIAL**: HIS BACKGROUND IN **KARATE**.

HIS **"STRONG STYLE"** WRESTLING AMPED UP THE **REALISM** OF MATCHES BY UTILIZING MORE MARTIAL ARTS–INFLUENCED **KICKS** AND **STRIKES**.

THE APPROACH LED TO A 1976 MATCH AGAINST **MUHAMMAD ALI**, WHICH MADE INOKI A MIXED MARTIAL ARTS **PIONEER**..

...THOUGH THE MATCH ITSELF WAS **PROFOUNDLY** DULL, DUE TO RULES THAT SERIOUSLY **HINDERED** INOKI'S **KICKING** AND **GRAPPLING**.

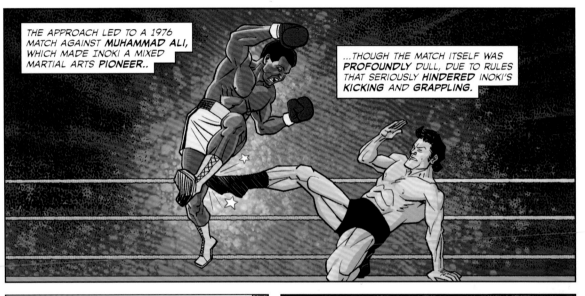

REALISM AND PERCEIVED **TOUGHNESS** BECAME SO **INGRAINED** IN STRONG STYLE WRESTLING THAT PROMOTIONS **ENCOURAGED** WRESTLERS TO COMPETE IN **MIXED MARTIAL ARTS** BOUTS.

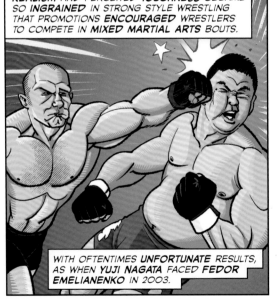

WITH OFTENTIMES **UNFORTUNATE** RESULTS, AS WHEN **YUJI NAGATA** FACED **FEDOR EMELIANENKO** IN 2003.

STRONG STYLE DREW INFLUENCE FROM NOT ONLY **KARATE** AND **JUDO**, BUT ALSO THE **WESTERN** MARTIAL ART OF **CATCH WRESTLING**.

THIS CONTRIBUTION CAME COURTESY OF THE MAN INOKI FACED IN THE MAIN EVENT OF THE **FIRST** NJPW EVENT: **KARL GOTCH**.

BORN **CHARLES ISTAZ** IN **BELGIUM**, GOTCH EXCELLED IN **GRECO-ROMAN WRESTLING**.

AND HE TOOK JUST AS QUICKLY TO **CATCH WRESTLING** UNDER THE TUTELAGE OF **BILLY RILEY** IN WIGAN'S RENOWNED **SNAKE PIT**.

LIKE **MANY** BRITISH WRESTLERS IN THE 1950s, HE TRAVELED TO **AMERICA**, AND BEGAN WRESTLING UNDER THE NAME **GOTCH**, A NOD TO THE LEGENDARY CHAMPION.

THIS **NOM DE GUERRE**, AS WELL AS GOTCH'S YOUTH IN **HAMBURG**, EXPLAINS HOW THE GERMAN SUPLEX CAME TO BE NAMED FOR A **BELGIAN** GRAPPLER.

IN 1962, GOTCH RAN **AFOUL** OF PROMOTERS AFTER **INJURING** NWA CHAMPION **BUDDY ROGERS** IN A LEGIT ALTERCATION.

OF COURSE, IT DIDN'T **HELP** THAT GOTCH'S APPROACH WASN'T **FLASHY** ENOUGH FOR WHERE **AMERICAN** WRESTLING WAS HEADING IN THE 1960s.

BUT **JAPANESE** AUDIENCES **ADORED** GOTCH, WHO BROUGHT TO STRONG STYLE WRESTLING HIS CATCH WRESTLING **SUBMISSIONS**, AS WELL AS HIS OWN VARIATION OF THE **PILEDRIVER**.

THOUGH **UNDERAPPRECIATED** IN **AMERICAN** WRESTLING, GOTCH BECAME A **LEGEND** IN JAPAN, WHERE HE IS KNOWN AS **KAMISAMA**, OR **GOD OF WRESTLING**.

NOT ONLY DID GOTCH TRAIN **INOKI** IN CATCH WRESTLING, BUT IN THE **1970s** HE BECAME THE **TRAINER** FOR ALL OF **NJPW**.

THROUGH **GOTCH**, THAT REGIONAL FORM OF ENGLISH **GRAPPLING** CONTINUED TO INFLUENCE **GENERATIONS** OF WRESTLERS ON THE OTHER SIDE OF THE **GLOBE**.

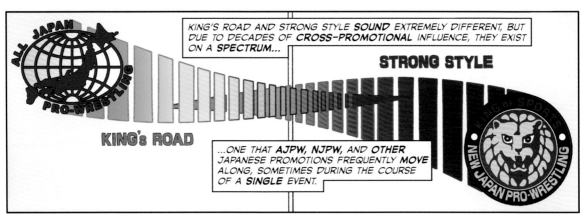

KING'S ROAD AND STRONG STYLE **SOUND** EXTREMELY DIFFERENT, BUT DUE TO DECADES OF **CROSS-PROMOTIONAL** INFLUENCE, THEY EXIST ON A **SPECTRUM**...

**STRONG STYLE**

KING's ROAD

...ONE THAT **AJPW, NJPW,** AND **OTHER** JAPANESE PROMOTIONS FREQUENTLY **MOVE** ALONG, SOMETIMES DURING THE COURSE OF A **SINGLE** EVENT.

NO MATTER **WHERE** THEY FALL, HOWEVER, **MOST** PURORESU PROMOTIONS CULTIVATE A MORE **SPORT-BASED** PRESENTATION THAN **AMERICAN** WRESTLING...

TATSUMI FUJINAMI

...AND OUTSIDE OF THE **FOREIGN INVADER** TROPE, THE FORM DOESN'T PLACE AS MUCH EMPHASIS ON **FACE** AND **HEEL** ROLES.

INSTEAD OF **MORALITY PLAYS,** JAPANESE WRESTLING TRADITIONALLY FOCUSES ON WRESTLERS' **"FIGHTING SPIRIT."**

RIKI CHOSHU

(THOUGH THERE ARE **NOTABLE** EXCEPTIONS TO THIS **GENERALIZATION,** LIKE THE DECIDEDLY **OUTLANDISH** DDT PRO-WRESTLING.)

AS A WHOLE, PURORESU IS SEEN AS MORE **GROUNDED** THAN OTHER FORMS OF **THE ONE TRUE SPORT.**

THIS DISTINCTION IMPACTS **RING GEAR** AND **APPEARANCES,** WHAT **MOVES** ARE USED, AND, MOST IMPORTANTLY, HOW MATCHES ARE **PACED** AND **PUT TOGETHER.**

(CHOSHU INVENTED THE **SASORI-GATAME,** BUT IT'S BETTER KNOWN AS THE **SHARPSHOOTER.**)

THIS DIFFERENCE **EVEN** EXTENDS TO PURORESU **AUDIENCES,** WHICH ARE MORE **RESTRAINED** THAN THEIR **WESTERN** COUNTERPARTS.

THOUGH LIKE **MOST** REGIONAL DIFFERENCES IN THE ONE TRUE SPORT, THESE **BROAD** CHARACTERIZATIONS ARE BECOMING **LESS ACCURATE** BY THE YEAR.

FIGHTING SPIRIT IS AN ENORMOUSLY IMPORTANT CONCEPT IN PURORESU, AS IT FORMS THE BASIS FOR TALENTS GETTING OVER.

IT ALSO EXPLAINS HOW TWO VICIOUS, MONSTROUS GAIJIN VILLAINS LIKE STAN HANSEN AND BRUISER BRODY...

...COULD BECOME BELOVED FIGURES IN JAPAN, NOT JUST DESPITE THEIR BRUTALITY, BUT BECAUSE OF IT, AS IT HELPED THEM PERSEVERE.

EVEN IF PERSEVERING MEANT BEATING THE TAR OUT OF JAPANESE HEROES LIKE GIANT BABA AND JUMBO TSURUTA.

THROUGH AJPW'S NWA CONNECTIONS AND NJPW'S PARTNERSHIP WITH WWWF/WWF, A PROCESSION OF GAIJIN HEAVYWEIGHTS MADE THEIR WAY TO JAPAN...

HULK HOGAN

ANDRE THE GIANT

ROAD WARRIOR HAWK

ROAD WARRIOR ANIMAL

TIGER JEET SINGH

...MOST STARTED AS VILLAINS, BUT THE BEST OF THEM WON OVER CROWDS WITH THEIR FIGHTING SPIRIT TO BECAME HEROES AND MASSIVE STARS.

BUT PERHAPS EVEN MORE INFLUENTIAL WERE THE GAIJIN JUNIOR HEAVYWEIGHTS, LIKE DYNAMITE KID.

IN HIS LEGENDARY FEUD AGAINST TIGER MASK, BEGINNING IN 1981, DYNAMITE COMBINED HIS URGENT, INTENSE, HARD-HITTING CATCH BACKGROUND...

...WITH TIGER MASK'S FAST-PACED, ACROBATIC MANEUVERS, EQUALLY INFLUENCED BY MARTIAL ARTS AND LUCHA LIBRE.

TOGETHER, THE TWO CODIFIED AND POPULARIZED JUNIOR HEAVYWEIGHT WRESTLING.

SATORU SAYAMA, THE FUTURE TIGER MASK, WAS SENT ABROAD TO **MEXICO** AND **ENGLAND**, WHERE HE APPEARED ON **WORLD OF SPORT** AS SAMMY LEE.

ON HIS EXCURSION, SAYAMA **BLENDED** HIS **NJPW DOJO** TRAINING WITH BRITISH **CATCH WRESTLING** AND HIGH-FLYING **LUCHA LIBRE** STYLES.

HE **RETURNED** TO JAPAN AS A HYBRID TALENT, TAKING ON THE NEW IDENTITY OF **TIGER MASK!**

BASED ON A CHARACTER FROM **IKKI KAJIWARA** AND **NAOKI TSUJI'S** MANGA, THE GIMMICK WAS MEANT TO APPEAL TO **YOUNGER FANS.**

**MASKED** WRESTLERS WERE NOTHING **NEW** IN JAPAN, BUT THE **ANIME** TIE-IN MADE THE CONCEPT EXPLICITLY **JAPANESE.**

BUT WITH SAYAMA'S **INNOVATIVE** STYLE, COMBINED WITH HIS **DYNAMITE KID** FEUD, TIGER MASK APPEALED TO **EVERYONE.**

TIGER MASK BECAME **SO** POPULAR THAT THE GIMMICK WAS CONTINUED THROUGH **MULTIPLE** WRESTLERS.

THERE HAVE BEEN **SIX**--ALL **JAPANESE**--TIGER MASKS, INCLUDING **MITSUHARU MISAWA, YOSHIHIRO YAMAZAKI,** AND **KOTA IBUSHI.**

AND THERE HAVE BEEN **SEVEN**--MOSTLY **GAIJIN**--WRESTLERS TO PORTRAY THE VILLAINOUS **BLACK TIGER,** INCLUDING **MARK "ROLLERBALL" ROCCO, EDDIE GUERRERO,** AND **ROCKY ROMERO.**

NJPW FOLLOWED UP ON **TIGER MASK'S** SUCCESS IN 1988 WITH **JUSHIN LIGER,** INSPIRED BY **GO NAGAI'S** ANIME.

TRAINED BY **STU HART,** LIGER'S SPECTACULAR **APPEARANCE** AND **SHOOTING STAR PRESS** THRILLED AUDIENCES IN JAPAN AND AMERICA, DUE TO A STINT IN **WCW.**

SENDING YOUNGER TALENTS TO **OTHER** PROMOTIONS FOR **"SEASONING"** IS A PRACTICE STILL UTILIZED BY **PURORESU** PROMOTIONS TODAY.

CURRENT NJPW STARS **KAZUCHIKA OKADA** AND **TETSUYA NAITO** SPENT TIME IN **AMERICA'S** TNA AND **MEXICO'S** CMLL, RESPECTIVELY.

THESE **EXCURSIONS** EXPOSE WRESTLERS TO OTHER **STYLES** OF WRESTLING...

...ALLOWING THEM TO **RETURN** HOME AS ENTIRELY **NEW** WRESTLERS, WITH JAPANESE FANS LARGELY **UNEXPOSED** TO THEIR **LEARNING PROCESS.**

THE **OTHER** BENEFIT OF JAPAN'S FREQUENT WRESTLER **EXPORTS** IS THE SPREADING OF **PURORESU** STYLES AND TECHNIQUES.

THE **GREAT KABUKI** ARRIVED IN TEXAS'S WCCW IN 1981, SHOCKING CROWDS WITH HIS **SAVAGERY**, HIS **MARTIAL ARTS**–BASED APPROACH, AND THE **POISON MIST** ATTACK THAT HE **INNOVATED.**

"GENTLEMAN" CHRIS ADAMS

EIGHT YEARS LATER, WHILE IN WCW, **KEIJI MUTOH** BECAME **THE GREAT MUTA**, KABUKI'S KAYFABE SON, WHO, **NATURALLY**, ALSO BLEW **POISON MIST.**

STING

AN **UPDATED** VERSION OF A **GIMMICK** GIVEN TO A **JAPANESE** WRESTLER IN AN **AMERICAN** PROMOTION MADE MUTOH ONE OF JAPAN'S MOST **POPULAR** WRESTLERS UPON HIS **RETURN** HOME.

**ÚLTIMO DRAGÓN** NOT ONLY LEARNED **LUCHA LIBRE** IN MEXICO, BUT HE STARTED HIS OWN **PROMOTION** THERE AND TRAINED WRESTLERS IN HIS **HYBRID** STYLE...

...THOUGH HE IS PROBABLY **BEST** KNOWN IN SOME CIRCLES AS THE GUY WHO HELD **TEN** CHAMPIONSHIPS **SIMULTANEOUSLY** BY WINNING THE **J-CROWN** TOURNAMENT.

IN 1989, FORMER AJPW WRESTLER **ATSUSHI ONITA** FORMED **FRONTIER MARTIAL ARTS WRESTLING**, BETTER KNOWN AS **FMW**.

BUT FMW DIDN'T FOCUS ON **KING'S ROAD** OR **STRONG STYLE**, IT OFFERED **SOMETHING ELSE** ENTIRELY:

**DEATH MATCHES.** ONITA HAD WITNESSED THE CHAOS OF **PUERTO RICAN** WRESTLING, AS WELL AS **HARDCORE** MATCHES IN **MEMPHIS**...

...BUT IN FMW HE TOOK THINGS TO **ANOTHER** LEVEL, FEATURING NOT JUST **CAGES** AND **WEAPONS** AND **FIRE** AND **BARBED WIRE**, BUT **EXPLOSIVES** AS WELL.

ONITA'S **RETIREMENT MATCH** WAS INSIDE A **STEEL CAGE**, WITH **BARBED WIRE** INSTEAD OF ROPES AND, FOR GOOD MEASURE, AN **EXPLODING** RING, AGAINST UP-AND-COMER **HAYABUSA**.

AS FMW TRANSITIONED **AWAY** FROM DEATH MATCHES IN 1995, THE HIGH-FLYING HAYABUSA BECAME AN EVEN **BIGGER** STAR, BEFORE BEING **TRAGICALLY** PARALYZED IN AN IN-RING ACCIDENT.

BUT THOUGH **FMW** WAS FINISHED WITH **DEATH MATCHES**, OTHER PROMOTIONS, LIKE **BIG JAPAN PRO WRESTLING** AND **ECW** IN PHILADELPHIA, WERE JUST GETTING **STARTED.**

ECW EVEN BROUGHT IN JAPANESE WRESTLERS LIKE **TAJIRI** AND **MASATO TANAKA**, AS WELL AS AMERICANS WHO HAD FOUND **SUCCESS** IN JAPANESE DEATH MATCHES, LIKE **MICK FOLEY** AND **SABU**.

PRIOR TO 1995, FMW **ALSO** GAVE FEMALE WRESTLERS A CHANCE TO GET **BRUTAL**, WITH A DIVISION **DOMINATED** BY MEGUMI KUDO.

SHE WRESTLED HER **RETIREMENT MATCH** AGAINST **SHARK TSUCHIYA**, WHO SET HER ABLAZE IN A **NO-ROPES EXPLODING BARBED WIRE DEATH MATCH.**

TYPICALLY, WOMEN'S WRESTLING, OR *JOSHI PURORESU*, HAS BEEN FEATURED IN PROMOTIONS WITH ONLY WOMEN.

THAT'S NOT TO SAY THAT WOMEN'S WRESTLING IN JAPAN IS *LOOKED DOWN* UPON, HOWEVER, AS IT'S BEEN *FAR MORE* RESPECTED, FOR *FAR LONGER*, THAN ELSEWHERE.

WHILE OTHER COUNTRIES HAVE *TRADITIONALLY* TREATED WOMEN'S WRESTLING AS A *TITILLATING* SIDESHOW, *PURORESU* HAS POSITIONED IT AS JUST AS *SERIOUS* AND *IMPORTANT* AS MEN'S WRESTLING.

JOSHI WAS FAR, FAR AHEAD OF THE CURVE IN TERMS OF *VALUING* FEMALE WRESTLERS-- LIKE *MANAMI TOYOTA* AND *AJA KONG*--FOR THEIR TALENT AND NOT THEIR *SEX APPEAL*.

BY THE 1990s, JOSHI HAD BECOME, IN *SOME* CIRCLES, MORE *WELL-RESPECTED* THAN MEN'S WRESTLING, DUE IN LARGE PART TO THE WOMEN OF *ALL JAPAN WOMEN'S PRO-WRESTLING*, OR *AJW*.

KYOKO INOUE

BULL NAKANO

DUMP MATSUMOTO

DYNAMITE KANSAI

ALONG WITH *TOYOTA* AND *KONG*, THEY USED AN ABUNDANCE OF *PHYSICALITY* TO MAKE UP FOR THEIR *SMALLER* SIZE COMPARED TO *MALE* WRESTLERS.

JOSHI FIRST STARTED LEAVING ITS MARK ON *AMERICAN* WRESTLING IN 1987, WHEN THE *JUMPING BOMB ANGELS*, NORIYO TATENO AND ITSUKI YAMAZAKI, APPEARED IN *WWF*.

AND IN 1994, THE PROMOTION BROUGHT IN *BULL NAKANO* TO FEUD WITH FORMER ALL JAPAN WOMEN'S *GAIJIN* STAR *ALUNDRA BLAYZE*.

MORE RECENTLY, WOMEN'S WRESTLING HAS EXPERIENCED A *SURGE* IN POPULARITY IN AMERICA, DUE IN NO SMALL PART TO *JOSHI-INFLUENCED INDIE PROMOTIONS...

...AND THE SUCCESS OF *ASUKA*, WHO WAS BROUGHT INTO WWE'S *DEVELOPMENTAL* PROGRAM IN 2015 AFTER MORE THAN A *DECADE* AS A JOSHI STAR.

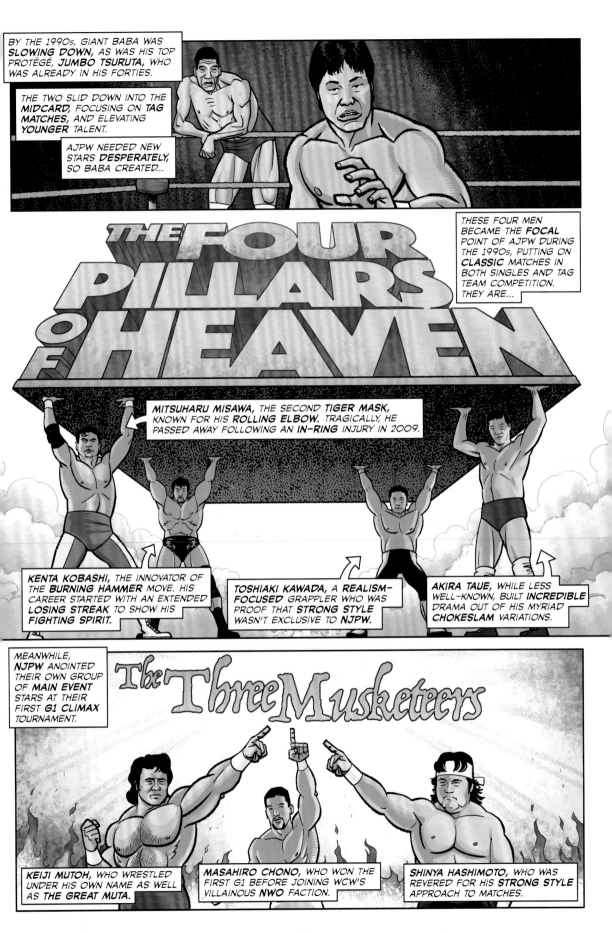

BY THE 1990s, GIANT BABA WAS **SLOWING DOWN,** AS WAS HIS TOP PROTÉGÉ, **JUMBO TSURUTA,** WHO WAS ALREADY IN HIS FORTIES.

THE TWO SLID DOWN INTO THE **MIDCARD,** FOCUSING ON **TAG MATCHES,** AND ELEVATING **YOUNGER** TALENT.

AJPW NEEDED NEW STARS **DESPERATELY,** SO BABA CREATED...

# THE FOUR PILLARS OF HEAVEN

THESE FOUR MEN BECAME THE **FOCAL** POINT OF AJPW DURING THE 1990s, PUTTING ON **CLASSIC** MATCHES IN BOTH SINGLES AND TAG TEAM COMPETITION. THEY ARE...

**MITSUHARU MISAWA,** THE SECOND **TIGER MASK,** KNOWN FOR HIS **ROLLING ELBOW.** TRAGICALLY, HE PASSED AWAY FOLLOWING AN **IN-RING** INJURY IN 2009.

**KENTA KOBASHI,** THE INNOVATOR OF THE **BURNING HAMMER** MOVE. HIS CAREER STARTED WITH AN EXTENDED **LOSING STREAK** TO SHOW HIS **FIGHTING SPIRIT.**

**TOSHIAKI KAWADA,** A REALISM-FOCUSED GRAPPLER WHO WAS PROOF THAT **STRONG STYLE** WASN'T EXCLUSIVE TO **NJPW.**

**AKIRA TAUE,** WHILE LESS WELL-KNOWN, BUILT **INCREDIBLE** DRAMA OUT OF HIS MYRIAD **CHOKESLAM** VARIATIONS.

MEANWHILE, **NJPW** ANOINTED THEIR OWN GROUP OF **MAIN EVENT** STARS AT THEIR FIRST **G1 CLIMAX** TOURNAMENT.

# The Three Musketeers

**KEIJI MUTOH,** WHO WRESTLED UNDER HIS OWN NAME AS WELL AS **THE GREAT MUTA.**

**MASAHIRO CHONO,** WHO WON THE FIRST G1 BEFORE JOINING WCW'S VILLAINOUS **NWO** FACTION.

**SHINYA HASHIMOTO,** WHO WAS REVERED FOR HIS **STRONG STYLE** APPROACH TO MATCHES.

THE 1990s WERE AN **INCREDIBLE** TIME FOR **PURORESU**, WITH AJW, AJPW, NJPW, AND FMW FIRING ON **ALL** CYLINDERS.

BUT IT WASN'T JUST **JAPANESE** AUDIENCES THAT THRILLED TO THESE INTENSE, **BELIEVABLE** MATCHES.

WRESTLING FANS IN OTHER COUNTRIES HAD LONG **HEARD** AND **READ** ABOUT **PURORESU**, BUT NOW THEY HAD AN OPPORTUNITY TO ACTUALLY **SEE** IT.

AN OPPORTUNITY MADE POSSIBLE BY THE **GROWING** INFLUENCE OF INTERNET **MESSAGE BOARDS** AND **CHATROOMS**, AS WELL AS AN **ACTIVE** VHS TAPE-TRADING SCENE.

**PURORESU** BECAME VIEWED AS A **PURER** FORM OF WRESTLING, AS IT TYPICALLY **ESCHEWED** THE **HISTRIONICS** AND **SPECTACLE** THAT HAS CAUSED AMERICAN WRESTLING TO BE SO OFTEN **DERIDED.**

SUPER J-CUP 1994

VHS TAPES OF **INCREDIBLE** MATCHES TRAVELED EVERYWHERE, BUT PERHAPS NO EVENT WAS AS **INFLUENTIAL** AS NJPW'S FIRST **SUPER J-CUP** IN 1994.

THE **JUNIOR HEAVYWEIGHT** TOURNAMENT WAS A LOOK INTO THE FUTURE OF WRESTLING, **BLENDING** CATCH, LUCHA LIBRE, STRONG STYLE, AND **MORE.**

IT FEATURED **EDDIE GUERRERO** AS BLACK TIGER, **JUSHIN THUNDER LIGER,** FUTURE NJPW BOOKER **GEDO,** WCW CRUISERWEIGHT **DEAN MALENKO**...

...LUCHADOR **NEGRO CASAS,** HAYABUSA, THE GREAT **SASUKE,** AND CHRIS BENOIT AS WILD PEGASUS.

ALL OF THAT **TAPE TRADING** ENDED UP INFLUENCING **GENERATIONS** OF WRESTLERS, AS PROMOTIONS LIKE **RING OF HONOR** IN THE 2000s BEGAN DISPLAYING A HEAVY **PURORESU** INFLUENCE...

...WHILE ALSO EMPLOYING **JAPANESE** WRESTLERS LIKE **KENTA** (THE FUTURE HIDEO ITAMI), AS IN HIS 2006 MATCH AGAINST **BRYAN DANIELSON** (THE FUTURE **DANIEL BRYAN**) AND SAMOA JOE.

PRESENTLY, JAPAN BOASTS A **SHOCKING** AMOUNT OF WRESTLING, WITH PROMOTIONS FOCUSING ON **EVERY VARIETY** OF THE ONE TRUE SPORT IMAGINABLE.

BUT THE CURRENT LEADER IS, WITHOUT A DOUBT, **NEW JAPAN PRO-WRESTLING.**

THE PROMOTION'S **ASCENSION** BEGAN IN THE 2000s, WITH THE MINTING OF THREE **NEW** STARS:

# The NEW Three Musketeers

SHINSUKE NAKAMURA, THE "**KING OF STRONG STYLE**," WHOSE FLASHY **CHARISMA** SAW HIM SNATCHED UP BY **WWE.**

**HIROSHI TANAHASHI,** WHO BECAME NJPW'S **TOP** AND MOST **RELIABLE** PERFORMER, THEIR **ACE.**

**KATSUYORI SHIBATA,** A **STRONG STYLE** GRAPPLER, WHO RETURNED TO WRESTLING AFTER AN **MMA** STINT ONLY TO BECOME A **VICTIM** OF HIS **HARD-HITTING** STYLE.

BUT THINGS WERE KICKED INTO **HIGH GEAR** IN THE 2010s, ONCE FORMER TAG TEAM PARTNERS **GEDO & JADO** WERE MADE THE PROMOTION'S **BOOKERS.**

THE **WELL-TRAVELED** WRESTLERS DID WHAT JAPANESE WRESTLING HAS **ALWAYS** DONE: THEY TOOK THREADS OF **DIFFERENT** TRADITIONS AND WOVE THEM INTO SOMETHING **NEW.**

WHILE **STRONG STYLE** IS STILL **PROMINENT,** IT'S NOT THE PROMOTION'S **ONLY** FOCUS, AS IT HAS LEANED INTO **STORYTELLING** APPROACHES THAT ARE MORE **KING'S ROAD** OR EVEN **AMERICAN.**

AND THERE IS NO **CLEARER** EXAMPLE OF THAT APPROACH THAN THE **MASSIVE** SUCCESS OF THE **BULLET CLUB.**

THE BULLET CLUB IS A **GAIJIN** HEEL FACTION THAT IS **HEAVILY** INFLUENCED BY WCW'S **NEW WORLD ORDER**, WHICH ITSELF WAS **INSPIRED** BY A 1996 NJPW STORYLINE.

THE FACTION PLAYED OFF **NOSTALGIA**, THE **FOREIGN INVADER** TROPE, AND A LOVE OF **COOL VILLAINS**. IT HAD **EVERYTHING**, AND PEOPLE ON **BOTH** SIDES OF THE PACIFIC RESPONDED EN MASSE.

THE BULLET CLUB WENT **MAINSTREAM** IN AMERICA WITH WWE'S **HIRING** OF A. J. STYLES, FINN BALOR, KARL ANDERSON, AND LUKE GALLOWS, AND THE COLOSSAL SUCCESS OF MATT & NICK JACKSON, THE **YOUNG BUCKS**, IN ROH AND ON THE **INDEPENDENT** CIRCUIT.

HOWEVER, EVEN WITH THE **LOSS** OF SO MANY BULLET CLUB MEMBERS, NJPW DIDN'T **HURT** FOR TALENT-- IT STILL HAD THE RAINMAKER, **KAZUCHIKA OKADA**...

...WHO WAS THE **FOCUS** OF A YEARS-LONG BUILD THAT **ELEVATED** THE MASSIVE, PRETERNATURALLY **TALENTED** YOUNG WRESTLER INTO NJPW'S **TOP STAR**.

NJPW EVEN FOUND A **PERFECT RIVAL** FOR OKADA IN CANADA NATIVE AND BULLET CLUB MEMBER **KENNY OMEGA**.

THE PROMOTION ALSO BOASTS A WEALTH OF OTHER **SEASONED-ABROAD** TALENT, LIKE THE MEMBERS OF **LOS INGOBERNABLES DE JAPON**...

TETSUYA NAITO

EVIL

BUSHI

SANADA

HIROMU TAKAHASHI

...THE **JAPANESE** CHAPTER OF THE VILLAINOUS **LOS INGOBERNABLES** FACTION THAT ORIGINATED IN MEXICO'S CMLL (DISCUSSED IN CHAPTER 4).

NJPW HAS GROWN TO BE SECOND ONLY TO **WWE** IN GLOBAL **POPULARITY**, WITH A **WEEKLY** AMERICAN **CABLE** SHOW, A PARTNERSHIP WITH ROH, AND **THEIR OWN** AMERICAN EVENTS.

FROM A **FORM** OF WRESTLING **BASED** ON **XENOPHOBIA**, PURORESU HAS EVOLVED INTO A **SYNTHESIS** OF MULTIPLE **INTERNATIONAL** TRADITIONS.

WHEN ASKED TO DESCRIBE HOW **"A WRESTLER"** LOOKS, MOST PEOPLE WILL COME BACK WITH SOMETHING **LOUD, GARISH,** AND LACKING IN **SUBTLETY.** IN OTHER WORDS...A **GIMMICK.**

"MACHO MAN" RANDY SAVAGE

BUT A GIMMICK DOES **A LOT** MORE THAN SIMPLY **GRAB** A VIEWER'S ATTENTION (THOUGH WHEN DONE **WELL,** IT CERTAINLY DOES THAT **TOO**).

A **GIMMICK** IS VISUAL SHORTHAND. IT'S A WELL-CURATED **AESTHETIC** THAT TELLS AUDIENCES **EXACTLY** HOW TO FEEL ABOUT A WRESTLER BEFORE A MATCH EVEN **STARTS.**

THE ROCK 'N' ROLL EXPRESS

**GOOD** LOOKING, **SMILING** WRESTLERS WITH **COOL MUSIC?** GO AHEAD AND **CHEER!**

BUT IF IT'S A **SCOWLING** MONSTER, WITH AN ARROGANT, **BIG-MOUTHED** MANAGER? YOU'RE **SUPPOSED** TO WANT TO SEE THEM GET **BEATEN UP.**

A **GOOD** GIMMICK IS A **GESAMTKUNSTWERK**--AN ALL-ENCOMPASSING WORK OF ART THAT INCLUDES **LOOKS, MOVEMENT,** TONE OF **VOICE, WRESTLING** STYLE, **ATTIRE,** AND **MORE.**

KING KONG BUNDY

BOBBY "THE BRAIN" HEENAN

GIMMICKS ALSO WORK TO SET UP **EXPECTATIONS** THAT CAN THEN BE **DELIVERED UPON...**

...**DENIED,** OR EVEN COMPLETELY **SUBVERTED.** WHICH IS HOW A **MEAN,** VICIOUS, **FOUL-MOUTHED,** VIOLENT **REDNECK** LIKE "STONE COLD" STEVE AUSTIN...

...COULD BECOME ONE OF THE **BIGGEST,** MOST **POPULAR,** MOST **BELOVED** BABYFACES IN PROFESSIONAL WRESTLING **HISTORY.**

AFTER BUYING **WWF** FROM HIS FATHER IN **1982**, VINCENT KENNEDY MCMAHON GREW THE REGIONAL OPERATION INTO THE **LARGEST** WRESTLING PROMOTION THE WORLD HAD **EVER** SEEN.

HIS **CONTRIBUTIONS** TO WRESTLING ARE **IMMENSE**, BUT MUCH OF WRESTLING **FANDOM** STILL SEES HIM...

...AS A **VILLAIN**. SOME OF THIS CHARACTERIZATION IS DUE TO MCMAHON'S **LATER** ON-CAMERA ROLE (SEE PAGE 138), BUT **MUCH** OF IT COMES FROM HIS **BUSINESS** PRACTICES.

HE'S OFTEN VIEWED AS A REMORSELESS, **AVARICIOUS** MONSTER WHO **BROKE** THE TERRITORY SYSTEM AND **GOBBLED UP** RIVAL BUSINESSES.

BUT BY THE EARLY 1980s, THE NWA WAS **ALREADY** STRUGGLING. AND THERE HAD BEEN IN-FIGHTING BETWEEN PROMOTERS FROM THE **BEGINNING**.

THINGS BECAME EVEN **MORE** HEATED WITH **SYNDICATED** TELEVISION DEALS THAT REACHED INTO **OTHER** TERRITORIES, LIKE **GEORGIA CHAMPIONSHIP WRESTLING**.

ALL OF THIS ON **TOP** OF **CONFLICTING** CLAIMS AND **DISPUTED** RUNS OF THE **NWA WORLD HEAVYWEIGHT TITLE**, GOING ALL THE WAY BACK TO THE **1950s**.

VINCE MCMAHON DIDN'T DO ANYTHING MORE **DEVIOUS** THAN OTHER PROMOTERS, OR EVEN ANYTHING **DIFFERENT** THAN WHAT HAD BEEN DONE BEFORE...

...HE JUST DID IT **BETTER**, DURING A PERIOD THAT, EVEN **DECADES** LATER, IS **STILL** REMEMBERED AS ONE OF PROFESSIONAL WRESTLING'S **BEST**.

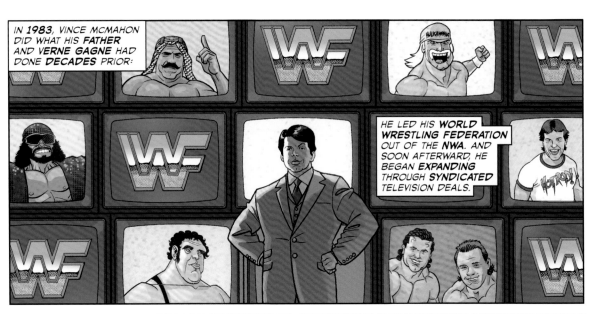

IN 1983, VINCE MCMAHON DID WHAT HIS FATHER AND VERNE GAGNE HAD DONE DECADES PRIOR:

HE LED HIS WORLD WRESTLING FEDERATION OUT OF THE NWA. AND SOON AFTERWARD, HE BEGAN EXPANDING THROUGH SYNDICATED TELEVISION DEALS.

NOT ONLY WAS MCMAHON'S MOVE OLD HAT, BUT OTHER PROMOTERS SOON FOLLOWED SUIT, LIKE FRITZ VON ERICH IN DALLAS.

BUILDING AROUND HIS CHARISMATIC SONS, VON ERICH'S WCCW ACHIEVED GLOBAL SYNDICATION AND APPEARED ON ESPN, WHICH ALSO HOSTED GAGNE'S AWA.

MEANWHILE, IN OKLAHOMA CITY, BILL WATTS ATTEMPTED TO TAKE HIS GRITTIER, MORE SPORT-BASED UWF NATIONAL.

THIS FOLLOWING AN EARLIER ATTEMPT WITH HIS MID-SOUTH WRESTLING IN 1979, WHICH WAS STYMIED WHEN HE LOST HIS SPOT ON TBS TO GCW.

THE GROWTH OF SYNDICATED TELEVISION MEANT THAT IF ANY PROMOTION HAD THE FAN AND PROFIT BASE TO FUND IT, AND THE CONNECTIONS TO SNAG A DEAL...

...THEY COULD GET EXPOSURE FAR BEYOND THEIR TERRITORY, EVEN GOING NATIONAL. AND MANY TRIED.

AND JUST AS IMPORTANT? CLOSED CIRCUIT TELEVISION, WHICH COULD SEND FEEDS OF BIG WRESTLING EVENTS TO ARENAS AND THEATERS AROUND THE COUNTRY.

WRESTLING EVENTS HAD BEEN SCREENED THIS WAY FOR YEARS, BUT IN 1983, JIM CROCKETT PROMOTIONS TRIED SOMETHING NEW...

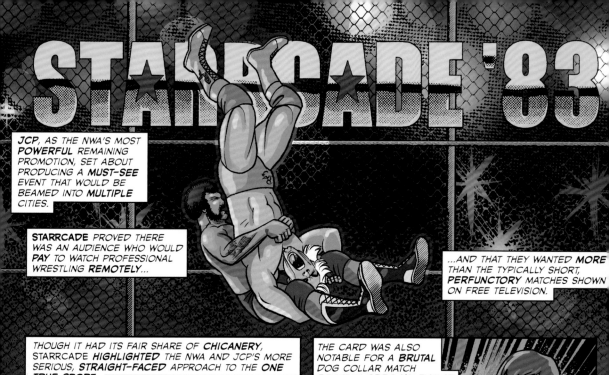

# STARRCADE '83

JCP, AS THE NWA'S MOST **POWERFUL** REMAINING PROMOTION, SET ABOUT PRODUCING A **MUST-SEE** EVENT THAT WOULD BE BEAMED INTO **MULTIPLE** CITIES.

**STARRCADE** PROVED THERE WAS AN AUDIENCE WHO WOULD **PAY** TO WATCH PROFESSIONAL WRESTLING **REMOTELY**...

...AND THAT THEY WANTED **MORE** THAN THE TYPICALLY SHORT, **PERFUNCTORY** MATCHES SHOWN ON FREE TELEVISION.

THOUGH IT HAD ITS FAIR SHARE OF **CHICANERY**, STARRCADE **HIGHLIGHTED** THE NWA AND JCP'S MORE SERIOUS, **STRAIGHT-FACED** APPROACH TO THE **ONE TRUE SPORT**.

AND THERE WAS NO **SMALL** AMOUNT OF **BLOOD**, MUCH OF WHICH WAS SPILLED DURING A **CONTINUATION** OF CARLOS CÓLON AND ABDULLAH THE BUTCHER'S **ONGOING** FEUD.

THE CARD WAS ALSO NOTABLE FOR A **BRUTAL** DOG COLLAR MATCH BETWEEN **GREG VALENTINE** AND **RODDY PIPER**.

**BOTH** MEN WOULD LATER WRESTLE IN WWF, WITH PIPER SERVING AS A CRUCIAL PIECE OF THE COMPANY'S **SUCCESS**.

JCP'S BOOKER AT THE TIME WAS **DUSTY RHODES**, WHO NOT ONLY MAPPED OUT A COMPELLING **BUILD** TO THE MAIN EVENT OF **STARRCADE 1983**...

...BUT, IN AN INSTANCE OF SUPERB LONG-TERM PLANNING, USED THE EVENT TO SET **HIMSELF** UP AS THE NUMBER ONE CONTENDER FOR **STARRCADE 1984**.

THE **MOST IMPORTANT** THING TO COME OUT OF **STARRCADE 1983**, HOWEVER, WAS **RIC FLAIR** AS NWA WORLD HEAVYWEIGHT CHAMPION.

THE EVENT, SUBTITLED **"A FLAIR FOR THE GOLD"** WAS A **CORONATION** FOR THE MAN WHO WOULD BE THE NWA'S **FOCUS** FOR THE REST OF THE **DECADE**.

BUT UP IN **NEW YORK**, THE WWF PREPARED TO USHER IN ITS **OWN** EPOCH-DEFINING STAR.

**HULK HOGAN!**

A FORMER **BODYBUILDER** AND MUSICIAN, HOGAN WAS URGED TO PURSUE WRESTLING BY FORMER **NWA** CHAMPION **JACK BRISCO** AND HIS BROTHER **GERALD**.

HOGAN'S TRAINER, **HIRO MATSUDA**, WAS A LEGIT JAPANESE SHOOTER WHO HAD BEEN TRAINED BY **RIKIDŌZAN** AND **KARL GOTCH**.

THE STORY GOES THAT HE **BROKE** HOGAN'S LEG ON THE **FIRST** DAY OF TRAINING, BUT THE YOUNG WRESTLER **RETURNED** AS SOON AS IT HAD **HEALED**.

HOGAN'S **GIMMICK**, INCLUDING HIS **BLOND** HAIR, **BODYBUILDER** PHYSIQUE, AND USE OF THE WORD **"BROTHER,"** WAS HEAVILY INFLUENCED BY **"SUPERSTAR"** BILLY GRAHAM.

GRAHAM WAS A FORMER **WWWF CHAMPION** WHO INSPIRED FUTURE GOVERNOR **JESSE "THE BODY" VENTURA** AND LIFTED WEIGHTS WITH FUTURE GOVERNOR **ARNOLD SCHWARZENEGGER**.

HULK--CALLED SUCH FOR HAVING **TOWERED** OVER **INCREDIBLE HULK** STAR LOU FERRIGNO--FIRST CAME TO THE **WWF** IN 1979.

VINCE SR. POSITIONED HIM AS **IRISH**, HENCE **HOGAN**, AND PLACED HIM WITH **HEEL MANAGER** AND FORMER DISPUTED WORLD CHAMPION, **FREDDIE BLASSIE**.

THE **FOLLOWING** YEAR, HOGAN WENT TO JAPAN, WHERE HE COMPETED IN NJPW AGAINST **ANTONIO INOKI**, **GREAT MUTA**, **TATSUMI FUJINAMI**, AND OTHERS.

KNOWN AS **ICHIBAN**, HE UTILIZED A STYLE THAT WAS **FAR** MORE TECHNICAL AND **WRESTLING**-BASED THAN WHAT HE **LATER** BECAME KNOWN FOR.

IN 1982, HOGAN APPEARED AS THE WRESTLER *THUNDERLIPS* IN ROCKY III, WHICH--IMPORTANT FOR LATER--ALSO FEATURED **MR. T.**

THE MOVIE'S MATCH WAS A **NOD** TO A BOUT BETWEEN **ANDRE THE GIANT** AND BOXER **CHUCK WEPNER**...

...WHICH WAS PROMOTED BY **VINCE SR.** AT THE SHEA STADIUM CLOSED CIRCUIT BROADCAST OF THE FAMOUS **ALI/INOKI** FIGHT.

BUT VINCE SR. WASN'T **THRILLED** ABOUT HIS **WRESTLERS** BECOMING **ACTORS**, SO AFTER FILMING THE PART, HOGAN WENT TO VERNE GAGNE'S **AWA**.

THOUGH INITIALLY **INTRODUCED** AS A VILLAIN IN 1981, HOGAN'S **UNDENIABLE** CHARISMA BEGAN TO **WIN OVER** THE AWA CROWDS.

ONLY **MONTHS** AFTER HIS DEBUT, HOGAN TURNED **FACE** BY ATTACKING THE VILLAINOUS **"CRUSHER" JERRY BLACKWELL**.

HOGAN WAS **MASSIVELY** POPULAR WITH THE AWA CROWDS, BUT GAGNE WAS **RELUCTANT** TO PUSH HIM DUE TO HIS LACK OF A **TRUE** WRESTLING BACKGROUND.

COMPLICATING THINGS EVEN FURTHER WAS THE FACT THAT **GAGNE** WANTED THE **BULK** OF HOGAN'S **CONSIDERABLE** NJPW EARNINGS...

...AS HE HAD CONTINUED TO **COMPETE** IN JAPAN WHILE WORKING FOR BOTH THE **WWF** AND **AWA**.

IN 1983, MONTHS BEFORE **STARRCADE**, WHEN **HOGAN** FACED **NICK BOCKWINKEL** FOR THE **AWA WORLD HEAVYWEIGHT CHAMPIONSHIP** AT THE **SUPER SUNDAY** EVENT...

...GAGNE **TEASED** PUTTING THE TITLE ON HOGAN, BEFORE **REVERSING** THE DECISION AND **LEAVING** IT ON THE VILLAINOUS **BOCKWINKEL**.

WITH **MAINSTREAM** PUBLICITY AND A **GROWING** FAN BASE, HOGAN KNEW HOW MUCH HE WAS **WORTH**.

AND SO, WHEN **VINCE MCMAHON, JR.** OFFERED HIM THE **WWF WORLD HEAVYWEIGHT TITLE**, HE RETURNED TO **NEW YORK**.

AT THE TIME, THE **CURRENT** TITLEHOLDER WAS NCAA CHAMPION GRAPPLER **BOB BACKLUND**, WHO HAD WON THE TITLE FROM **BILLY GRAHAM** IN 1978.

**BACKLUND**, WHO **DEBUTED** IN THE AWA, WAS OF THE SAME MOLD AS **GAGNE**, AND DIDN'T WANT TO LOSE THE TITLE TO A **"NON-WRESTLER."**

ENTER **THE IRON SHEIK**, AN IRANIAN GRAPPLER WHO COACHED UNITED STATES **OLYMPIC GRECO-ROMAN** WRESTLING TEAMS IN THE 1970S...

...AND RECEIVED **PROFESSIONAL** TRAINING FROM GAGNE AND **SNAKE PIT** GRADUATE **BILLY ROBINSON**. HE **BEAT** BACKLUND WITH HIS **CAMEL CLUTCH** IN LATE 1983.

LESS THAN A **MONTH** LATER, ON JANUARY 23, 1984, HULK HOGAN **DEFEATED** THE IRON SHEIK IN A **FIVE-MINUTE** MATCH AT **MADISON SQUARE GARDEN**. THE CROWD **EXPLODED**.

THE IRON SHEIK MAY HAVE ONLY BEEN A **TRANSITIONAL** CHAMPION, BUT COMING ON THE HEELS OF THE **IRAN HOSTAGE CRISIS**, HE MADE THE **PERFECT** VILLAIN FOR THE **PATRIOTIC** HOGAN.

IT WAS A **PERFECT STORM** OF EXCITEMENT, DUE IN **LARGE** PART TO THE VERY THINGS THAT HAD MADE GAGNE **RELUCTANT** TO PUSH HOGAN.

THE MOMENT MARKED THE **BEGINNING** OF **HULKAMANIA**, THE **UNPRECEDENTED** EXPANSION OF WWF AND PROFESSIONAL WRESTLING'S **TRIUMPHANT** RETURN TO THE **MAINSTREAM**.

HULKAMANIA WAS **REAL**. HOGAN WAS A **CROSSOVER** SENSATION, WITH ALL THE MERCHANDISE TO **PROVE** IT.

BUT A **GOOD** WRESTLING PROMOTION CAN'T **SURVIVE** WITH ONLY A **SINGLE** STAR, SO THE WWF **PLUNDERED** THE ROSTERS OF OTHER PROMOTIONS.

AWA WAS HIT **PARTICULARLY** HARD, AS IT LOS NOT ONLY **WRESTLERS**, BUT AN **INTERVIEWE** AND THE GREATEST WRESTLING **MANAGER** OF ALL TIME.

KEN PATERA

ADRIAN ADONIS

JESSE "THE BODY" VENTURA

RICK MARTEL

BOBBY "THE BRAIN" HEENAN

"MEAN" GENE OKERLUND

NATURALLY, WWF **ALSO** WENT AFTER NWA TALENT, ESPECIALLY THOSE AFFILIATED WITH JCP, THE ORGANIZATION BEHIND **STARRCADE**.

HARLEY RACE

"ROWDY" RODDY PIPER

GREG "THE HAMMER" VALENTINE

RICKY "THE DRAGON" STEAMBOAT

"COWBOY" BOB ORTON

WATTS'S **MID-SOUTH** WAS **ALSO** TARGETED, AS MANY OF HIS **TOUGH-GUY** BRAWLERS LEFT TO BECOME MORE **CARTOONISH** CHARACTERS IN WWF.

JUNKYARD DOG

"THE MILLION DOLLAR MAN" TED DIBIASE

WITH THIS **INFLUX** OF TALENT, WWF COULD **INCREASE** THEIR TOURING AND BRANCH OUT **FURTHER** FROM THEIR **NORTHEAST** STRONGHOLD.

AND WITH **COLISEUM VIDEO**, WHICH SOLD WWF VHS AND BETAMAX **TAPES**, FANS WERE **READY** WHEN THE SHOW CAME TO TOWN.

JAKE "THE SNAKE" ROBERTS

"THE NATURAL" BUTCH REED

ONE MAN GANG

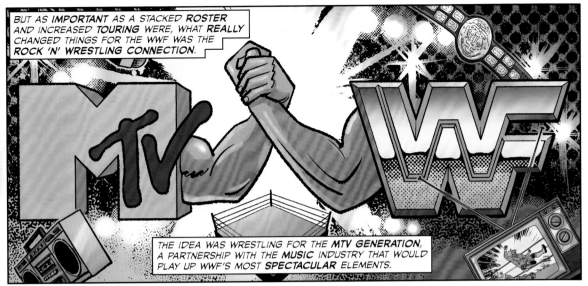

BUT AS **IMPORTANT** AS A STACKED **ROSTER** AND INCREASED **TOURING** WERE, WHAT **REALLY** CHANGED THINGS FOR THE WWF WAS THE **ROCK 'N' WRESTLING CONNECTION.**

THE IDEA WAS WRESTLING FOR THE **MTV GENERATION,** A PARTNERSHIP WITH THE **MUSIC** INDUSTRY THAT WOULD PLAY UP WWF'S MOST **SPECTACULAR** ELEMENTS.

IT ALL STARTED WITH **CYNDI LAUPER,** WHO MET LEGENDARY WWF MANAGER **CAPTAIN LOU ALBANO** ON A FLIGHT TO **PUERTO RICO.**

THE TWO STRUCK UP A **FRIENDSHIP,** WHICH LED TO ALBANO APPEARING AS LAUPER'S **FATHER** IN THE VIDEO FOR "GIRLS JUST WANT TO HAVE FUN."

AN **ANGLE** FOLLOWED, WITH THE TWO MANAGING PROXY GRAPPLERS **WENDI RICHTER** AND **THE FABULOUS MOOLAH.**

AND MOST **IMPORTANTLY?** THE MATCH WAS AIRED **LIVE** ON MTV AS **THE BRAWL TO END IT ALL** ON JULY 23, 1984.

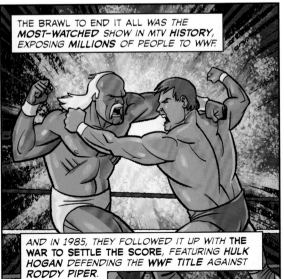

THE **BRAWL TO END IT ALL** WAS THE **MOST-WATCHED** SHOW IN MTV **HISTORY,** EXPOSING **MILLIONS** OF PEOPLE TO WWF.

AND IN 1985, THEY FOLLOWED IT UP WITH **THE WAR TO SETTLE THE SCORE,** FEATURING **HULK HOGAN** DEFENDING THE **WWF TITLE** AGAINST **RODDY PIPER.**

LATER THAT **SAME YEAR,** A CARTOON FEATURING THE WWF ROSTER DEBUTED ON **CBS,** EXPOSING AN EVEN **YOUNGER** FAN BASE TO THE PROMOTION'S CAST OF **CHARACTERS...**

...INCLUDING, MOST **PROMINENTLY,** PIPER AND A REMARKABLY **WELL-COIFFED** HOGAN.

MCMAHON KNEW IT WAS TIME TO **BUILD** UPON WHAT THE NWA HAD DONE WITH **STARRCADE**. IT WAS TIME FOR A **MEGA EVENT** OF HIS OWN.

WWF WRESTLEMANIA

NAMED BY LEGENDARY RING ANNOUNCER **HOWARD FINKEL**, THE FIRST **WRESTLEMANIA** TOOK PLACE ON **MARCH 31, 1985**, JUST A MONTH AFTER **THE WAR TO SETTLE THE SCORE**.

IN A **RARE** MISSTEP, THE WWF HAD EXPERIENCED **BACKLASH** IN 1984, WHEN THEY RAN **THEIR** WRESTLING IN THE TBS SPOT THAT HAD FEATURED **GCW** SINCE 1979.

ASSUMING HE HAD THE **BEST** END OF THE DEAL, JIM CROCKETT, JR., PURCHASED THE SLOT FOR **$1 MILLION**, WHICH **FINANCED** WRESTLEMANIA.

THE **INAUGURAL** EVENT LEANED IN TO THE **POP CULTURE** LINK **FORGED** WITH THE **ROCK 'N' WRESTLING CONNECTION**...

...BY FEATURING CELEBRITY GUESTS LIKE **CYNDI LAUPER, MUHAMMAD ALI, LIBERACE, THE ROCKETTES**, AND, MOST **IMPORTANTLY**...

...**MR. T**, WHO HAD NOT ONLY BEEN INVOLVED IN **THE WAR TO SETTLE THE SCORE**, BUT HAD APPEARED WITH HOGAN IN **ROCKY III**.

IN THE MAIN EVENT OF THE **FIRST** WRESTLEMANIA, MR. T, A **MASSIVE** STAR AT THE TIME, JOINED WITH **HOGAN** TO FACE **RODDY PIPER & PAUL ORNDORFF**.

19,121 PACKED **MADISON SQUARE GARDEN**, THE **ANCESTRAL** HOME OF NEW YORK WRESTLING...

...AND MORE THAN **ONE MILLION** PEOPLE WATCHED **REMOTELY**, MAKING WRESTLEMANIA THE BIGGEST CLOSED CIRCUIT EVENT **EVER** AT THAT POINT.

MCMAHON'S **EMBRACE** OF SPECTACLE AND **ARTIFICE** HAD MADE WRESTLING MORE **POPULAR** THAN IT HAD BEEN IN **DECADES...**

...BUT THE **ONE TRUE SPORT** HAS A LONG HISTORY OF PROTECTING ITS **LEGITIMACY,** AND THERE WERE **PLENTY** OF WRESTLERS WHO FELT THEY NEEDED TO **CONTINUE** THAT TRADITION.

YOU THINK THIS IS **FAKE?**

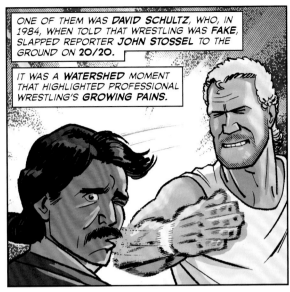

ONE OF THEM WAS **DAVID SCHULTZ,** WHO, IN 1984, WHEN TOLD THAT WRESTLING WAS **FAKE,** SLAPPED REPORTER **JOHN STOSSEL** TO THE GROUND ON **20/20.**

IT WAS A **WATERSHED** MOMENT THAT HIGHLIGHTED PROFESSIONAL WRESTLING'S **GROWING PAINS.**

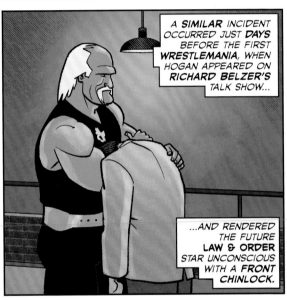

A **SIMILAR** INCIDENT OCCURRED JUST **DAYS** BEFORE THE FIRST **WRESTLEMANIA,** WHEN HOGAN APPEARED ON **RICHARD BELZER'S** TALK SHOW...

...AND RENDERED THE FUTURE **LAW & ORDER** STAR UNCONSCIOUS WITH A **FRONT CHINLOCK.**

IN 1982, WRESTLER JERRY LAWLER HAD SLAPPED COMEDIAN **ANDY KAUFMAN** SILLY ON **LATE NIGHT WITH DAVID LETTERMAN.**

BUT THAT ATTACK WAS **PLANNED,** PART OF A **GROUNDBREAKING** FEUD THAT KAUFMAN HAD **UNSUCCESSFULLY** PITCHED TO **WWF** AND **VINCE SR.**

BY THE MIDDLE OF THE DECADE, A **RIFT** HAD APPEARED, SEPARATING THE MORE **SPORT-BASED,** TRADITIONAL APPROACH FROM **WWF'S** PATH.

IN THE LATE 1980s, IN AN EFFORT TO **ESCAPE** STATE SPORT REGULATION (SEE PAGE 121), WWF CAME UP WITH A **NAME** FOR THEIR APPROACH: **SPORTS ENTERTAINMENT.**

MANY FANS SEE THIS AS THE **DEATH OF KAYFABE,** BUT **PFEFER'S** EXPOSÉ (SEE PAGE 31) CAME OUT **FIFTY** YEARS PRIOR, AND THERE WERE EVEN **SUSPICIONS** ABOUT **GOTCH/HACKENSCHMIDT!**

IN THE WAKE OF **WRESTLEMANIA**, THE WWF **PRESSED** THEIR ADVANTAGE, WITH THE EVENT'S **SECOND** ITERATION MADE WIDELY AVAILABLE ON **PAY-PER-VIEW**.

BUT THINGS WERE ONLY GOING TO GET **BIGGER** AND **BETTER** FOR THE COMPANY, DUE TO MCMAHON'S RELATIONSHIP WITH A **NEW** BUSINESS PARTNER...

...DICK EBERSOL, THE **VICE PRESIDENT** OF LATE NIGHT PROGRAMMING AT **NBC**, WHO HAD DEVELOPED **SATURDAY NIGHT LIVE** WITH **LORNE MICHAELS**.

TOGETHER, THE TWO CAME UP WITH A **CONCEPT** THAT, STARTING IN **1985**, WOULD AIR DURING **SNL'S** OFF WEEKS...

SATURDAY NIGHT'S MAIN EVENT (SNME) WAS ON **NETWORK TELEVISION**, GIVING THE ONE TRUE SPORT THE TYPE OF **MAINSTREAM** EXPOSURE IT HADN'T ENJOYED SINCE THE **1950S**.

PLUS, UNLIKE **OTHER** TELEVISED EVENTS, SNME FEATURED NOTHING BUT THE PROMOTION'S **BIGGEST** NAMES IN FRONT OF **PACKED** ARENAS.

WITH **EBERSOL'S** EXPERIENCE IN **FILMING** LIVE ENTERTAINMENT, **SNME** QUICKLY BECAME THE **SLICKEST**, BEST-LOOKING, MOST **PROFESSIONAL** WRESTLING SHOW IN **HISTORY**...

...ALL WHILE PROMOTING **HUGE** ANGLES, LIKE "MACHO MAN" RANDY SAVAGE'S TRANSFORMATION INTO A **HERO** AND SUBSEQUENT PARTNERSHIP WITH **HULK HOGAN** IN 1987.

NOT ONLY DID **SNME** PUT WWF'S BRAND OF WRESTLING IN FRONT OF **MILLIONS** OF PEOPLE, IT SHOWCASED A **QUANTUM LEAP** IN PRODUCTION VALUES.

AFTERWARD, **CAMERAS** AND **LIGHTING** BECAME A PRIORITY FOR MCMAHON, AND THE CRISP **SLICKNESS** OF THE WWF PRODUCT IS STILL ONE OF THE PROMOTION'S **HALLMARKS**.

WWF'S **UNPRECEDENTED** EXPANSION TOOK THE INDUSTRY BY **STORM**, BUT IN THE DECADES PRIOR, **AWA** HAD BECOME ONE OF THE COUNTRY'S MOST **SUCCESSFUL** PROMOTIONS.

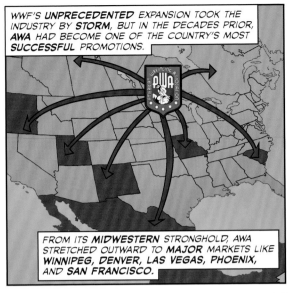

FROM ITS **MIDWESTERN** STRONGHOLD, AWA STRETCHED OUTWARD TO **MAJOR** MARKETS LIKE **WINNIPEG, DENVER, LAS VEGAS, PHOENIX,** AND **SAN FRANCISCO.**

BUT BY THE MID-1980S, THE AWA HAD LOST **SO MUCH** TALENT TO THE WWF THAT GAGNE HAD TO RELY ON **EXPERIENCED**, BUT **OLDER**, TALENT AND HIS OWN SON, **GREG GAGNE.**

IN A DECADE WHEN WRESTLING WAS AIMING FOR A **YOUNGER** AUDIENCE, THIS PUT THE AWA AT A **DISTINCT** DISADVANTAGE, ONE THAT WASN'T AIDED BY ACCUSATIONS OF **NEPOTISM.**

IN 1984, GAGNE BANDED TOGETHER WITH A GROUP OF **NWA** PROMOTERS FOR THEIR OWN ATTEMPT AT A **NATIONAL** EXPANSION, **PRO WRESTLING USA.**

BUT **JUST** LIKE THE NWA, THE GROUP STRUGGLED FROM A **DIFFUSE** FOCUS, **CONFLICTING** INTERESTS, AND **GENERAL** DISTRUST. IT FELL APART WITHIN **TWO YEARS.**

VERNE GAGNE, AWA

JIM CROCKETT, JR., JCP

FRITZ VON ERICH, WCCW

BILL WATTS, MID-SOUTH

JERRY LAWLER & JERRY JARRETT, CWA

IN 1985, THE PROMOTION INKED A DEAL WITH **ESPN** TO AIR **AWA CHAMPIONSHIP WRESTLING**, FILMED IN **LAS VEGAS.**

HOWEVER, OUTSIDE THE AWA'S MIDWESTERN **HOME TURF**, LIVE AUDIENCES WERE **SMALL** AND **UNENTHUSIASTIC**, HINDERING THE SHOW'S **SUCCESS.**

THE AWA WENT OUT OF BUSINESS IN **1991**, BUT NOT BEFORE THE COMPANY ATTEMPTED A **PAY-PER-VIEW** OF ITS OWN WITH 1988'S **SUPERCLASH III.**

THE SHOW WAS A FINANCIAL **DISASTER**, DESPITE FEATURING TALENT FROM OTHER PROMOTIONS, LIKE CWA'S **JERRY LAWLER** AND WCCW'S **KERRY VON ERICH.**

KERRY WAS THE SON OF **FRITZ VON ERICH**, WHO, AFTER BEING TRAINED BY **STU HART**, PORTRAYED A GOOSE-STEPPING **NAZI** VILLAIN IN THE 1950s.

BUT IN THE MID-1960s, VON ERICH BECAME A **HEROIC** FIGURE IN HIS OWN DALLAS PROMOTION, ONE THAT WOULD BECOME **WORLD CLASS CHAMPIONSHIP WRESTLING.**

IN THE LATE **1970s**, THE ELDER VON ERICH STARTED BUILDING WCCW AROUND HIS **CHARISMATIC**, TALENTED SONS, **KEVIN**, **DAVID**, AND **KERRY**.

THIS LED TO A **LEGENDARY**, LONG-RUNNING, **VIOLENT** FEUD WITH THE **FABULOUS FREEBIRDS**, MICHAEL "P.S." HAYES, TERRY "BAM BAM" GORDY, AND BUDDY "JACK" ROBERTS.

THE VON ERICHS AND THE FREEBIRDS WERE **ROCK STARS** WHO ENTERED TO CONTEMPORARY **ROCK MUSIC**--A **FIRST** IN WRESTLING.

THE **TALENT**, THE **MUSIC**, THE **INNOVATIVE** FILMING AND PRODUCTION TECHNIQUES...IT ALL BROUGHT **YOUNGER** AUDIENCES TO WCCW'S **SYNDICATED** TELEVISION SHOW.

BUT THE VON ERICH FAMILY WAS **PLAGUED** BY **MISFORTUNE**, WITH ALL THE SONS BUT **KEVIN** MEETING **TRAGIC** ENDS.

DAVID: HEART ATTACK. 1984.

FRITZ

MIKE: SUICIDE. 1987.

KEVIN

KERRY: SUICIDE. 1993.

CHRIS: SUICIDE. 1991.

THE TRAGEDIES TOOK THEIR TOLL NOT ONLY ON THE **VON ERICH FAMILY**, BUT ON WCCW FANS, WHO WERE **DEVASTATED** BY **EACH** OF THE DEATHS.

AFTER **SUPERCLASH III** IN 1989, **JERRY JARRETT** BOUGHT WCCW TO ATTEMPT HIS OWN **NATIONAL** PROMOTION, **THE UNITED STATES WRESTLING ASSOCIATION** (USWA).

OF THE OTHER PROMOTIONS THAT PERSISTED THROUGH THE 1980s, THE MOST **SIGNIFICANT** AND **SUCCESSFUL** WAS **JIM CROCKETT PROMOTIONS.**

RUN BY **JIM CROCKETT, JR.,** THE **SON** OF THE PROMOTION'S FOUNDER, JCP WAS THE **STANDARD BEARER** FOR THE **NWA.**

BY BUYING WWF'S **SATURDAY NIGHT** SLOT ON **TBS,** JCP COULD **PLACATE** SOUTHERN WRESTLING FANS MADE FURIOUS OVER THE LOSS OF **GCW.**

THE EARLY SUCCESS OF **TED TURNER'S** TBS WAS LARGELY BUILT ON **WRESTLING**--IT WAS **POPULAR,** BUT **CHEAP,** PROGRAMMING.

AND AS THE CHANNEL **GREW,** MORE PEOPLE WERE EXPOSED TO THE **JCP** PROGRAM, **WORLD** CHAMPIONSHIP WRESTLING.

CROCKETT WAS THE **NWA PRESIDENT** FOR MUCH OF THE DECADE, WHICH MADE IT EASIER TO LEAVE THE NWA TITLE **ENSCONCED** ON THE WAIST OF JCP TALENT **RIC FLAIR.**

WITH SO MUCH **POWER** AND AN EAGERNESS TO GO NATIONAL AND **COMPETE** WITH THE WWF, JCP **GOBBLED UP** STRUGGLING PROMOTIONS, MAKING IT THE **FACE** OF THE NWA.

UNFORTUNATELY, THESE PROMOTIONS' **BEST** ASSETS, THEIR **WRESTLERS,** OFTEN WENT **UNDERUTILIZED** OR WERE USED SOLELY TO **ELEVATE** OTHER TALENTS.

A **NOTABLE** EXCEPTION IS **STING,** WHO RECEIVED A **MASSIVE** PUSH AFTER COMING TO JCP FROM MID-SOUTH IN **1987.**

PREVIOUSLY, JCP HAD ELEVATED THE YOUNG, HANDSOME, BELIEVABLE **MAGNUM T.A.,** WHO HAD **ALSO** SPENT TIME IN **MID-SOUTH.**

HE ROSE TO PROMINENCE THROUGH A **BLOODY** AND **PERSONAL** FEUD WITH TULLY BLANCHARD, CULMINATING IN A **BRUTAL** "I QUIT" MATCH INSIDE A **STEEL CAGE** AT **STARRCADE 1985.**

BUT THE FEUD THAT **DEFINED** JCP DURING THE 1980s WAS THE **SON OF A PLUMBER**, FRIEND TO THE COMMON MAN AND JCP BOOKER, **DUSTY RHODES** VS....

...THE **STYLIN'**, PROFILIN', **LIMOUSINE RIDIN'**, JET FLYIN', **KISS-STEALIN'**, WHEELIN' N' DEALIN' SON OF A GUN, **RIC FLAIR.**

THE TWO WERE A **STUDY** IN CONTRASTS, AND JCP SET ABOUT **HEIGHTENING** THEIR ANIMOSITY THROUGH THE PROMOTION'S **VISCERAL** BRAND OF STORYTELLING.

BUT WHAT **REALLY** KICKED THE FEUD INTO HIGH GEAR WERE THE **VILLAINOUS** TACTICS OF FLAIR'S **ASSOCIATES**...

...**THE FOUR HORSEMEN!** RIC FLAIR, OLE ANDERSON, ARN ANDERSON, TULLY BLANCHARD, AND MANAGER J.J. DILLON WERE A **PIONEERING** HEEL FACTION...

...NOT ONLY BECAUSE OF THEIR **PRODIGIOUS** TALENTS, BUT BECAUSE THEY **POPULARIZED** THE **COOL HEEL** TROPE THAT WOULD BECOME **CRUCIAL** TO WRESTLING IN THE 1990s.

THE GROUP HAD **MULTIPLE** LINEUPS, WITH **SOME** REPLACEMENTS MORE **WELL-RECEIVED** THAN **OTHERS.**

BUT THE **NUCLEUS** OF THE GROUP WAS ALWAYS **FLAIR** AND **ARN ANDERSON**, EVEN IN **REVIVALS** UP THROUGH THE **1990s.**

THE HORSEMEN WERE **INFAMOUS** FOR FULLY **EMBRACING** THEIR GIMMICK **OUTSIDE** OF THE RING.

THE **PARTIES**, LIMOUSINES, **EXPENSIVE** CLOTHES, AND, OF COURSE, **WOMEN**, THAT THE HORSEMEN ENJOYED DURING THIS ERA HAVE BECOME THE STUFF OF **LEGEND.**

BOTH *JCP* AND *WWF* WERE RUN BY THE **SCIONS** OF PROMOTERS. THEY HAD **TELEVISION** EXPOSURE, **PAY-PER-VIEWS**, DEEP **ROSTERS**, AND EACH HAD **CONSUMED** RIVAL PROMOTIONS.

BUT FOR ALL THEIR **SIMILARITIES**, THE TWO WERE **VASTLY DIFFERENT** PROMOTIONS AT **FOUNDATIONAL** LEVELS.

THE MOST **OBVIOUS** DIFFERENCE WAS THE NWA AFFILIATION, WHICH WAS A **DOUBLE-EDGED** SWORD.

IT BROUGHT **CREDIBILITY**, BUT MEANT THAT **CROCKETT** COULDN'T ACT AS **UNILATERALLY** AS **MCMAHON**.

WITH NO **RESPONSIBILITY** TO ANYONE BUT HIMSELF, MCMAHON COULD SIMPLY RUN **RIVALS** OUT OF BUSINESS IF THEY WOULDN'T PLAY **BALL**.

THERE WAS ALSO THE **WRESTLING** ITSELF. WHILE NOT AS "**REALISTIC**" AS AWA, JCP HAD MUCH MORE **GRIT** THAN THE **FLASHY**, FAMILY-FRIENDLY **SPECTACLE** OF WWF.

WHILE WWF FEATURED **SUPERHEROES**, JCP HAD WRESTLERS WHO, EVEN WHEN **SPECTACULAR**, WERE **PRESENTED** AS MEN MADE OF **BLOOD** AND **GUTS**.

THESE DIFFERENCES IMPACTED WHO WAS ON **TOP**: CONSUMMATE VILLAIN **FLAIR** OR HERO-TO-MILLIONS **HOGAN**.

THE NWA STILL NEEDED A **HEEL CHAMPION** TO PROP UP MEMBER PROMOTIONS AND **LOCAL FACES**, BUT THE WWF COULD PUT **ALL** THEIR ENERGY BEHIND **HOGAN**.

THIS **STARK** CONTRAST IS A **RESULT** OF THE SWITCH IN PHILOSOPHY THAT WWF UNDERWENT WHEN MOVING FROM **BUDDY ROGERS** TO **BRUNO SAMMARTINO**.

JCP **DID** MAKE BABYFACE STARS: YOUNG MEN WITH **HERCULEAN** PHYSIQUES LIKE **MAGNUM T.A.**, **STING**, **LEX LUGER**, AND **NIKITA KOLOFF**.

BUT GETTING THEM TO **MEGASTAR** STATUS WAS MORE **DIFFICULT**, AS THEY WERE **SUBJUGATED** TO THE **VILLAINS** THAT DEFINED THIS **STYLE** OF WRESTLING.

WHILE JCP'S HOME OF **CHARLOTTE** IS, WITHOUT A DOUBT, A MAJOR CITY, IT ALSO COULDN'T COMPETE WITH **NEW YORK** IN TERMS OF POPULATION.

**WRESTLEMANIA SOLD OUT**

AS IT HAD ALWAYS BEEN FOR **NYC** PROMOTIONS, THE **SIZE** OF THE **POTENTIAL** AUDIENCE PROVIDED A **MASSIVE** EDGE FOR WWF IN THE FORM OF **GATE RECEIPTS.**

BUT A **BASE** IN NEW YORK CITY, OR EVEN NEARBY **STAMFORD, CONNECTICUT,** ALSO PROVIDED WWF WITH **ANOTHER** ADVANTAGE:

THE PROXIMITY TO **MAINSTREAM,** POP CULTURE **POWERHOUSES,** IN THE FORM OF **CELEBRITIES,** AS WELL AS TELEVISION **NETWORKS.**

IN 1986, JCP ELEVATED **MAGNUM T.A.,** A WRESTLER WHO, WITH HIS **MUSCULAR** PHYSIQUE AND SOUTHERN **GRIT,** COULD HAVE GIVEN THEM THEIR VERSION OF **HULKAMANIA.**

BUT A **CAR ACCIDENT** FORCED HIM INTO **RETIREMENT** MONTHS BEFORE STARRCADE AND AN **NWA TITLE MATCH** AGAINST **RIC FLAIR** THAT WOULD HAVE MADE HIM A **STAR.**

IN 1987, JCP BRANCHED OUT TO **CHICAGO** FOR **STARRCADE,** BUT IN AN **AGGRESSIVE** MOVE, WWF SCHEDULED THEIR NEW PAY-PER-VIEW, **SURVIVOR SERIES,** FOR THE SAME NIGHT...

...AND EVEN FORCED **CABLE PROVIDERS** TO CHOOSE BETWEEN CARRYING **STARRCADE** OR THE **MUCH** MORE POPULAR AND PROFITABLE **WRESTLEMANIA** THE FOLLOWING YEAR.

THEN, **TWO** MONTHS LATER, WWF CUT THE LEGS OUT FROM UNDER JCP ONCE **AGAIN,** SCHEDULING THE FIRST **ROYAL RUMBLE** ON **FREE** TELEVISION...

...AT THE SAME TIME AS JCP'S **BUNKHOUSE STAMPEDE,** AN EVENT WITH A **SIMILAR** CONCEPT, FOR WHICH THE PROMOTION HAD VENTURED INTO **LONG ISLAND,** WWF'S **BACKYARD.**

AS THEY **BLOCKED** JCP AT EVERY TURN, THE WWF REFINED THEIR **OWN** APPROACH TO PROFESSIONAL WRESTLING, CULMINATING WITH **WRESTLEMANIA III** IN 1987.

IT AIRED AT **160** CLOSED CIRCUIT LOCATIONS, AND WAS WATCHED BY **MILLIONS** ON PAY-PER-VIEW, AND THE WWF CLAIMED TO PACK MORE THAN **93,000** INTO THE **PONTIAC SILVERDOME**.

**WRESTLEMANIA III** WAS A **HUMONGOUS** FINANCIAL SUCCESS, DUE IN **LARGE** PART TO THE **MUST-SEE** NATURE OF ITS MAIN EVENT: **HULK HOGAN** VS. **ANDRE THE GIANT**.

HULKAMANIA WAS A **PHENOMENON** AND **ANDRE** HAD BEEN A **BELOVED** STAR AND SPECTACLE FOR **DECADES** (SO WHEN HE TURNED INTO A **VILLAIN**, IT WAS **BIG** NEWS).

BUT WWF'S **THREE-RING CIRCUS** APPROACH AIMED TO GIVE SOMETHING TO **EVERYONE**, INCLUDING FANS WHO PREFERRED **GRAPPLING** TO **SPECTACLE**.

WRESTLEMANIA III ALSO FEATURED **"MACHO MAN" RANDY SAVAGE** VERSUS **RICKY "THE DRAGON" STEAMBOAT** IN A MATCH STILL CONSIDERED ONE OF THE **BEST** OF ALL TIME.

AND THE SAVVY WWF MACHINE ENSURED THAT THEY WOULD RECEIVE **MAINSTREAM** ATTENTION FROM **CELEBRITY** INVOLVEMENT...

...LIKE THAT OF LEGENDARY SHOCK ROCKER **ALICE COOPER** ACCOMPANYING **JAKE "THE SNAKE" ROBERTS** TO THE RING AND LENDING A HAND AGAINST THE VILLAINOUS **JIMMY HART**.

IN 1988, WWF HELD **SUMMERSLAM**, WITH A MAIN EVENT FEATURING **HOGAN**, **SAVAGE**, AND HIS VALET **MISS ELIZABETH** AS THE **MEGA POWERS**.

THE EVENT JOINED **WRESTLEMANIA**, **SURVIVOR SERIES**, AND THE **ROYAL RUMBLE** ON THE ANNUAL PPV SCHEDULE, ALL **FOUR** OF WHICH ARE STILL GOING STRONG **TODAY**.

JCP **TRIED** TO COMPETE WITH WWF, BUT IT WAS AN **UPHILL** BATTLE DUE TO **STRUCTURAL** DIFFERENCES IN THE COMPANIES AND MCMAHON'S **MERCILESS** MANEUVERING...

...AS WELL AS SEVERAL CRITICAL **BUSINESS** MISTAKES AND A FAILURE TO **ADAPT** TO A MARKETPLACE THAT WAS MORE INTERESTED IN WWF'S NORTHERN **SHEEN** THAN JCP'S SOUTHERN **GRIT**.

THE PROMOTION ALSO SUFFERED FROM **CREATIVE** MISSTEPS, SUCH AS **HASTILY** PUSHING **MIDDLE-AGED** MIDCARDER **RONNIE GARVIN** INTO THE MAIN EVENT OF **STARRCADE 1987**...

...AND TOO MANY **BIG** MATCHES THAT ENDED WITH **INCONCLUSIVE** OR **DISAPPOINTING** FINISHES, JUST AS THE HOGAN/BOCKWINKEL MATCH HAD AT **AWA** SUPER SUNDAY.

BY 1988, JCP WAS ON ITS **LAST LEGS**, BUT THE PROMOTION WAS STILL CRUCIAL TO **TBS** FOR ITS RELATIVELY **INEXPENSIVE** BUT **POPULAR** PROGRAMMING.

SO, TED TURNER STEPPED IN AND **PURCHASED** THE PROMOTION, BRINGING THE ONE TRUE SPORT IN-HOUSE AT **TURNER BROADCASTING**.

AND AMONG THE **FIRST** CHANGES TURNER MADE WAS MATCHING THE PROMOTION'S **NAME** TO THAT OF ITS MOST **POPULAR** TELEVISION SHOW: **WORLD CHAMPIONSHIP WRESTLING**.

THE **JOINED** LINEAGES OF **SOUTHERN** AND **NWA** WRESTLING STILL HAD **FURTHER** TO FALL, BUT IN THE **NEXT** DECADE, WITH **TURNER'S** BACKING AND **DEEP** POCKETS, THEY WOULD **RISE** AGAIN.

MEANWHILE, WWF CONTINUED TO **DOMINATE**, POACHING WRESTLERS FROM **DYING** TERRITORIES, THEN **REPACKAGING** THEM IN THEIR BRIGHT, **EXPLOSIVE** STYLE.

ONE OF THE MOST **NOTABLE**, A WRESTLER DESIGNED TO BE THE **NEXT** HOGAN, WAS THE **ULTIMATE WARRIOR**, WHO HAD PREVIOUSLY TAGGED WITH **STING** IN CWA AND **MID-SOUTH**.

WRESTLING WAS AT THE **PEAK** OF ITS POWERS: THE INDUSTRY **LEADER**, WWF, HAD ACHIEVED MAINSTREAM **APPEAL** THE LIKES OF WHICH HADN'T BEEN SEEN IN **DECADES**...

...AND THE PROMOTION'S SLICK, **PROFESSIONAL** PRODUCTION MADE THE **ONE TRUE SPORT** MORE **ACCESSIBLE** THAN EVER...

...ESPECIALLY TO **CHILDREN**. THEY ADORED **ASPIRATIONAL** CHARACTERS LIKE **HOGAN**, WHO IMPLORED THEM TO TRAIN **HARD**, SAY THEIR **PRAYERS**, AND EAT THEIR **VITAMINS**.

THIS **CAMPY**, OVER-THE-TOP, BUT STILL SHOCKINGLY **SINCERE-FEELING** APPROACH **DEFINED** WRESTLING FOR **GENERATIONS** OF FANS.

IT WAS ALSO THE ERA WHEN MCMAHON BEGAN TO **POPULARIZE** PERHAPS THE MOST **ACCURATE** DESCRIPTION OF THE ONE TRUE SPORT: **SPORTS ENTERTAINMENT**.

SPORTS ENTERTAINMENT

THE PHRASE ITSELF **WINKED** AT WRESTLING'S **ARTIFICE**, WHICH HAS LED TO **DECADES** OF IT BEING REVILED BY **PURIST** FANS.

BUT AS SHOWN **PREVIOUSLY**, WRESTLING HADN'T BEEN A **TRUE** SPORT FOR A FULL **CENTURY** AT THAT POINT.

AND THE **GOLD DUST TRIO**--INCLUDING **TOOTS MONDT**, WHO MENTORED VINCE'S **FATHER**--HAD BEEN PRIORITIZING **ENTERTAINMENT** SINCE THE **1920S**.

BUT NOW THERE WAS **REASON** FOR WWF TO **EMBRACE** THIS TRUTH, AS MCMAHON WISHED TO **ESCAPE** THE SUPERVISION OF **STATE ATHLETIC COMMISSIONS**...

...AND MORE **IMPORTANTLY**, IT WAS THE **SPECTACLE** OF WRESTLING, **NOT** THE REALISM, THAT HAD BROUGHT WWF ITS **COLOSSAL** SUCCESS.

AND SO, IN 1989, IN FRONT OF NEW JERSEY'S **STATE SENATE**, MCMAHON DID WHAT HAD BEEN **ANATHEMA** TO SO MANY PROMOTERS **BEFORE** HIM.

HE **ACKNOWLEDGED** WRESTLING'S **ARTIFICE**, SO HE COULD **BETTER** PURSUE THE ONLY **REAL** GOAL THAT WRESTLING HAS **EVER** HAD, GOING ALL THE WAY BACK TO THE **CARNIVAL** DAYS...

...PUTTING **BUTTS** IN **SEATS** AND MAKING **MONEY**.

# CARICATURE, STEREOTYPE, AND REPRESENTATION

WRESTLING HAS LONG USED ETHNIC IDENTITY TO SELL TICKETS, AS WITH *ITALIAN IMMIGRANT* BRUNO SAMMARTINO...

...AND "THE RUSSIAN BEAR" IVAN KOLOFF.

THESE IDENTITIES ARE OFTEN *CARICATURES,* LIKE WHEN THE MEXICAN-AMERICAN *TITO SANTANA* BECAME EL MATADOR.

GIMMICKS WORK AS **SHORTHAND** IN **BIG** ARENAS, SO THEY'RE OFTEN **BROAD,** REDUCTIVE, AND NOT **INFREQUENTLY...**

...**OFFENSIVE,** ESPECIALLY WHEN LOOKED BACK UPON WITH A **CONTEMPORARY** AWARENESS OF RACIAL AND ETHNIC **REPRESENTATION.**

THOUGH **SOME** GIMMICKS, LIKE WHEN THE **WHITE** ONE MAN GANG BECAME AKEEM, **THE AFRICAN DREAM** IN 1988, WERE ILL-ADVISED EVEN IN **CONTEXT.**

LIKE **MANY** FORMS OF **ENTERTAINMENT,** WRESTLING HAS LONG HAD A PROBLEM WITH **REPRESENTATION,** SUFFERING FROM A **LACK** OF IT AND A **RELIANCE** UPON **STEREOTYPES.**

...BUT WHILE THE PROBLEM IS MADE MORE **DIFFICULT** BY THE ONE TRUE SPORT'S **PECULIARITIES...**

...AND THE SOMETIMES **BLURRED** LINES BETWEEN CARICATURE, STEREOTYPE, AND REPRESENTATION...

...IT'S ALSO **AIDED** BY THE FACT THAT WHILE A GIMMICK IS HOW FANS **INITIALLY** PROCESS A WRESTLER, STEREOTYPES ARE **ALWAYS** TRUMPED...

I'm your papi!

...BY WRESTLING'S **UNIQUE** MORAL CODE, WHICH IS HOW **EDDIE GUERRERO,** AS A MEXICAN-AMERICAN STEREOTYPE THAT PROUDLY CLAIMED TO **LIE, CHEAT,** AND **STEAL...**

...COULD BECOME A **HERO.**

WHILE PROFESSIONAL WRESTLING STILL HAS **SIGNIFICANT** AND **IMPORTANT** GROUND TO COVER IN TERMS OF **REPRESENTATION...**

...IN RECENT YEARS IT'S MADE **VITAL** PROGRESS, WITH MORE **DIVERSE** TALENTS OCCUPYING MORE **IMPORTANT** SPOTS ON THE CARD THAN **EVER** BEFORE.

A MONTH AFTER TURNER **PURCHASED** JCP, DUSTY RHODES WAS **FIRED** FOR A BLOODY INCIDENT WITH THE **ROAD WARRIORS**...

...IN WHICH THE **BOOKER** AND STAR WAS KAYFABE **BLINDED** IN A VIOLATION OF TURNER'S NEW **"NO BLOOD"** POLICY.

WHEN HE BECAME THE **NEW** HEAD BOOKER IN 1989, **RIC FLAIR** LEANED INTO WHAT MADE THE NEWLY CHRISTENED WCW **UNIQUE** FROM WWF: **WRESTLING.**

TO DO SO, HE BROUGHT IN REVERED COMPETITORS LIKE **RICKY STEAMBOAT** AND **TERRY FUNK** TO WORK **WELL-RECEIVED** ANGLES WITH HIM.

FLAIR'S BRIEF **REIGN** AS WCW BOOKER IS ALSO **NOTABLE** FOR THE YOUNGER STARS THAT WERE **DEVELOPED**, WRESTLERS WHO MATCHED WWF'S **SPECTACLE** WITHOUT BECOMING **CARTOONISH.**

THE GREAT MUTA

BRIAN PILLMAN

STING

RICK & SCOTT STEINER

LEX LUGER

BUT THERE WAS **PRESSURE** FROM ABOVE TO COMPETE WITH WWF ON **ALL** FRONTS, INCLUDING **POP CULTURE** TIE-INS.

THESE WERE GENERALLY **CORNY** AND **RIDICULOUS**, AND NONE MORE SO THAN **ROBOCOP'S** APPEARANCE AT **CAPITAL COMBAT** IN 1990.

THE **BAD IDEAS** STARTED COMING **HARDER** AND **FASTER** WHEN **JIM HERD**, AN EXECUTIVE WITH **NO** WRESTLING EXPERIENCE, WAS PLACED IN **CHARGE.**

SOME OF HIS GEMS INCLUDED THE BELL-WIELDING **DING DONGS** AND **THE HUNCHBACKS**, WHOSE **DEFORMITIES** WOULD PREVENT THEM FROM BEING **PINNED.**

BUT THE **WORST** THING ABOUT HERD'S TENURE IS THAT HE COULDN'T GET ALONG WITH WCW'S TOP STAR, **RIC FLAIR**.

THE TWO **BUTTED HEADS** OVER **MONEY**, FLAIR'S **GIMMICK**, AND **MORE**, UNTIL HERD **FIRED** FLAIR IN 1991. BUT THERE WAS A **PROBLEM**...

...FLAIR STILL HELD WCW'S **WORLD HEAVYWEIGHT TITLE**. AND HE BROUGHT THE **PHYSICAL BELT** WITH HIM...

...WHEN HE APPEARED ON **WWF** TELEVISION WITH **BOBBY HEENAN** AND **MR. PERFECT**, PROCLAIMING HIMSELF "THE **REAL WORLD CHAMPION**."

...IT WAS A PROMOTER'S **BIGGEST** FEAR: LOSING THEIR **TOP** TITLE TO A **RIVAL** PROMOTION. PROMOTERS LIKE GAGNE **STILL** FAVORED LEGIT **SHOOTERS**...

...BECAUSE OF **STANISLAUS ZBYSZKO'S** BETRAYAL OF **THE GOLD DUST TRIO** BACK IN 1925!

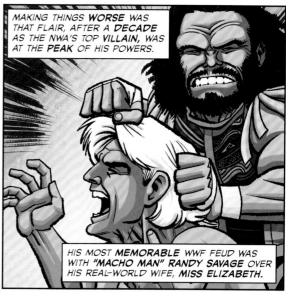

MAKING THINGS **WORSE** WAS THAT FLAIR, AFTER A **DECADE** AS THE NWA'S TOP VILLAIN, WAS AT THE **PEAK** OF HIS POWERS.

HIS MOST **MEMORABLE** WWF FEUD WAS WITH "**MACHO MAN**" RANDY SAVAGE OVER HIS REAL-WORLD WIFE, **MISS ELIZABETH**.

...WERE PART OF ONE OF THE MOST ~~M~~ESSIVE ROSTERS IN WWF HISTORY.

ESTABLISHED DRAWS LIKE **HULK HOGAN** AND **SGT. SLAUGHTER**...

...**FUTURE** STARS LIKE **BRET HART** AND **SHAWN MICHAELS**...

...AND TALENT PULLED FROM **WCW**, LIKE THE **ROAD WARRIORS**.

WWF SEEMED **UNSTOPPABLE**. THEY HAD MEDIA **SATURATION**, A **MURDERER'S** ROW OF **TALENT**, AND NO **REAL** COMPETITION.

WHICH IS WHY WHAT CAME **NEXT** WAS SUCH A **MASSIVE** BLOW.

BEGINNING IN **1991**, THE SAME YEAR THAT **FLAIR** JOINED THE COMPANY, WWF WAS **ROCKED** BY A **DRUG SCANDAL**.

DOCTOR **GEORGE ZAHORIAN** WAS CHARGED WITH **ILLEGALLY** DISTRIBUTING **STEROIDS**, AND CALLED TO **TESTIFY** WERE **FIVE** WWF WRESTLERS, INCLUDING **HULK HOGAN**.

THEN, IN 1993, **VINCE MCMAHON** HIMSELF WAS **IMPLICATED**, AS THE PROSECUTION CLAIMED THAT HE DIDN'T JUST **KNOW** ABOUT THE DISTRIBUTION OF **STEROIDS**...

...BUT THAT HE **CREATED** AN ENVIRONMENT WHERE THEY WERE **DE FACTO** OBLIGATORY AND THAT HE EVEN **ENCOURAGED** WRESTLERS TO USE THEM.

A **KEY** PILLAR OF WWF'S SUCCESS WAS ITS **KID-FRIENDLY** IMAGE, CONTRASTED WITH THE GRITTIER, **BLOODIER** JCP PRODUCT.

BUT NOW, THE ILLUSION OF THESE **NATURALLY** MUSCULAR, **IMPECCABLY** SCULPTED **SUPERHEROES** HAD BEEN **SHATTERED**.

EVEN **WORSE**, THEIR BIGGEST STAR HAD BEEN **IMPLICATED**, AFTER **YEARS** OF ENCOURAGING KIDS TO **TRAIN**, SAY THEIR **PRAYERS**, AND TAKE THEIR **VITAMINS**...

...WITHOUT **ANY** MENTION OF **ILLEGAL** DRUG USE.

ULTIMATELY, MCMAHON WAS **ACQUITTED** OF ALL CHARGES, BUT THE **DAMAGE** HAD BEEN **DONE** IN THE PUBLIC EYE.

THE TIME OF **MASSIVE**, VASCULAR, SOMETIMES **LUMBERING** MAIN EVENTERS WAS COMING TO A **CLOSE**, AS WWF BEGAN TO CHAMPION LESS **ENHANCED** PHYSIQUES.

AMONG THESE NEWER, **SMALLER** WRESTLERS WAS **BRET "THE HITMAN" HART**, WHO WAS **FORMERLY** A TAG TEAM CHAMPION WITH JIM "THE ANVIL" NEIDHART.

TRAINED BY HIS LEGENDARY FATHER, **STU HART**, BRET WAS A **SHOCKINGLY** SMOOTH AND **BELIEVABLE** PERFORMER.

THE MAN WHO WOULD BECOME HART'S **GREATEST** RIVAL, **SHAWN MICHAELS**, WAS A **BRASH**, ARROGANT, **FLASHY** VILLAIN IN THE **RIC FLAIR** MOLD.

HE HAD TURNED **HEEL** BY PUTTING HIS ERSTWHILE TAG TEAM PARTNER, **MARTY JANNETTY**, THROUGH A **WINDOW** DURING AN INTERVIEW SEGMENT.

MICHAELS ALSO FEUDED WITH THE **UNDERTAKER**, WHO CREATED **LEGITIMATE** FEAR OUT OF AN **OUTLANDISH** SUPERNATURAL GIMMICK.

THE UNDERTAKER WOULD COMPETE IN WWF FOR A **STUNNING** PERIOD OF TIME-- MORE THAN **TWENTY-SEVEN YEARS**.

IN 1993, THEY ALL BECAME **CRUCIAL** COMPONENTS OF WWF'S **NEWEST** INDUSTRY-CHANGING **INNOVATION**...

...A **WEEKLY** TELEVISION SHOW THAT WAS SHOT AND AIRED **LIVE**.

# WWF
# MONDAY NIGHT
# RAW

WHILE **OTHER** SHOWS WERE SHOT ON A **SOUNDSTAGE** AND **EDITED** TOGETHER, **RAW** WAS FILMED AND BROADCAST **LIVE** FROM NEW YORK'S **MANHATTAN CENTER**.

EVERYTHING HAPPENED IN **REAL TIME**, WHICH GAVE THE **SHOW**, THE **WRESTLERS**, AND THE WWF AS A **WHOLE** A NEW SENSE **IMMEDIACY** AND **URGENCY**.

RAW WAS **ALSO** DIFFERENT FOR ANOTHER IMPORTANT **REASON**: THE **TYPES** OF MATCHES SHOWN.

**OTHER** WEEKLY SHOWS WERE MOSTLY **SQUASH** MATCHES, BUT RAW HAD **COMPETITIVE** MATCH-UPS, **TITLE** CHANGES, AND EVEN **SHOCKING** UPSETS.

RAW WAS A **RUNAWAY** SUCCESS. BUT **BIG THINGS** WERE BREWING IN WCW AND THEY WERE ALL **CENTERED** AROUND **ERIC BISCHOFF**.

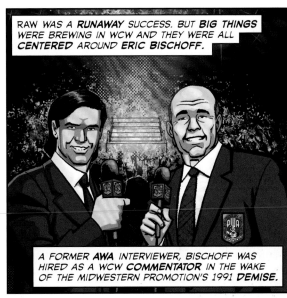

A FORMER **AWA** INTERVIEWER, BISCHOFF WAS HIRED AS A WCW **COMMENTATOR** IN THE WAKE OF THE MIDWESTERN PROMOTION'S 1991 **DEMISE**.

THE WCW THAT BISCHOFF CAME INTO WAS **FLOUNDERING**, SUFFERING FROM A SERIES OF BAD **BUSINESS** AND CREATIVE **DECISIONS**, LIKE THE INFAMOUS **SHOCKMASTER**...

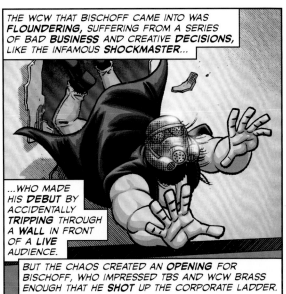

...WHO MADE HIS **DEBUT** BY ACCIDENTALLY **TRIPPING** THROUGH A **WALL** IN FRONT OF A **LIVE** AUDIENCE.

BUT THE CHAOS CREATED AN **OPENING** FOR BISCHOFF, WHO IMPRESSED TBS AND WCW BRASS ENOUGH THAT HE **SHOT** UP THE CORPORATE LADDER.

BY **1994**, BISCHOFF WAS IN **CONTROL**, USING **TURNER** MONEY TO **EMULATE** WWF'S **PRODUCTION** VALUES, **SPECTACLE**, PAY-PER-VIEW **FREQUENCY**, AND EVEN...

...**TALENT**. HE SPENT **WHATEVER** IT TOOK TO HIRE KEY WRESTLERS **AWAY** FROM WWF, EVEN OFFERING THE BIGGEST NAMES UNPRECEDENTED **CREATIVE CONTROL**.

BUT BISCHOFF'S **BIGGEST** IMPACT ON WCW CAME IN 1995, WHEN HE CONVINCED TURNER THAT THE **ONLY** WAY TO COMPETE WITH WWF WAS BY GOING **LIVE**.

TURNER **AGREED,** AND WCW MONDAY NITRO DEBUTED ON TNT ON SEPTEMBER 4, 1995, COUNTERPROGRAMMED **AGAINST** RAW, KICK-STARTING THE **MONDAY NIGHT WARS.**

NITRO'S FIRST EPISODE, AIRED **LIVE** FROM THE **MALL OF AMERICA,** OPENED WITH **BRIAN PILLMAN** VS. **JUSHIN LIGER,** AND ALSO FEATURED HULK HOGAN, RIC FLAIR, AND STING.

AND SINCE RAW HAD BEEN **PREEMPTED** THAT NIGHT, NITRO WAS THE **ONLY** PLACE FOR WRESTLING FANS TO GET THEIR MONDAY NIGHT **FIX.**

THE DEBUT EPISODE SCORED **ANOTHER** COUP WITH THE **SURPRISE** RETURN OF **LEX LUGER,** WHO HAD SPENT THE LAST **THREE YEARS** WORKING FOR MCMAHON.

HIS **HOMECOMING** WAS A **THUMB** IN WWF'S **EYE,** AS LUGER HAD JUST RECEIVED A **MASSIVE** MONTHS-LONG PUSH FROM THE COMPANY.

BUT AN EVEN **BIGGER** SHOT ACROSS THE BOW CAME **TWO** MONTHS LATER, WHEN WWF CHAMPION **ALUNDRA BLAYZE** APPEARED ON NITRO AND THREW HER **TITLE** IN THE **GARBAGE.**

IN A WAY, THIS WAS EVEN **WORSE** THAN FLAIR IN 1991, AS BLAYZE PUBLICLY **DENIGRATED** THE TITLE AND THE **WWF** BEFORE RETURNING TO HER WCW NAME, **MADUSA.**

MEANWHILE, IN WWF, **SHAWN MICHAELS, DIESEL, RAZOR RAMON, HUNTER HEARST HELMSLEY,** AND **SEAN WALTMAN** FORMED A BACKSTAGE ALLIANCE CALLED THE **KLIQ.**

BY **COORDINATING** TOGETHER, THEY SOUGHT TO EXERT **INFLUENCE** OVER WWF'S **BOOKING,** THOUGH HOW MUCH **CLOUT** THEY HAD DEPENDS ON **WHOM** YOU ASK.

THEY EVEN HAD THEIR OWN **HAND GESTURE,** WHICH WAS LATER APPROPRIATED BY NJPW'S **BULLET CLUB.**

**TALES** OF THEIR **MACHIAVELLIAN** SCHEMING BECAME KNOWN TO **FANS,** WHICH LED TO THEIR BACKSTAGE **POWER** BECOMING PART OF THEIR **CHARACTERS.**

THE KLIQ ALLOWED **PERCEPTION** AND **REALITY** TO INFORM ONE ANOTHER, TAKING ADVANTAGE OF THE **SHIFTING** GOALPOSTS OF WHAT'S **REAL** AND WHAT'S **FAKE.**

IN 1996, **DIESEL** AND **RAZOR RAMON** WERE TWO OF THE BIGGEST STARS IN **WWF,** BUT WCW HAD COME CALLING WITH **TURNER** MONEY.

THEY WERE **LURED AWAY** BY **GUARANTEED** CONTRACTS, MEANING THEY GOT **PAID** NO MATTER HOW **MANY** DATES THEY WORKED--ANOTHER **INNOVATION** FOR PROFESSIONAL WRESTLING.

DIESEL AND RAZOR'S **LAST** NIGHT IN WWF WAS MAY 19, 1996, AND AFTERWARD, DIESEL AND HELMSLEY, **VILLAINS,** EMBRACED RAMON AND MICHAELS, **HEROES.**

IT WAS A **SCANDALOUS** MOMENT, AS IT ACKNOWLEDGED AND TACITLY **PROMOTED** A COMPETITOR IN WWF'S **ANCESTRAL** HOME OF **MADISON SQUARE GARDEN.**

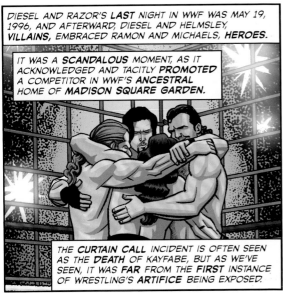

THE **CURTAIN CALL** INCIDENT IS OFTEN SEEN AS THE **DEATH** OF KAYFABE, BUT AS WE'VE SEEN, IT WAS **FAR** FROM THE **FIRST** INSTANCE OF WRESTLING'S **ARTIFICE** BEING EXPOSED.

SOMEONE NEEDED TO TAKE THE **FALL,** BUT **SHAWN MICHAELS** HAD JUST WON THE WWF TITLE AT **WRESTLEMANIA XII.**

SO THE **BLAME** FELL **SOLELY** UPON HUNTER HEARST HELMSLEY, WITH A 1996 **KING OF THE RING** VICTORY EARMARKED FOR HIM GOING **ELSEWHERE.**

MEANWHILE, RAMON, UNDER HIS REAL NAME, **SCOTT HALL,** DEBUTED ON NITRO THE WEEK **AFTER** THE **CURTAIN CALL.**

COMING OUT THROUGH THE **CROWD,** HALL **IMPLIED** THAT HE WAS STILL WITH THE **WWF,** TEASING AN INTERPROMOTIONAL **WAR.**

TWO WEEKS LATER, DIESEL APPEARED UNDER **HIS** REAL NAME, **KEVIN NASH,** FORMING THE VILLAINOUS **OUTSIDERS** TEAM.

FANS WERE **CAPTIVATED,** UNABLE TO SEPARATE **FACT** FROM **FICTION.** IT'S THE **EXACT** TYPE OF THING THAT THE **ONE TRUE SPORT** EXCELS AT.

THEN, AT THE 1996 **BASH AT THE BEACH,** TWO YEARS AFTER HE DEFEATED **RIC FLAIR** FOR THE WCW TITLE, **HULK HOGAN** JOINED THE VILLAINOUS GROUP.

YOU CAN CALL THIS THE **NEW WORLD ORDER** OF WRESTLING, BROTHER!

HOGAN HAD BEEN A **VILLAIN** IN AWA AND EVEN WWF, BUT THIS WAS **DIFFERENT.** HIS ATTACK ON **RANDY SAVAGE** WAS SEEN AS A **COLOSSAL** BETRAYAL...

...FROM A MAN WHO, EVEN IN THE WAKE OF THE **STEROID SCANDAL,** WAS STILL A **MAINSTREAM,** POP CULTURE **HERO** TO **GENERATIONS** OF KIDS.

HOWEVER, WHILE FANS WERE **BEYOND** OUTRAGED, THEIR **VENOM** DIDN'T **HURT** WCW, AND IN FACT...

...THE FACTION, DUBBED THE **NEW WORLD ORDER,** EXPLODED IN *POPULARITY.*

THE NWO WASN'T COMPRISED OF **TERRIFYING** MONSTERS OR **SNIVELING** COWARDS, BUT OF **COOL HEELS** THAT FANS **LOVED** TO HATE. AND **INCREASINGLY** JUST *LOVED.*

AND THEY **ALSO** LOVED TO SPEND **MONEY** ON MERCHANDISE FROM THE **ANTI-AUTHORITY** GROUP WHO WERE MORE **ANTIHEROES** THAN PURE **VILLAINS.**

THE NWO WAS A **REPUDIATION** OF NOT JUST **STODGY** WCW, BUT ALSO, SEEMINGLY, WRESTLING'S **GUIDING PHILOSOPHY.** THEY FELT **DANGEROUS,** NEW, AND **EXCITING.**

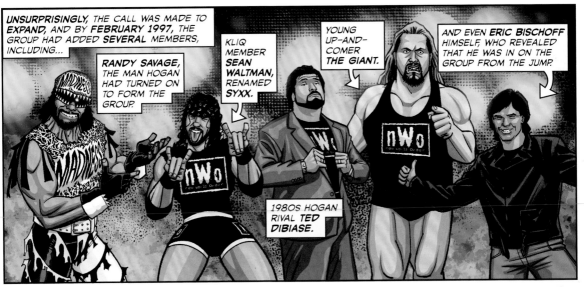

**UNSURPRISINGLY,** THE CALL WAS MADE TO **EXPAND,** AND BY **FEBRUARY 1997,** THE GROUP HAD ADDED **SEVERAL** MEMBERS, INCLUDING...

**RANDY SAVAGE,** THE MAN HOGAN HAD TURNED ON TO FORM THE GROUP.

KLIQ MEMBER **SEAN WALTMAN,** RENAMED **SYXX.**

YOUNG UP-AND-COMER **THE GIANT.**

AND EVEN **ERIC BISCHOFF** HIMSELF, WHO REVEALED THAT HE WAS IN ON THE GROUP FROM THE JUMP.

1980S HOGAN RIVAL **TED DIBIASE.**

THE NWO'S **WAR** AGAINST WCW, INCLUDING **WRESTLERS** AND EVEN **REFEREES,** CONSUMED NITRO, WHICH GREW TO **TWO** HOURS IN 1996 AND A WHOPPING **THREE** IN 1998.

THE FANS **LOVED** IT, AS THE ONGOING **DRAMA** OF WHOM THE NWO WOULD ATTACK NEXT WAS **HEIGHTENED** BY THE FACT THAT NITRO, UNLIKE RAW, WAS **ALWAYS** LIVE.

THE **STRENGTH** OF THE NWO FACTION AND NITRO'S **UNPREDICTABILITY** LED TO RATINGS VICTORIES OVER RAW EVERY WEEK FOR ALMOST **TWO** YEARS.

**EVERYTHING** REVOLVED AROUND THE NWO, EVEN THE FACTION'S **RIVALS** AND THEIR **REFUSAL** TO JOIN.

IN RESPONSE, **STING** TOOK ON A **DARKER** GIMMICK, INFLUENCED BY THE MOVIE, **THE CROW.**

WCW HAD HIRED AWAY SOME OF THE WWF'S **BIGGEST** NAMES AND TURNED THEM INTO **COOL HEELS** OR **ANTIHEROES**, DEPENDING ON YOUR POINT OF VIEW.

BUT THERE WAS **HOPE** FOR THE WWF, AND IT WAS, **IRONICALLY,** BASED ON SEVERAL WRESTLERS THAT WCW **CAST ASIDE** BUT WOULD BECOME WWF'S **OWN** ANTIHEROES.

THERE WAS "STONE COLD" STEVE AUSTIN, A **TRASH-TALKING,** VIOLENT **REDNECK** WHO WON THE **KING OF THE RING** TOURNAMENT MEANT FOR **HUNTER HEARST HELMSLEY**...

...AND PROCEEDED TO GIVE HIS LEGENDARY **AUSTIN 3:16** PROMO, WHICH LED TO A **MERCHANDISING** BONANZA.

AUSTIN 3:16 SAYS I JUST **WHOOPED** YOUR ASS!

BISCHOFF **FIRED** AN INJURED AUSTIN VIA **FEDEX,** PROMPTING HIM TO SPEND A **BRIEF** PERIOD IN **ECW,** LAYING GROUNDWORK FOR THE "STONE COLD" PERSONA.

IN 1997, AUSTIN ENTERED **WRESTLEMANIA 13** AS A VILLAIN, SQUARING OFF AGAINST THE HEROIC **BRET HART** IN A **SUBMISSION MATCH.**

VIA SOME **EXQUISITE** RING WORK AND NO SMALL AMOUNT OF **BLOOD** FOR SYMPATHY, THE TWO **SWITCHED** ALIGNMENTS, WITH AUSTIN BECOMING, **INCONGRUOUSLY,** A **BABYFACE.**

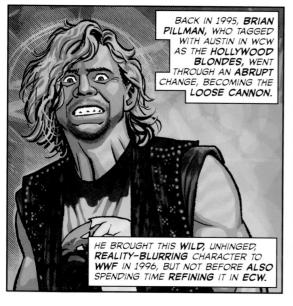

BACK IN 1995, **BRIAN PILLMAN,** WHO TAGGED WITH AUSTIN IN WCW AS THE **HOLLYWOOD BLONDES,** WENT THROUGH AN **ABRUPT** CHANGE, BECOMING THE **LOOSE CANNON.**

HE BROUGHT THIS **WILD,** UNHINGED, **REALITY-BLURRING** CHARACTER TO WWF IN 1996, BUT NOT BEFORE **ALSO** SPENDING TIME **REFINING** IT IN ECW.

AND IN 1996 **MICK FOLEY** TRANSFORMED FROM THE VICIOUS **CACTUS JACK** THAT HE PORTRAYED IN **WCW,** TO **MANKIND,** WHO WAS SO **DERANGED** HE BECAME **BELOVED.**

WHAT WAS THE **COMMON** THREAD? LIKE AUSTIN AND PILLMAN, **FOLEY** LEFT WCW AND SPENT TIME IN **ECW.** BUT WHAT **WAS** ECW?

IN 1992, **TOD GORDON** PURCHASED PHILADELPHIA'S **TRI-STATE WRESTLING ALLIANCE**, TRANSFORMING IT INTO **EASTERN CHAMPIONSHIP WRESTLING**.

THE PROMOTION WAS **NWA**-AFFILIATED AND BOOKED BY "HOT STUFF" **EDDIE GILBERT**.

BUT IN 1993, GORDON **REPLACED** GILBERT WITH CWA, AWA, AND WCW ALUM **PAUL HEYMAN**, BETTER KNOWN AT THE TIME AS **PAUL E. DANGEROUSLY**.

BEGINNING AS A TEENAGE **PHOTOGRAPHER** FOR WWF, HEYMAN BECAME ONE OF THE INDUSTRY'S MOST **HATEABLE** MANAGERS AND **SAVVIEST** BOOKERS.

IN 1994, **SHANE DOUGLAS** WAS SCHEDULED TO WIN THE **NWA WORLD HEAVYWEIGHT TITLE** BY DEFEATING **2 COLD SCORPIO** IN THE FINALS OF A **TOURNAMENT** IN ECW.

BUT **GORDON** AND **HEYMAN** HAD A PLAN TO GET EYES ON THEIR **FLEDGLING** PROMOTION...

AFTER **WINNING** THE **PRESTIGIOUS** TITLE, DOUGLAS THREW IT TO THE GROUND, TELLING **PREVIOUS** CHAMPIONS TO KISS HIS **HINDQUARTERS!**

HE WENT ON TO CLAIM TO A SHOCKED, BUT NOT **DISPLEASED**, CROWD THAT THE NWA **DIED** SEVEN YEARS PRIOR...

...BEFORE HOLDING UP THE **ECW TITLE**, PROCLAIMING HIMSELF **CHAMPION** AND ANNOUNCING THAT THE TITLE WAS A **WORLD CHAMPIONSHIP**, NOT JUST A **REGIONAL** ONE.

LET THE NEW ERA **BEGIN!** THE ERA OF THE **SPORT** OF **PROFESSIONAL WRESTLING!**

SOON AFTERWARD, GORDON ANNOUNCED THE COMPANY'S **NEW** IDENTITY: **EXTREME** CHAMPIONSHIP WRESTLING.

AND FROM AN **UNASSUMING** WAREHOUSE IN PHILADELPHIA, DUBBED THE **ECW ARENA**, THE PROMOTION **EXPLODED** IN POPULARITY.

UNLIKE **WWF** AND **WCW**, WHICH COUNTED ON **KIDS** FOR THEIR **MAINSTREAM** APPEAL, ECW TARGETED **HARDCORE**, MOSTLY **MALE**, **TEENAGE**, AND **YOUNG ADULT** FANS.

THAT MEANT COURTING **CONTROVERSY**, LIKE WITH THE **CRUCIFIXION** OF THE SANDMAN, WHICH COST ECW A **PARTNERSHIP** WITH OLYMPIC **GOLD MEDALIST** KURT ANGLE.

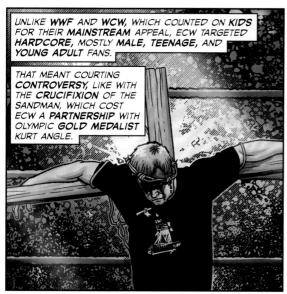

ECW ALSO FEATURED A **LIBERAL** DOSAGE OF **PROFANITY**, WHICH, IN ITS EARLIEST DAYS, WASN'T EVEN EDITED OFF THE PROMOTION'S **SYNDICATED** TELEVISION SHOW.

BEGINNING IN **1993**, **HARDCORE TV** WAS FEATURED **LATE NIGHTS** ON LOCAL TELEVISION, GROWING SO **POPULAR** THAT TNN OFFERED THE PROMOTION A **CABLE** SHOW IN 1999.

THERE WAS ALSO **SEXUAL** CONTENT, THE LIKES OF WHICH HAD **NEVER** BEEN SEEN ON WRESTLING **TELEVISION**.

LIKE WHEN FORMER **PENTHOUSE** MODEL **BEULAH MCGILLICUTTY** MADE OUT IN THE RING WITH FORMER **GO-GO** DANCER **KIMONA WANALAYA** (SAY IT OUT **LOUD**).

AND THERE WAS THE **VIOLENCE**, AS ECW SHOWCASED THE TYPE OF **HARDCORE** MATCHES MADE POPULAR IN **PUERTO RICO** AND **JAPAN**.

NOT EVEN **LIVING LEGENDS** WERE SAFE FROM THESE **BRUTAL** STIPULATIONS, AS SEEN FROM **TERRY FUNK'S** BARBED WIRE MATCH AGAINST HIGH-FLYING DAREDEVIL **SABU**.

IN **1995**, GORDON SOLD THE PROMOTION TO **HEYMAN**, WHO SET ABOUT MAKING SURE THAT ECW WAS **UNLIKE** ANY OTHER WRESTLING PROMOTION IN HISTORY.

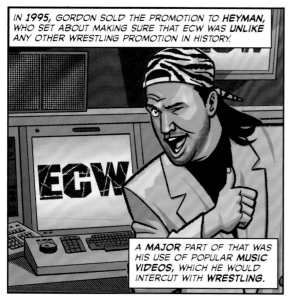

A **MAJOR** PART OF THAT WAS HIS USE OF POPULAR **MUSIC VIDEOS**, WHICH HE WOULD INTERCUT WITH **WRESTLING**.

THE PROMOTION TOOK LESSONS FROM **MTV**, PICKING UP ON THE **AESTHETICS** OF TWO OF THE ERA'S MOST POPULAR **MUSIC GENRES** AND FASHIONS:

GRUNGE AND HIP-HOP.

WHILE ECW IS REMEMBERED FOR ITS **VIOLENCE**, THE PROMOTION WAS ALSO **GROUNDBREAKING** IN THE WAY IT SHOWCASED **OTHER STYLES** OF THE **ONE TRUE SPORT.**

THEY WERE THE **FIRST** AMERICAN PROMOTION TO HEAVILY FEATURE **LUCHADORES** LIKE **PSICOSIS, REY MYSTERIO,** AND **EDDIE GUERRERO,** WHO WERE ALL LATER **PICKED UP** BY WCW.

ECW ALSO FEATURED UP-AND-COMING **JAPANESE** WRESTLERS, LIKE **TAJIRI...**

...MASHING UP THEIR **PURORESU** WITH LUCHADORES SUCH AS **SUPER CRAZY,** ALONG WITH THE REST OF THE **ROSTER.**

ANOTHER **KEY** TO THEIR **POPULARITY?** HEYMAN'S BOOKING, WHICH WAS ALL ABOUT **EMPHASIZING** STRENGTHS AND **DOWNPLAYING** WEAKNESSES.

ECW MADE STARS LIKE **TAZ** AND **TOMMY DREAMER** AT AN **ASTONISHING** RATE, WHICH WAS **IMPORTANT,** AS THEIR ROSTER WAS **FREQUENTLY** PILLAGED BY LARGER PROMOTIONS.

BUT THE TALENT EXCHANGE WENT BOTH WAYS, AS ECW WELCOMED **ESTABLISHED** STARS LIKE **TERRY FUNK** AND **BAM BAM BIGELOW...**

...AS WELL AS YOUNGER WRESTLERS, LIKE **AUSTIN,** WHO WERE EAGER TO **REINVENT** THEMSELVES IN THE WORKED SHOOT, **INSIDE-BASEBALL** STYLE THAT ECW USED SO WELL.

ECW WAS ALSO THE **LAUNCHING PAD** FOR NEW **NORTH AMERICAN** WRESTLERS, MANY OF WHOM HAD **PRIMARILY** WRESTLED **ABROAD.**

THESE INCLUDED, AMONG **OTHERS,** FUTURE MEGASTARS **CHRIS JERICHO, ROB VAN DAM,** AND **CHRIS BENOIT.**

ECW'S **POPULARITY** WAS **DRIVEN** BY A **NEW** TYPE OF FAN, ONE **ENAMORED** WITH THE **INNER WORKINGS** OF THE ONE TRUE SPORT.

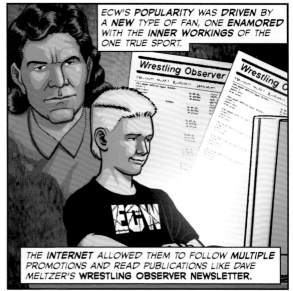

THE **INTERNET** ALLOWED THEM TO FOLLOW **MULTIPLE** PROMOTIONS AND READ PUBLICATIONS LIKE DAVE MELTZER'S **WRESTLING OBSERVER NEWSLETTER.**

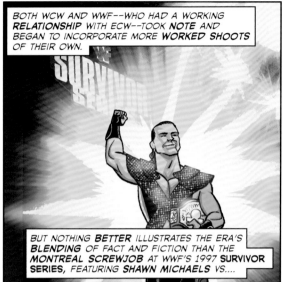

BOTH WCW AND WWF--WHO HAD A WORKING **RELATIONSHIP** WITH ECW--TOOK **NOTE** AND BEGAN TO INCORPORATE MORE **WORKED SHOOTS** OF THEIR OWN.

BUT NOTHING **BETTER** ILLUSTRATES THE ERA'S **BLENDING** OF FACT AND FICTION THAN THE **MONTREAL SCREWJOB** AT WWF'S 1997 **SURVIVOR SERIES**, FEATURING **SHAWN MICHAELS** VS....

...WWF WORLD HEAVYWEIGHT CHAMPION **BRET HART**. HART WAS ONE OF WWF'S **TOP** STARS, BUT THEY COULD NO LONGER AFFORD TO PAY HIS **MASSIVE** CONTRACT.

SO, HART DECIDED TO LEAVE FOR **GUARANTEED** MONEY AT **WCW**, AND MCMAHON, **AWARE** OF HIS PLANS, WANTED HART TO DROP THE TITLE TO **MICHAELS**.

BUT **HART**, WHOSE CHARACTER WAS BUILT AROUND **CANADIAN** PRIDE, DIDN'T WANT TO LOSE THE CHAMPIONSHIP IN HIS **HOME** COUNTRY...

...AND **ESPECIALLY** NOT TO **MICHAELS**, WITH WHOM HE HAD ISSUES IN BOTH **STORYLINES** AND **REAL LIFE**.

FEARING A **REPEAT** OF WHAT **MADUSA** HAD DONE TO THE **WOMEN'S TITLE**, THE DECISION WAS MADE TO HAVE HART **LOSE** THE TITLE WHETHER HE **WANTED** TO OR NOT.

IN THE **PAST**, SCREWJOBS WOULD OCCUR AS THE RESULT OF A **SHOOT**, AS WITH **ZBYSZKO** AND **MUNN**...

...BUT **THIS** SCREWJOB TOOK PLACE WITH HELP FROM REFEREE **EARL HEBNER**, WHO CALLED FOR THE **BELL** ONCE MICHAELS LOCKED HIS RIVAL INTO HART'S **OWN** MOVE, THE **SHARPSHOOTER**.

EVEN THOUGH THE DEPARTING HART NEVER **TAPPED** OR **SUBMITTED**, MICHAELS WAS AWARDED THE **WWF WORLD TITLE**.

IT SEEMED ALMOST **TOO** PERFECT, ESPECIALLY SINCE THE **BACKSTAGE** RESPONSE WAS **RECORDED** FOR THE DOCUMENTARY **WRESTLING WITH SHADOWS**.

BUT WHETHER IT WAS **LEGITIMATE** OR NOT (MANY FANS, JOURNALISTS, AND EVEN **WRESTLERS** CLAIM IT **WASN'T**) IS BESIDE THE POINT, AS THE FALLOUT WAS **ENORMOUS**.

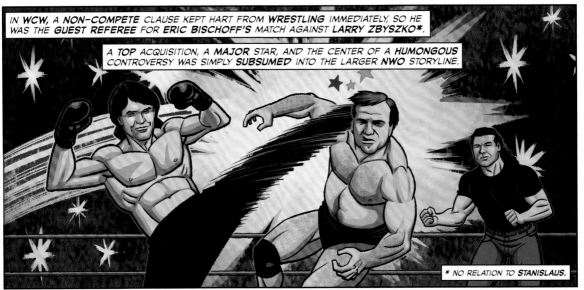

IN **WCW**, A **NON-COMPETE** CLAUSE KEPT HART FROM **WRESTLING** IMMEDIATELY, SO HE WAS THE **GUEST REFEREE** FOR ERIC BISCHOFF'S MATCH AGAINST **LARRY ZBYSZKO\***.

A **TOP** ACQUISITION, A **MAJOR** STAR, AND THE CENTER OF A **HUMONGOUS** CONTROVERSY WAS SIMPLY **SUBSUMED** INTO THE LARGER **NWO** STORYLINE.

\* NO RELATION TO **STANISLAUS**.

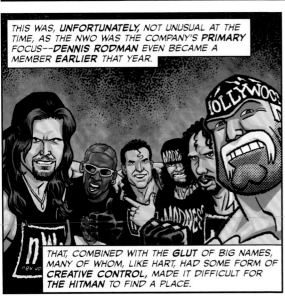

THIS WAS, **UNFORTUNATELY**, NOT UNUSUAL AT THE TIME, AS THE NWO WAS THE COMPANY'S **PRIMARY** FOCUS--**DENNIS RODMAN** EVEN BECAME A MEMBER **EARLIER** THAT YEAR.

THAT, COMBINED WITH THE **GLUT** OF BIG NAMES, MANY OF WHOM, LIKE HART, HAD SOME FORM OF **CREATIVE CONTROL**, MADE IT DIFFICULT FOR **THE HITMAN** TO FIND A PLACE.

AND FOR WHAT LITTLE **NON-NWO** SPACE THERE WAS ON EACH EPISODE OF **NITRO?** COMPETITION WAS **STIFF**...

...AS WCW BOASTED THE **FAN-FAVORITE** CRUISERWEIGHT DIVISION, FEATURING NAMES LIKE **CHRIS JERICHO** AND **EDDIE GUERRERO**.

PLUS, THE PROMOTION HAD **ALSO** BUILT NEWER **HEAVYWEIGHT** STARS, INCLUDING **DIAMOND DALLAS PAGE**.

A FORMER **MANAGER** IN WCW AND THE AWA, PAGE WAS **ELEVATED** BY A FEUD WITH **RANDY SAVAGE** IN 1997.

**BILL GOLDBERG**, A FORMER **ATLANTA FALCON**, BECAME AN **INSTANT SENSATION** WITH HIS **POWER MOVES** AND A WINNING STREAK THAT, THOUGH **INFLATED**, WAS STILL **UNPRECEDENTED**.

TRUTHFULLY, HART'S ARRIVAL CHANGED VERY **LITTLE** IN WCW. BUT IN **WWF** THE **MONTREAL SCREWJOB** HAD A **SEISMIC** IMPACT.

FOR THE **VAST** MAJORITY OF **CASUAL** FANS, **VINCE MCMAHON** HAD ALWAYS BEEN JUST WHAT HE WAS **PORTRAYED** AS ON TELEVISION:

AN **ANNOUNCER, INTERVIEWER,** AND **UNDERRATED** PLAY-BY-PLAY MAN (AS SEEN HERE WITH JERRY LAWLER AND **LEGENDARY** COMMENTATOR, **JIM ROSS**).

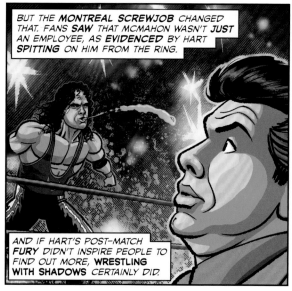

BUT THE **MONTREAL SCREWJOB** CHANGED THAT. FANS **SAW** THAT MCMAHON WASN'T **JUST** AN EMPLOYEE, AS **EVIDENCED** BY HART **SPITTING** ON HIM FROM THE RING.

AND IF HART'S POST-MATCH **FURY** DIDN'T INSPIRE PEOPLE TO FIND OUT MORE, **WRESTLING WITH SHADOWS** CERTAINLY DID.

FANS BEGAN TO SEE THE **THIRD-GENERATION** PROMOTER AS A VILLAIN, SO THE WWF **LEANED** IN, CREATING THE DASTARDLY **MR. MCMAHON** CHARACTER.

THE **SHOCKINGLY** MUSCULAR MR. MCMAHON WAS A VICIOUS, SADISTIC BOSS, SOMETHING THAT **EVERYONE** CAN RELATE TO AND WHO JUST HAPPENED TO BE **THE PERFECT FOIL**...

...FOR THE **BEER**-CHUGGING, **FOUL**-MOUTHED EVERYMAN, "STONE COLD" STEVE AUSTIN.

THE TWO WERE **IDEAL** RIVALS, AND THEIR **LONG-RUNNING** FEUD BECAME ONE OF THE **GREATEST** AND MOST **SUCCESSFUL** OF ALL TIME.

IT WAS **WISH** FULFILLMENT: A NO-NONSENSE **BADASS** FINALLY **SNAPS** AND GOES TO **WAR** WITH HIS **BOSS.**

IT **CONNECTED** WITH AUDIENCES IN A **PROFOUND** WAY, USHERING IN THE MOST **SUCCESSFUL** PERIOD IN PROFESSIONAL WRESTLING'S **HISTORY**...

...THE **ATTITUDE ERA!** OPINIONS **VARY** ABOUT WHEN IT **OFFICIALLY** BEGAN, BUT IN DECEMBER OF 1997, MCMAHON **ANNOUNCED** AND **EXPLAINED** THE NEW DIRECTION ON RAW.

HE ADMITTED THAT THE WWF WAS **ENTERTAINMENT** FIRST, COMPARING THE SHOW TO **SOAP OPERAS, MUSIC VIDEOS, CARTOONS,** AND **SITCOMS.**

MCMAHON PROMISED A MORE **ADULT** PRODUCT, AND THE WWF **DELIVERED** IN SPADES, WITH MORE **MATURE** THEMES...

...LIKE THE UNDERTAKER'S **TRANSFORMATION** FROM A MACABRE **WESTERN** CHARACTER, TO A MORE **EVIL,** EVEN **SATANIC** GIMMICK.

MCMAHON ENCOURAGED WRESTLERS TO PUT MORE OF **THEMSELVES** INTO THEIR **GIMMICKS,** WHICH LED **MICK FOLEY** TO TAKE MORE RISKS **CREATIVELY...**

...AND **PHYSICALLY,** TAPPING INTO HIS **DEATH MATCH** HERITAGE BY GETTING THROWN OFF THE **HELL IN A CELL** BY **UNDERTAKER** IN 1998.

WWF PUSHED EVERY ENVELOPE WITH **PORN STAR VAL VENIS, CROSS-DRESSER** GOLDUST (THE SON OF **DUSTY RHODES**), THE **VAMPIRE** GANGREL...

...UNDERTAKER'S **DEFORMED** AND **DEMONIC** HALF-BROTHER KANE, AND EVEN A **PIMP** WITH A **"HO TRAIN,"** THE GODFATHER.

MEANWHILE, **SHAWN MICHAELS,** HUNTER HEARST HELMSLEY (AS **TRIPLE H**), AND WALTMAN (AS **X-PAC**) FORMED **D-GENERATION X** WITH **CHYNA** AND THE **NEW AGE OUTLAWS.**

IN KEEPING WITH THE **SPIRIT** OF THE ERA, THEIR SIGNATURE PHRASE WAS **"SUCK IT,"** ACCOMPANIED BY A **CROTCH CHOP.**

IN A WAY, THEY WERE **WWF'S** VERSION OF THAT **OTHER** FACTION THAT GREW OUT OF THE **KLIQ:** THE **NEW WORLD ORDER.**

THE **ATTITUDE ERA** ALSO BROUGHT THE WORLD A MAN WHO WOULD LATER BECOME ONE OF ITS **BIGGEST** MOVIE STARS: **DWAYNE "THE ROCK" JOHNSON.**

ALTHOUGH WHEN HE FIRST DEBUTED IN **1996** AS SMILING BABYFACE **ROCKY MAIVIA,** THE WWF AUDIENCE **BOOED** HIM.

HIS PARENTS WERE WRESTLER **ROCKY JOHNSON** AND ATA MAIVIA, THE DAUGHTER OF WRESTLER AND HAWAIIAN NWA PROMOTER **"HIGH CHIEF" PETER MAIVIA.**

HE WAS PUSHED AS A **THIRD-GENERATION** WRESTLER, BUT AUDIENCES DIDN'T WANT TO BE **TOLD** WHAT TO LIKE.

SO, IN 1997, THE WWF PLACED JOHNSON IN THE **NATION OF ISLAM** AND BLACK PANTHER–INFLUENCED **NATION OF DOMINATION** FACTION.

REFERRING TO HIMSELF IN THIRD PERSON AS **THE ROCK,** HE LEANED INTO THE GROUP'S **VILLAINOUS** TENDENCIES, BECOMING **INCREASINGLY** ARROGANT, INSULTING, AND **ABRASIVE.**

HE WAS LIKE **HOGAN:** A LARGER-THAN-LIFE **SUPERHERO** WITH **CATCHPHRASES** TO SPARE. BUT IN THE **ATTITUDE ERA,** WWF FANS DIDN'T WANT **ASPIRATIONAL** HEROES...

...THEY WANTED **ANTIHEROES,** AND THEY SOON FELL IN LOVE WITH THE ROCK'S BITING **WIT** AND **NATURAL CHARISMA,** LEADING TO A **FACE** RUN.

BUT WHETHER AS A **FACE** OR A HEEL, THE ROCK'S MOST MEMORABLE **MATCHES** AND **MOMENTS** CAME AS THE SLICK, MOVIE-STAR FOIL TO **"STONE COLD" STEVE AUSTIN.**

THE **ATTITUDE ERA** APPEARED TO HAVE TURNED TRADITIONAL WRESTLING LOGIC ON ITS **HEAD**...

...AS THE **INSULTING BRAGGART** AND THE **UNHINGED ROUGHNECK** BECAME TWO OF THE MOST-**BELOVED** STARS IN THE INDUSTRY.

IT WAS AN ERA WHEN EVEN AMERICAN HERO KURT ANGLE, WHO HAD WON AN OLYMPIC GOLD MEDAL WITH A BROKEN NECK, COULD BE BOOED.

ANGLE WOULD GO ON TO BECOME ONE OF THE ERA'S BIGGEST STARS AND BEST PERFORMERS, LARGELY AS A VILLAIN.

BUT HOW DIFFERENT WAS IT? WRESTLING MATCHES ARE MORALITY TALES, BUT MORAL ABSOLUTES FREQUENTLY TAKE A BACKSEAT TO A TYPE OF TRIBALISM.

AUDIENCES CHEER WHO THEY LIKE, WHICH IS HOW A CHEAT LIKE RIC FLAIR AND A MONSTER LIKE BRUISER BRODY COULD BECOME BELOVED.

THE WWF SIMPLY DID WHAT THE ONE TRUE SPORT WAS DESIGNED TO DO. THEY GAVE THE AUDIENCE WHAT THEY WANTED: ANTIHEROES...

...AND AN UPTICK IN VIOLENCE, MIRRORING THE APPROACHES OF ECW, FMW, WWC, AND EVEN BRITISH ALL-IN WRESTLING.

WWF MATCHES BEGAN FEATURING MORE FOREIGN OBJECTS, AS WELL AS HARDCORE STIPULATIONS, LIKE AT THE 2000 SUMMERSLAM...

...WHEN BUBBA RAY & D-VON DUDLEY, MATT & JEFF HARDY, AND EDGE & CHRISTIAN MET IN THE FIRST TABLES, LADDERS, AND CHAIRS MATCH.

ALSO LIKE ALL-IN WRESTLING, WWF BEGAN TO RELY ON TITILLATION, SEXING UP FEMALE COMPETITORS, NEWLY RENAMED DIVAS.

INTO THE 2000s, WRESTLERS LIKE TRISH STRATUS AND LITA WERE ROUTINELY OBJECTIFIED AND USED IN HYPERSEXUALIZED WAYS, LIKE BRA AND PANTIES MATCHES.

MEANWHILE, WCW WAS **STILL** PUSHING THE **NWO**, AND HAD INDUCTED **MULTIPLE** NEW MEMBERS TO **DIMINISHING** RETURNS.

THOSE NEW NAMES INCLUDED **THE GREAT MUTA, SCOTT STEINER, MASAHIRO CHONO, HIROYOSHI TENZAN, KONNAN, RICK RUDE, CURT HENNIG,** AND **MORE.**

IN 1998, THE FACTION **SPLIT** INTO THE **HEROIC** NWO WOLFPAC (WHICH UTILIZED THE **KLIQ** GESTURE) AND THE **VILLAINOUS** NWO HOLLYWOOD.

THE SHOW HAD **LITERALLY** BECOME THE **NEW WORLD ORDER** VS. THE **NEW WORLD ORDER.**

WHILE WWF PUSHED **NEW** STARS, WCW BUILT AROUND **VETERAN** NAMES, SOME OF WHOM HAD FIRST RISEN TO PROMINENCE BACK IN THE **1980s.**

AND THEIR **EXPENSIVE** CONTRACTS, SOME WITH GUARANTEES OF **CREATIVE CONTROL,** MADE IT **DIFFICULT** TO RIGHT THE SHIP.

THE NWO WASN'T JUST THE **FOCUS,** IT WAS PRACTICALLY THE **SOLE** FOCUS OF WCW, TO THE DETRIMENT OF **OTHER** WRESTLERS, ESPECIALLY YOUNGER **CRUISERWEIGHT** TALENTS.

**EDDIE GUERRERO** AND MOST LUCHADORES WERE PLACED IN THE **LATINO WORLD ORDER,** A FONDLY REMEMBERED **PARODY** OF THE NWO.

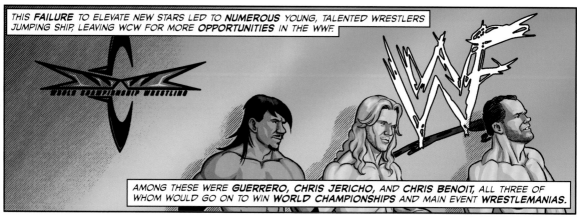

THIS **FAILURE** TO ELEVATE NEW STARS LED TO **NUMEROUS** YOUNG, TALENTED WRESTLERS JUMPING SHIP, LEAVING WCW FOR MORE **OPPORTUNITIES** IN THE WWF.

AMONG THESE WERE **GUERRERO, CHRIS JERICHO,** AND **CHRIS BENOIT,** ALL THREE OF WHOM WOULD GO ON TO WIN **WORLD CHAMPIONSHIPS** AND MAIN EVENT **WRESTLEMANIAS.**

BUT WHEN IT COMES TO WCW'S FAILURE TO **PROPERLY** CAPITALIZE ON A WRESTLER'S **POPULARITY**, THERE'S NO **BIGGER** EXAMPLE THAN **GOLDBERG**.

THOUGH HIS WINNING STREAK WAS **INFLATED**, IT HAD TURNED HIM INTO A **MASSIVELY** POPULAR STAR, ONE OF WCW'S FEW TRUE **HOMEGROWN** BREAK-OUTS.

ON JULY 6, 1998, GOLDBERG **FINALLY** FACED HULK HOGAN WITH THE **WCW WORLD HEAVYWEIGHT TITLE** ON THE LINE, LIVE ON **NITRO**.

WCW'S MOST **ANTICIPATED** MATCH WAS GIVEN AWAY FOR **FREE**, WHICH SCORED THEM A **MASSIVE** 6.91 RATING, BUT DID **NOTHING** FOR THE MORE PROFITABLE **PAY-PER-VIEW** MODEL.

BUT WCW STILL HAD GOLDBERG'S **STREAK** TO MARKET BEHIND AND POTENTIALLY, **BREAK**, TO CREATE A **BRAND-NEW** STAR.

INSTEAD, THE STREAK WAS BROKEN BY THE ALREADY **ESTABLISHED** KEVIN NASH AT **STARRCADE 1998**, AFTER GOLDBERG WAS ZAPPED BY A **STUN GUN**.

THEN A **MONTH** LATER, IN A MATCH THAT SHOULD HAVE BEEN **HUGE**, NASH DEFENDED THE TITLE AGAINST HIS **ERSTWHILE** ALLY **HOGAN**. BUT INSTEAD OF A **MATCH**...

...HOGAN WON WITH THE INFAMOUS **FINGERPOKE OF DOOM**. NASH LAID DOWN, **REUNITING** THEIR FACTION AND MAKING THE SHOW **ONCE AGAIN** ALL ABOUT THE **NWO**.

poke.

FOR YEARS, BISCHOFF, ON THE **LIVE** NITRO, HAD GIVEN AWAY THE RESULTS TO **RAW** ON WEEKS THAT IT WAS **PRE-TAPED**. IT WAS A WAY OF PREVENTING FANS FROM **CHANGING** CHANNELS.

ON THE NIGHT OF THE **FINGERPOKE OF DOOM**, COMMENTATOR **TONY SCHIAVONE** REVEALED THAT **MICK FOLEY** WOULD **WIN** THE WWF TITLE, SARCASTICALLY REMARKING...

THAT'S GONNA PUT SOME **BUTTS** IN THE SEATS.

BUT SCHIAVONE WAS **RIGHT**: IT **DID** PUT BUTTS IN SEATS, AS **HUNDREDS** OF **THOUSANDS** SWITCHED OVER TO SEE **MANKIND** DEFEAT **THE ROCK** FOR THE **WWF WORLD TITLE**.

THE WWF HAD **ALREADY** WON THE WEEKLY RATINGS BATTLES FOR **TWO MONTHS**, AND WCW WOULD **NEVER** WIN AGAIN. THE **MONDAY NIGHT WARS** WERE ALL BUT **OVER**.

WITH NITRO *AND* WCW THUNDER ON TURNER *NETWORKS*, WITH *TRUCKLOADS* OF TURNER *CASH*, THE MONDAY NIGHT WARS HAD BEEN WCW'S TO LOSE.

BUT WCW'S **PROBLEM** WAS NEVER A **LACK** OF MONEY, RATHER, IT WAS HOW THEY CHOSE TO **SPEND** IT.

THE **GUARANTEED** CONTRACTS THAT BROUGHT THEM THEIR **TALENT** TURNED INTO A **LIABILITY**. BRET HART AND GOLDBERG **BOTH** MADE **$2.5 MILLION** PER YEAR.

EVEN **WORSE**, WCW SIGNED **HUNDREDS** OF WRESTLERS--MANY OF WHOM DIDN'T EVEN APPEAR ON **TELEVISION**--SIMPLY TO KEEP **WWF** FROM GETTING THEM.

AND AS WWF WAS TAKING THE **LEAD**, WCW WAS SPENDING **EXORBITANT** AMOUNTS OF MONEY ON **POORLY** RECEIVED **CELEBRITY** AND **MUSICIAN-DRIVEN** STORYLINES AND MATCHES...

...FEATURING NAMES LIKE **KISS**, **MASTER P**, **JAY LENO**, **CHUCKY** FROM **CHILD'S PLAY**, AND EVEN THE **INSANE CLOWN POSSE**.

IN 1999, WCW BROUGHT IN WWF WRITERS **VINCE RUSSO** AND **ED FERRARA** TO **REPLICATE** RAW'S **SUCCESS**.

BUT THEIR APPROACH WAS **CHAOTIC**, RELYING TOO HEAVILY ON **WORKED SHOOTS** AND **INSIDE-BASEBALL** STORYLINES.

**RUSSO**, WHO HAD **NEVER** WRESTLED AND CERTAINLY DIDN'T **LOOK** THE PART, EVEN BOOKED **HIMSELF** TO WIN THE **WCW WORLD HEAVYWEIGHT CHAMPIONSHIP.**

BUT FOR **MANY** FANS, THE **FINAL STRAW** WAS IN 2000, WHEN ACTOR **DAVID ARQUETTE** WON THE WCW TITLE TO PROMOTE HIS MOVIE **READY TO RUMBLE.**

THE MOVE **DEVALUED** WCW'S **GREATEST** PRIZE AND WAS A **PERFECT** EXAMPLE OF HOW THE PROMOTION HAD **LOST** ITS WAY.

TED TURNER BUILT HIS EMPIRE UPON THE FOUNDATION OF TBS, AND MUCH OF THE SUPERSTATION'S ORIGINAL SUCCESS WAS BASED ON THE POPULARITY OF WRESTLING.

AS A RESULT, TURNER WAS OKAY WITH POURING MONEY INTO WCW, EVEN IF IT WASN'T AS PROFITABLE AS ITS COMPETITORS.

IN 1996 TURNER BROADCASTING SYSTEM MERGED WITH TIME WARNER. AT THE TIME, WCW WAS LOSING $12 TO $17 MILLION ANNUALLY.

THE COMPANY WASN'T THRILLED, BUT TURNER WAS STILL THE BIGGEST SINGLE SHAREHOLDER AND COULD SHIELD WCW FROM CUTS.

THAT CHANGED IN 2001, WHEN TIME WARNER WAS PURCHASED BY AOL AND TURNER WAS NO LONGER ABLE TO PROTECT WCW...

...ESPECIALLY SINCE IN THE PREVIOUS YEAR, THE PROMOTION HAD LOST MORE THAN $60 MILLION.

WCW FOUND ITSELF IN THE SIGHTS OF COST-CUTTING EXECUTIVES, WHO REMOVED IT FROM AOL-TIME WARNER CHANNELS.

TELEVISION HAD BECOME AN INTEGRAL PART OF SUCCESSFUL WRESTLING PROMOTIONS, AND WITHOUT IT, ANY POTENTIAL BUYERS IMMEDIATELY LOST INTEREST.

ALL THAT WAS LEFT WAS A CONSIDERABLE TAPE LIBRARY, A SLEW OF TRADEMARKS, AND A MIXED BAG OF WRESTLER CONTRACTS, ALL ESSENTIALLY WORTHLESS...

...UNLESS YOU ALREADY HAD A SUCCESSFUL, VICTORIOUS WRESTLING PROMOTION WITH SECURE TELEVISION SLOTS.

UNLESS YOU WERE VINCE MCMAHON AND THE WWF.

CONTEMPORARY **BURLESQUE** IS, IN MOST CASES, A **PERFORMANCE** OF **FEMININITY.**

ONE WHERE THE **MALE GAZE** IS DISREGARDED IN FAVOR OF **EXPLORING** FEMININITY AND ITS **BOUNDARIES.**

SIMILARLY, WRESTLING IS A PERFORMANCE OF **MASCULINITY,** BOTH IN TERMS OF ITS STARS' **APPEARANCES...**

...AS WELL AS THE FACT THAT **EVERY** CONCEIVABLE PROBLEM IS SOLVED WITH THE **SAME** THING...

...**VIOLENCE.** VIOLENCE THAT IS **CATHARTIC,** SHOCKING, AND, MOST **IMPORTANTLY,** WELL–**DESERVED.**

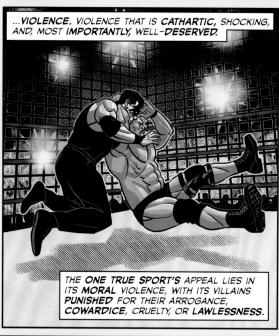

THE **ONE TRUE SPORT'S** APPEAL LIES IN ITS **MORAL** VIOLENCE, WITH ITS VILLAINS **PUNISHED** FOR THEIR ARROGANCE, **COWARDICE,** CRUELTY, OR **LAWLESSNESS.**

AND JUST AS **BURLESQUE** SEPARATES **SENSUALITY** FROM **SEX,** SO TOO DOES WRESTLING **ABSTRACT** VIOLENCE AWAY FROM ITS **REAL-WORLD** CONSEQUENCES.

IT IS **CRASS** AND **REDUCTIVE** TO BE SURE, BUT **ALL** STORIES OPERATE THIS WAY: **SIMPLIFYING THE REAL WORLD** TO MAKE A **LARGER** POINT ABOUT IT.

BUT WHAT **SEPARATES** PROFESSIONAL WRESTLING FROM **OTHER** MEDIUMS IS ITS WILLINGNESS TO **LEAN IN** TO THIS **CRASS** AND **REDUCTIVE** VIEW OF **MASCULINITY...**

...AND IN THE **PROCESS,** CREATE SOMETHING THAT APPEALS TO MEN, WOMEN, AND CHILDREN ALIKE.

IN WCW'S **DYING** DAYS, ERIC BISCHOFF TRIED TO **PURCHASE** THE PROMOTION FROM AOL TIME WARNER.

BUT WHEN WCW'S TELEVISION **TIME SLOTS** WERE PULLED, HIS **INVESTORS** QUICKLY LOST INTEREST.

MEANWHILE, ECW **ALSO** STRUGGLED, EVEN WITH THE **BACKING** OF WWF, WHO **FEATURED** THE PROMOTION ON **RAW**...

...AND GAVE ECW **MONEY** TO STAY **AFLOAT**, RECOGNIZING ITS VALUE AS A **FARM TEAM**, AS WELL AS AN **ALLY** IN THE WAR AGAINST **WCW**.

BUT IN LATE **2000**, WITH **WCW** NO LONGER A **THREAT**, WWF MOVED **RAW** TO **TNN**, WHICH THEN **CANCELED** ECW ON TNN.

ONLY **THEN** DID THE WWF SWOOP IN AND PURCHASE THE PROMOTIONS' **TRADEMARKS**, TAPE **LIBRARIES**, AND **REMAINING** ASSETS.

WITH NO **NATIONAL** TELEVISION, THINGS ONLY GOT **WORSE**. THE SYNDICATED **HARDCORE TV** ENDED IN **DECEMBER** AND THE COMPANY **FOLDED** IN EARLY 2001.

WWE REPORTEDLY PURCHASED **WCW** FOR AROUND **$4 MILLION**, A **PALTRY** SUM FOR WHAT HAD BEEN THE **TOP** PROMOTION IN THE WORLD A **FEW** YEARS EARLIER.

THE WWF WAS THE **LAST** PROMOTION STANDING. VINCE MCMAHON HAD **WON**, ACHIEVING THE DREAMS OF BOTH THE **GOLD DUST TRIO** AND THE EARLY **NWA**.

HIS WWF WAS A **NATIONAL** PROMOTION WITH A DE FACTO **MONOPOLY** ON THE ONE TRUE SPORT, WITH NOT A **SINGLE** POTENTIAL **CHALLENGER** IN SIGHT.

THOUGH THEY **WON** THE MONDAY NIGHT WARS, THE WWF WAS NOT **UNCHANGED.**

IT HAD BECOME MORE **VIOLENT, SEXUAL, VULGAR,** AND ALL-AROUND **EDGIER.**

ADDITIONALLY, INSTEAD OF **SQUASHES** MEANT TO TEASE BIG **PAY-PER-VIEW** MATCHES...

...AUDIENCES **EXPECTED** BIG, EXCITING, **PPV-QUALITY** MATCHES BETWEEN **TOP STARS** ON A **WEEKLY** BASIS.

AND THE PROMOTION NEEDED **TWICE** AS MANY WEEKLY MATCHES, AS **SMACKDOWN** LAUNCHED IN 1999.

A REFERENCE TO THE ROCK'S "LAY THE SMACK DOWN!" CATCHPHRASE, THE SHOW RAN AGAINST **WCW THUNDER.**

THE **COMPETITION** BETWEEN WWF AND WCW CREATED **MAINSTREAM** ATTENTION, BUT WITHOUT SOMEONE TO **BEAT...**

...WITHOUT **TWO** PROGRAMS TO **SWITCH** BETWEEN, COULD WWF RETAIN THE **MASSIVE** AUDIENCE THAT WAS **THEIRS** TO **LOSE?**

FORTUNATELY, THE WWF HAD THE **PERFECT** STORYLINE IN THEIR BACK POCKET, THE SAME TACTIC THAT **PROPELLED** WCW TO SUCCESS, THE ANGLE FANS WANTED MORE THAN **ANYTHING:**

A WCW **INVASION** OF WWF.

INVASION

ON A **SIMULCAST** OF RAW AND THE **FINAL** EPISODE OF NITRO, VINCE MCMAHON'S SON, **SHANE**, REVEALED THAT--IN WWF **STORYLINES**-- IT WAS **HE** WHO **PURCHASED** WCW.

THIS KICKED OFF AN ANGLE WHERE WCW **INVADED** WWF (IRONIC, AS THE **NWO** BEGAN AS AN **IMPLIED** INVASION FROM THE **WWF**).

FANS HAD **DREAMT** OF THIS ANGLE FOR **YEARS**, BUT MANY OF WCW'S TOP NAMES WEREN'T EVEN **INVOLVED**...

...AS THEY WERE **STILL** SIGNED TO **LUCRATIVE** CONTRACTS WITH **AOL-TIME WARNER**.

PLUS, WHILE THE STORY WAS **OSTENSIBLY** THE WWF FENDING OFF THE **ALLIANCE** OF WCW AND ECW...

...THE PROMOTIONS WERE JUST **PROXIES** FOR VINCE MCMAHON AND HIS CHILDREN, **SHANE** AND **STEPHANIE**, WHO BECAME **CENTRAL** TO THE STORY.

WHAT FANS **WANTED** WAS **COMPETITIVE** BACK-AND-FORTH BETWEEN **WWF** WRESTLERS AND THEIR FAVORITES FROM **OTHER** PROMOTIONS.

BUT THEY GOT A MOSTLY **ONE-SIDED** FEUD, WITH WWF WRESTLERS REIGNING **SUPREME**, AS WHEN THE ROCK BEAT **BOOKER** T FOR THE **WCW** TITLE.

IN ORDER TO **COMPENSATE** FOR MISSING STARS, **WWF** WRESTLERS JOINED THE ALLIANCE, TYPICALLY COMING OFF **BETTER** THAN THE WCW AND ECW WRESTLERS.

IN FACT, THE ALLIANCE WRESTLER THAT LOOKED THE BEST WAS **"STONE COLD"** STEVE AUSTIN, WHO HAD HELPED WWF **BEAT** WCW JUST A **FEW** YEARS EARLIER!

INSTEAD OF SHOWCASING A **HEATED** COMPETITION, THE LARGELY **DISLIKED** INVASION ANGLE SENT THE MESSAGE THAT WCW AND ECW **WEREN'T** ANY COMPETITION ITS AT **ALL.**

BUT IN ALL LIKELIHOOD ...THAT WAS THE **POINT.** IT WAS A **SUCCESSFUL** CAMPAIGN TO **SUBJUGATE** THE RIVAL BRANDS IN THE EYES OF WRESTLING FANDOM...

...AN OPPORTUNITY FOR THE **VICTORS,** WWF, TO WRITE THE **HISTORY** BOOKS.

BY **BUYING** WCW AND ECW, THEN **HIRING** MANY OF THEIR WRESTLERS, WWF GREW ITS ROSTER **DRAMATICALLY...**

...MAKING IT **DIFFICULT** FOR ANYONE BUT THE **TOP** STARS TO GET **ANY** ATTENTION. BUT THERE WAS A SOLUTION: THE **BRAND EXTENSION.**

THE WWF **SPLIT** THEIR ROSTER IN **TWO** AND BEGAN TREATING RAW AND SMACKDOWN AS **SEPARATE** PROMOTIONS.

EACH HAD ITS OWN **WRESTLERS, STORYLINES, AUTHORITY FIGURES,** AND EVEN TITLES. IN THE **ABSENCE** OF COMPETITION, WWF CREATED ITS **OWN.**

INITIALLY, THE **UNDISPUTED TITLE**--THE RESULT OF **UNIFICATION** WITH THE WCW CHAMPIONSHIP--WAS DEFENDED ON **BOTH** SHOWS.

BUT IN 2002, **CHAMPION** (AND **FUTURE** UFC STAR) **BROCK LESNAR** BECAME **EXCLUSIVE** TO SMACKDOWN, AND THE NEW **WORLD HEAVYWEIGHT** TITLE WENT TO **TRIPLE H.**

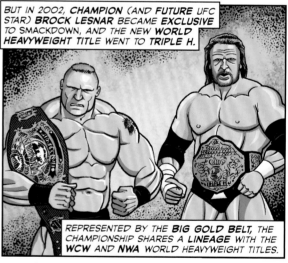

REPRESENTED BY THE **BIG GOLD BELT,** THE CHAMPIONSHIP SHARES A **LINEAGE** WITH THE **WCW** AND **NWA** WORLD HEAVYWEIGHT TITLES.

THE WWF WAS **REDEFINING** ITSELF FOR THE **NEW** MILLENNIUM. BUT A 2002 LAWSUIT FROM THE **WORLD WILDLIFE FUND** NECESSITATED THAT THEY DO IT UNDER A **NEW** NAME.

SO, WWF TRANSFORMED INTO **WORLD WRESTLING ENTERTAINMENT** (WWE), FURTHER DRIVING HOME THEIR "**ENTERTAINMENT**" FOCUS.

BUT JUST BECAUSE WWE WAS THE **ONLY** PROMOTION WITH **NATIONAL** TELEVISION, DIDN'T MEAN IT WAS THE **ONLY** PURVEYOR OF THE **ONE TRUE SPORT.**

IN FACT, FORMER **MEMPHIS** PROMOTER **JERRY JARRETT** AND HIS SON, **JEFF,** A FORMER **WWE** AND **WCW** WRESTLER, WERE READY TO TAKE **ADVANTAGE** OF THE **VACUUM** CREATED BY WCW'S CLOSURE.

THE FAMILY'S **TOTAL NONSTOP ACTION** BEGAN IN 2002 AS AN **NWA-AFFILIATED** GROUP, AIRING **WEEKLY** PAY-PER-VIEWS WITH **NO** FREE TELEVISION...

...UNTIL 2004, WHEN THEY OBTAINED A **WEEKLY** TELEVISION DEAL FOR THEIR SHOW **IMPACT!** AND DITCHED THEIR **NWA** AFFILIATION.

THE GROUP **KEPT** THE **NWA** TITLE, HOWEVER, ALLOWING THE PROMOTION TO BECOME A **SPIRITUAL SUCCESSOR** TO THE SOUTHERN WRESTLING **TRADITION.**

THE CONNECTION WAS **STRENGTHENED** BY THE PRESENCE OF NWA LEGENDS LIKE **DUSTY RHODES,** THE **JARRETTS'** INVOLVEMENT, AND EVEN ITS **HEELS-ON-TOP** BOOKING.

WHILE WCW HAD THE **CRUISERWEIGHTS,** TNA BOASTED THE **X-DIVISION,** FEATURING SMALLER, **FASTER,** AND **YOUNGER** COMPETITORS.

FOR **YEARS,** IT WAS A **FAN-FAVORITE** PART OF THE SHOW, FEATURING NAMES LIKE **SAMOA JOE, CHRISTOPHER DANIELS,** AND **A.J. STYLES.**

TNA **ALSO** STOOD OUT FROM WWE IN THE WAY IT TREATED THE **WOMEN** IN ITS KNOCKOUTS DIVISION.

LIKE WWE, THEY STILL **SEXUALIZED** THE WRESTLERS, BUT IN TNA WOMEN LIKE **AWESOME KONG** AND **GAIL KIM** WERE **GENERALLY** TREATED LIKE **SERIOUS** COMPETITORS.

TALENT WASN'T A PROBLEM FOR TNA, WHO INTRODUCED FANS TO NAMES LIKE **BOBBY ROODE, ABYSS, ODB, THE MOTOR CITY MACHINE GUNS,** AND **JAY LETHAL.**

BUT THE PROMOTION **REPEATED** MANY OF WCW'S **MISTAKES,** LIKE A FAILURE TO PUSH THESE **YOUNGER** NAMES...

...IN FAVOR OF MORE **ESTABLISHED** TALENTS WHO HAD COMPETED IN WCW AND WWE.

NAMES LIKE **STING, KURT ANGLE, THE HARDYS, BOOKER T,** AND **KEVIN NASH** BROUGHT **ATTENTION** TO THE PRODUCT, BUT **TOO** OFTEN MADE IT SEEM LIKE **WWE-LITE.**

THE TENDENCY TO **LEAN** ON FORMER WWF AND WCW TALENT ALSO EXTENDED TO THE **CREATIVE** SIDE, WITH **VINCE RUSSO** WORKING WITH THE COMPANY OFF-AND-ON.

AND IN **2010,** TRYING TO START A NEW **MONDAY NIGHT WAR,** TNA BROUGHT IN **ERIC BISCHOFF** AND **HULK HOGAN** AND MOVED IMPACT! TO RUN **OPPOSITE** OF RAW.

THOUGH IT HAD BEEN **FIFTEEN YEARS** SINCE THEY HAD **TRANSFORMED** THE INDUSTRY, THEY WEREN'T INTERESTED IN TRYING ANYTHING **NEW.**

INSTEAD, TNA BROUGHT IN **MORE** WCW AND WWF TALENT, **REVISITING** WHAT WORKED IN THE **PAST,** INCLUDING MASSIVE, UNWIELDY **FACTIONS** LIKE **ACES & EIGHTS.**

BY 2014, HOGAN AND BISCHOFF WERE **OUT,** BUT TNA WAS STILL **PLAGUED** BY **FREQUENT** CHANGES IN DIRECTION AND EVEN TELEVISION CHANNELS.

TNA HAD BEEN RUN BY **PRESIDENT DIXIE CARTER** SINCE 2002, WHEN HER FAMILY BOUGHT A **CONTROLLING** INTEREST IN THE COMPANY.

BUT IN 2016, SHE BECAME **CHAIRWOMAN,** AS **SMASHING PUMPKINS** FRONTMAN AND TNA INVESTOR **BILLY CORGAN** BECAME THE PROMOTION'S **PRESIDENT.**

THE **FOLLOWING** YEAR, AMID A **LAWSUIT** FROM CORGAN, **ANTHEM SPORTS & ENTERTAINMENT** GAINED CONTROL, MAKING CARTER A **MINORITY** OWNER.

LIKE JCP CHANGING TO **WCW,** TNA WAS REBRANDED TO **IMPACT WRESTLING,** A NAME THAT **STUCK** EVEN AFTER A TEASED MERGER WITH JEFF JARRETT'S **GLOBAL FORCE WRESTLING.**

THOUGH **BOTH** CONTINUED TO APPEAR **INTERMITTENTLY**, FOLLOWING THE **BRAND EXTENSION**, WWE LOST ITS TWO **BIGGEST** ATTITUDE-ERA STARS.

"STONE COLD" STEVE AUSTIN RETIRED ON THE ADVICE OF HIS **DOCTORS** IN 2003, AND **THE ROCK** LEFT TO PURSUE A **STAGGERINGLY** SUCCESSFUL **ACTING** CAREER IN 2004.

THE **LAST** MAJOR STARS OF THE ATTITUDE ERA STILL **ACTIVELY** COMPETING WERE THE **UNDERTAKER**, WHOSE **UNDEFEATED** STREAK BECAME A SELLING POINT FOR **WRESTLEMANIA**...

...AND **TRIPLE H**, WHO BEGAN TAKING ON A MORE **CORPORATE** ROLE AS HIS **ON-SCREEN** ROMANCE WITH **STEPHANIE MCMAHON** BECAME A **REAL-LIFE** ONE. THEY **MARRIED** IN 2003.

BUT WWE DIDN'T RELY **SOLELY** ON **ESTABLISHED** NAMES, AS THEY USED **TRIPLE H** AND **RIC FLAIR** TO ELEVATE **NEW** TALENT THROUGH THEIR FACTION, **EVOLUTION**.

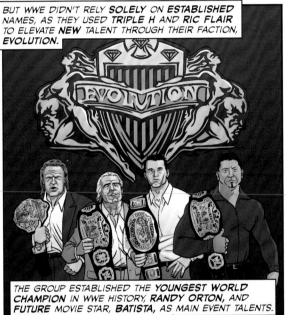

THE GROUP ESTABLISHED THE **YOUNGEST WORLD CHAMPION** IN WWE HISTORY, **RANDY ORTON**, AND **FUTURE** MOVIE STAR, **BATISTA**, AS MAIN EVENT TALENTS.

AND **WRESTLEMANIA XX** WAS A **CORONATION** FOR TWO **BELOVED** GRAPPLERS: WORLD HEAVYWEIGHT CHAMPION **CHRIS BENOIT** AND WWE CHAMPION **EDDIE GUERRERO**.

BUT THE **JOY** OF THAT MOMENT GAVE WAY TO **TRAGEDY** THE FOLLOWING YEAR WHEN GUERRERO PASSED AWAY SUDDENLY FROM **HEART FAILURE**.

THE PERIOD, OFTEN DUBBED THE "RUTHLESS AGGRESSION" ERA, ALSO SAW THE RISE OF FORMER **WCW** CRUISERWEIGHT **REY MYSTERIO**, FORMER **ECW** CHAMPION **ROB VAN DAM**...

...**RATED-R** BAD BOY **EDGE**, AND THE RICH, **ARROGANT**, ARCH-CONSERVATIVE **JBL**. BUT THE **BIGGEST**, MOST **SIGNIFICANT** NAME TO ARISE DURING THE PERIOD WAS...

...JOHN CENA, WHO FIRST ROSE TO **PROMINENCE** WITH A **RAPPER** GIMMICK, HIS "YOU CAN'T SEE ME" CATCHPHRASE, AND A CUSTOMIZED **SPINNER** CHAMPIONSHIP BELT.

CENA'S **ABRASIVE**, SOMETIMES **RISQUÉ** AND OFF-COLOR CHARACTER WOULD SERVE AS A **BRIDGE** FROM THE **ATTITUDE ERA** TO WHAT WOULD COME **NEXT**.

CENA WAS THE **CONTINUATION** OF AN OLD, CONSISTENTLY SUCCESSFUL WWE **TROPE**: THE **BIG**, BRAWLING **SUPERHERO** WITH **MAINSTREAM** APPEAL.

LIKE **BRUNO SAMMARTINO**, **HULK HOGAN**, AND **THE ROCK** BEFORE HIM, CENA PROVED A HIGHLY **CHARISMATIC** PRESENCE, CAPABLE OF WORKING THE CROWD INTO A **FEVER PITCH**.

OVER TIME, THE **ROUGHER** ASPECTS OF CENA'S CHARACTER **SOFTENED**, A RESULT OF A **GENERAL** WWE TREND TOWARD MORE **FAMILY-FRIENDLY** ENTERTAINMENT.

...OR HIS **ATTITUDE ADJUSTMENT**, WHICH WAS ORIGINALLY KNOWN AS THE **F-U**.

THOUGH SOME FANS **BLANCHED** AT THE CHANGES, THEY ENABLED CENA TO TAKE ON THE **ASPIRATIONAL** ROLE THAT HOGAN HAD MADE SO **SUCCESSFUL** IN THE 1980s.

A **CLEAR** EXAMPLE CAN BE SEEN IN THE **NAMES** OF CENA'S **FINISHING** MOVES, LIKE THE STFU, WHICH WAS SHORTENED TO THE STF...

CENA'S **CHARISMA**, **BROAD** APPEAL, AND, OF COURSE, RELIABLY **EXCELLENT** RINGWORK MADE HIM THE **BIGGEST** WRESTLING STAR OF THE TWENTY-FIRST CENTURY.

THE CHAMP IS HERE

HIS **CROSSOVER** SUCCESS EXTENDS TO **MOVIES**, TELEVISION APPEARANCES, **SATURDAY NIGHT LIVE**, AWARD SHOW **HOSTING**, A **RAP ALBUM**, AND EVEN **CEREAL**.

IN 2007, IN THE **MAIN EVENT** OF **WRESTLEMANIA 23**, CENA DEFENDED HIS **WWE CHAMPIONSHIP** AGAINST ONE OF THE MEN WHO HAD **KICK-STARTED** THE **ATTITUDE ERA**...

...**SHAWN MICHAELS**, WHO HAD RETURNED TO THE RING IN **2002** AFTER RECOVERING FROM WHAT WAS **THOUGHT** TO BE A **CAREER-ENDING** BACK INJURY.

BUT THAT WASN'T THE **ONLY** MATCH PITTING A **2000s** STAR AGAINST ONE FROM THE **ATTITUDE ERA**...

...AS THE **UNDERTAKER** CHALLENGED **BATISTA** FOR HIS **WORLD HEAVYWEIGHT CHAMPIONSHIP**, BUT THE MATCH WITH THE MOST **OUTSIDE** APPEAL...

...WAS **UMAGA** VS. **BOBBY LASHLEY**, PROXIES FOR **MR. McMAHON** AND **DONALD TRUMP**, WITH **BOTH** MEN'S **HAIR** ON THE LINE.

THE **MAINSTREAM** ATTENTION GARNERED BY THE MATCH MADE THE EVENT **MASSIVELY** SUCCESSFUL, THE MOST **WELL-ATTENDED** AND **BOUGHT** UP TO THAT POINT.

IT MIGHT SEEM **ODD** TO THINK OF THE FORTY-FIFTH **PRESIDENT** OF THE UNITED STATES APPEARING AT **WRESTLEMANIA**, BUT TRUMP'S **HISTORY** WITH **WWE** GOES BACK TO THE 1980s.

HIS TRUMP PLAZA HOSTED **BACK-TO-BACK** WRESTLEMANIAS, WHILE **WWE** AND THE McMAHONS DONATED **MILLIONS** TO THE **TRUMP FOUNDATION** AND TRUMP'S ELECTION **SUPER PAC**.

RELATIONSHIPS BETWEEN **PROMOTERS** AND **POLITICIANS** WERE COMMON GOING BACK TO THE DAYS OF **SAM MUCHNICK**, BUT THE TWO **MERGED** IN 2017...

...WHEN **LINDA McMAHON**, AFTER TWO **FAILED** U.S. SENATE RUNS AND $7 MILLION IN DONATIONS TO TRUMP'S CAMPAIGN...

...BECAME HIS **ADMINISTRATOR** OF THE **SMALL BUSINESS ADMINISTRATION**.

THOUGH **NOT** ONE OF THE SHOW'S **THREE** MAIN EVENTS, MANY **DEDICATED** WRESTLING FANS WERE MOST EXCITED ABOUT **ANOTHER** MATCH AT WRESTLEMANIA 23...

...ONE THAT SAW UP-AND-COMER **MVP** CHALLENGE FOR THE **UNITED STATES** TITLE AGAINST **CHRIS BENOIT.**

BENOIT WAS **BELOVED** BY **HARDCORE** FANS, WHO HAD WATCHED HIM AS **WILD PEGASUS** ON VHS TAPES OF THE **1994 SUPER J-CUP.**

HIS WRESTLING WAS A BLEND OF **MULTIPLE** STYLES, WITH AN **IMPRESSIVE** PEDIGREE INCLUDING STU HART'S **DUNGEON** AND THE **NJPW DOJO.**

FANS HAD WATCHED AS HE, **EDDIE GUERRERO, PERRY SATURN,** AND **DEAN MALENKO,** UNAPPRECIATED IN WCW, FORMED THE **RADICALZ** IN WWF.

AND THEY **REJOICED** WHEN BENOIT BECAME **WORLD CHAMPION.** HE WAS AN **UNDERDOG** STORY THAT ALSO ACTED AS **VINDICATION** FOR A CERTAIN **TYPE** OF WRESTLING AND **FAN.**

AND ABOVE ALL, HE WAS **EXQUISITE** IN THE RING, ONE OF WWE'S **BEST** PERFORMERS, WITH UNRIVALED **INTENSITY** AND **URGENCY.**

BENOIT MATCHES WERE **SHOCKINGLY** BELIEVABLE, TRADING OFF THE PERCEPTION OF HIM AS **VIOLENT** AND **DANGEROUS.**

AND ALL OF THAT **TOGETHER** IS WHY WHAT HAPPENED NEXT WAS SO **UTTERLY DEVASTATING** TO THE WRESTLING **INDUSTRY** AND **FANDOM.**

ON JUNE 22, 2007, CHRIS BENOIT **MURDERED** HIS **WIFE** AND SEVEN-YEAR-OLD **SON.**

HE TOOK HIS **OWN** LIFE **TWO** DAYS LATER.

IT WAS A HORRIFIC, **UNTHINKABLE** CRIME, AND TRYING TO MAKE **SENSE** OF IT, PEOPLE FIRST ATTRIBUTED THE ACT TO STEROID-INDUCED **"ROID RAGE."**

BUT WHILE BENOIT WAS ON SYNTHETIC **TESTOSTERONE** AT THE TIME (NOT **UNCOMMON** FOR THOSE WHO HAD **PREVIOUSLY** TAKEN STEROIDS, AS BENOIT HAD)...

...THERE WERE NO **DRUGS** IN HIS SYSTEM THAT COULD **EXPLAIN** HIS ACTIONS.

BUT A LATER EXAMINATION OF HIS **BRAIN** REVEALED AN **EXPLANATION:** IT HAD SUFFERED SO MUCH **DAMAGE** AS TO BE **COMPARABLE** TO THE BRAIN OF AN **OCTOGENARIAN** ALZHEIMER'S PATIENT.

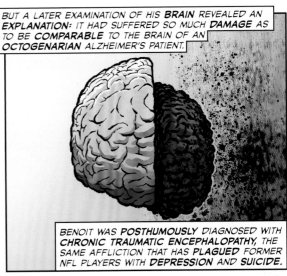

BENOIT WAS **POSTHUMOUSLY** DIAGNOSED WITH **CHRONIC TRAUMATIC ENCEPHALOPATHY,** THE SAME AFFLICTION THAT HAS **PLAGUED** FORMER NFL PLAYERS WITH **DEPRESSION** AND **SUICIDE.**

BENOIT'S HARD-HITTING, **AGGRESSIVE** STYLE--ONE OF THE THINGS PEOPLE **LOVED** ABOUT HIM--HAD **CAUGHT** UP WITH HIM.

YEARS OF **CONCUSSIONS** AND **HEAD** INJURIES FROM **CHAIR SHOTS,** HIS SIGNATURE **DIVING HEADBUTT,** AND **MORE** HAD LEFT HIM **DEPRESSED,** UNSTABLE, AND **BRAIN-DAMAGED.**

BY 2007, **FAR** TOO MANY WRESTLERS HAD **DIED** FROM SOME COMBINATION OF **WEAR AND TEAR, STEROID** ABUSE, PRESCRIPTION **PAINKILLERS,** AND **RECREATIONAL** DRUG USE...

...INCLUDING BENOIT'S LONGTIME FRIEND **EDDIE GUERRERO,** WHO HAD PASSED AWAY LESS THAN **TWO YEARS** EARLIER, POSSIBLY **EXACERBATING** BENOIT'S **DEPRESSION.**

BRIAN PILLMAN, 1997

RICK RUDE, 1999

EDDIE GUERRERO, 2005

CURT HENNIG, 2003

DAVEY BOY SMITH, 2002

TWO MONTHS AFTER THE BENOIT **MURDER-SUICIDE,** A GROUP OF WWE WRESTLERS--

--INCLUDING **BENOIT** AND **GUERRERO--** WERE IMPLICATED IN AN **ILLEGAL PHARMACY** SCANDAL.

AS A **RESULT,** WWE BEGAN TAKING A MORE **SERIOUS** APPROACH TO THE **WELLNESS** POLICY THEY HAD INSTITUTED IN THE WAKE OF **GUERRERO'S** DEATH.

IN ADDITION TO A **STANDING** OFFER TO PAY FOR **REHAB,** WWE ALSO BEGAN ISSUING **SUSPENSIONS** FOR THE USE OF **STEROIDS** AND **UNAUTHORIZED** PAINKILLERS.

THEY ALSO BEGAN **TESTING** AND **BENCHING** WRESTLERS AFTER **CONCUSSIONS.**

THIS INCREASED **AWARENESS** AND **PROTECTION** OF WRESTLERS' SAFETY WAS A TINY, **INSUFFICIENT** SILVER LINING TO WRESTLING'S **DARKEST** CHAPTER.

DURING THE **MONDAY NIGHT WARS**, TAPE TRADING GAVE WAY TO TAPE **SELLING**, WITH **RF VIDEO** SELLING MORE ECW THAN **ANYTHING** ELSE.

WHEN ECW WENT **UNDER** IN 2001, RF VIDEO NEEDED A **NEW** TOP-SELLER, SO THE COMPANY DECIDED TO **CREATE** THEIR OWN.

THE NEW PROMOTION, DUBBED **RING OF HONOR**, MADE ITS EVENTS AVAILABLE **EXCLUSIVELY** THROUGH **RF VIDEO**.

THOUGH IT WAS **INITIALLY** CREATED MERELY TO FILL THE **VOID** OF ECW, ROH WENT ON TO BECOME ONE OF THE NEW MILLENNIUM'S MOST **INFLUENTIAL** AND **IMPORTANT** PROMOTIONS.

ROH'S VERY FIRST SHOW WAS **CLEARLY** DESIGNED TO PICK UP **ECW** FANS. IT TOOK PLACE IN A **PHILADELPHIA** RECREATIONAL CENTER...

...AND FEATURED AN IWA TITLE MATCH BETWEEN ECW ALUMNI **EDDIE GUERRERO** AND **SUPER CRAZY**.

BUT MORE **IMPORTANTLY**, THE SHOW FEATURED AND HIGHLIGHTED **NEW** NAMES IN ITS **MAIN EVENT:**

A **TRIPLE-THREAT MATCH** BETWEEN FUTURE TNA STARS **CHRISTOPHER DANIELS** AND **LOW KI**...

...AND "AMERICAN DRAGON" **BRYAN DANIELSON**, WHO WOULD BECOME BEST KNOWN AS **DANIEL BRYAN** IN WWE.

THESE **THREE** MEN BECAME KNOWN AS RING OF HONOR'S **FOUNDING FATHERS**, NOT JUST BECAUSE THEY **MAIN EVENTED** THE FIRST SHOW...

...BUT BECAUSE THEIR WORK WAS **EMBLEMATIC** OF THE PROMOTION'S **UNIQUE** APPEAL, WHICH BROUGHT IT ITS **BIGGEST** SUCCESS AND ALLOWED IT TO HAVE SUCH A **LASTING** IMPACT.

WITH ITS **"REAL WRESTLING** FOR **REAL FANS"** TAGLINE, ROH SET ITSELF IN **STARK** OPPOSITION TO WWE'S **SPORTS ENTERTAINMENT.**

WRESTLERS LIKE **CM PUNK,** WHO WERE SEEN AS **TOO FAR** AFIELD FROM WWE'S **TYPICAL** HIRES, **EMBRACED** THIS ROLE.

LIKE THE **FANS** IT WAS AIMED AT, ROH WRESTLERS HAD BEEN EXPOSED TO **DIVERSE** STYLES OF THE **ONE TRUE SPORT,** SYNTHESIZING SOMETHING **NEW** THAT ROH THEN **POPULARIZED.**

**INNOVATIVE** TALENTS LIKE THE MMA-INFLUENCED **SAMOA JOE** DRILLED THAT POINT **HOME.**

ROH INSTITUTED A **CODE OF HONOR,** STIPULATING PRE-MATCH **HANDSHAKES** AND **FORBIDDING** INTERFERENCE AND ATTACKS ON **OFFICIALS** THAT HAD BECOME SO **COMMON.**

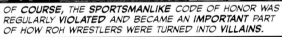

OF **COURSE,** THE **SPORTSMANLIKE** CODE OF HONOR WAS REGULARLY **VIOLATED** AND BECAME AN **IMPORTANT** PART OF HOW ROH WRESTLERS WERE TURNED INTO **VILLAINS.**

FROM **PURORESU,** ROH TOOK NOT ONLY ITS MORE **SPORT**-BASED PRESENTATION, BUT ALSO ITS **FAST-PACED** STRIKES AND KICKS.

IT MADE FOR A **QUICKER,** MORE **INTENSE,** MORE **BELIEVABLE** FORM OF GRAPPLING THAN FANS **TYPICALLY** SAW FROM WWE'S MORE **MUSCLE-BOUND** ROSTER.

THE PROMOTION ALSO FEATURED MORE ACTUAL **GRAPPLING** IN GENERALLY **LONGER** MATCHES, WITH **MAT WRESTLING** EXCHANGES AND A **WIDE** VARIETY OF **SUBMISSIONS.**

IT ALL PLAYED INTO ROH'S **MARKETING:** THIS IS WHAT **WRESTLING** WAS **SUPPOSED** TO BE. IT WAS THE **REAL** WRESTLING THAT WWE DIDN'T **WANT** YOU TO SEE.

IT WAS **MARKETING**, BUT IT WAS ALSO **EXTREMELY** EFFECTIVE AT ATTRACTING THE SAME TYPE OF **YOUNG, MALE, HARDCORE** FANS THAT **ECW** HAD HELD **ENTHRALLED.**

BUT THESE **HARDCORE** FANS WEREN'T AS INTERESTED IN **HARDCORE** WRESTLING--THE PENDULUM HAD SWUNG IN THE **OTHER** DIRECTION.

IN 2004, ROH LEANED **FURTHER** INTO THIS NOTION WITH THE CREATION OF ITS **PURE CHAMPIONSHIP.**

HELD MOST **FAMOUSLY** BY **NIGEL MCGUINNESS**, THE TITLE COULD BE CONTESTED ONLY UNDER **RULES** THAT MADE MATCHES EVEN MORE **SPORT**-LIKE.

IN 2004, ROH WAS PURCHASED BY **CARY SILKIN**, AND BY 2007, IT WAS RUNNING ITS OWN **PAY-PER-VIEWS...**

...WHILE FEATURING A **BROADER** VARIETY OF **TALENT**, INCLUDING **HARDCORE** AND **INTERNATIONAL** GRAPPLERS AS WELL AS A **PROCESSION** OF **INNOVATIVE** YOUNG WRESTLERS.

THE NECRO BUTCHER | TAKESHI MORISHIMA | DOUGLAS WILLIAMS | RODERICK STRONG | THE BRISCOE BROTHERS

AS WRESTLERS LEFT FOR **OTHER** PROMOTIONS, ROH REPEATEDLY **REPLENISHED** ITS **TALENT** POOL, **DIVERSIFYING** IN THE PROCESS.

MOOSE

CODY RHODES

DALTON CASTLE

ADAM COLE

THE YOUNG BUCKS

ROH FIRST AIRED WEEKLY **TELEVISION** IN 2009, AND TWO YEARS LATER THEY WERE PURCHASED BY **SINCLAIR BROADCAST GROUP.**

ROH CONTINUES TO PRODUCE **TELEVISION**, TOUR, PUT ON **PAY-PER-VIEWS**, AND PARTNER WITH **INTERNATIONAL** PROMOTIONS, LIKE **NJPW** (SEE PAGE 98)...

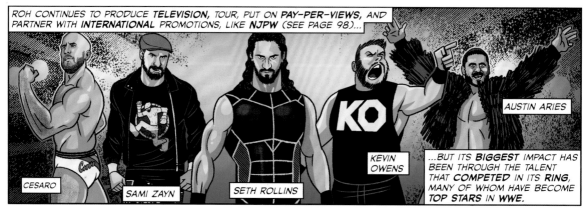

AUSTIN ARIES

KEVIN OWENS

CESARO

SAMI ZAYN

SETH ROLLINS

...BUT ITS **BIGGEST** IMPACT HAS BEEN THROUGH THE TALENT THAT **COMPETED** IN ITS **RING**, MANY OF WHOM HAVE BECOME **TOP STARS** IN WWE.

ROH SUCCEEDED BY CATERING TO AN **UNDERSERVED** AUDIENCE: **HARDCORE** FANS, MANY OF WHOM FOLLOWED WRESTLING **NEWS** AND **RUMORS** ON THE **INTERNET**.

WHILE THEY SAW ROH AS **EXCITING** AND **NEW**, WWE SEEMED LIKE IT WAS SPINNING ITS **WHEELS**, COMPLACENT IN AN **UNCHALLENGED** SPOT.

NAMES LIKE THE **UNDERTAKER, TRIPLE H,** AND **SHAWN MICHAELS** WERE STILL **ON TOP** A **DECADE** AFTER THE **ATTITUDE ERA** HAD BEGUN.

THEY WERE STILL **BELOVED,** BUT HARDCORE FANS FOUND THE APPROACH **STALE,** DIRECTING SPECIAL IRE TOWARD **TRIPLE H** FOR HOW HE WAS **PERCEIVED** AS USING HIS INCREASING **POWER** IN THE COMPANY.

ALTHOUGH TRIPLE H IS **OFTEN** ACCUSED OF HOLDING OTHER WRESTLERS **DOWN,** THE LATE **2000s** DID HAVE OTHER **MAJOR** STARS.

BUT MANY OF THOSE HAD **ALSO** BEEN WITH THE COMPANY SINCE THE **ATTITUDE ERA,** ALBEIT NOT ALWAYS IN A **MAIN EVENT** CAPACITY.

JEFF HARDY | REY MYSTERIO | EDGE | CHRIS JERICHO | JBL

AND THE **BRAND-NEW** TALENTS DIDN'T DO MUCH FOR **HARDCORE** FANS, AS THEY WERE IN THE **ESTABLISHED** WWE MOLD OF **BRAWLING BODYBUILDERS.**

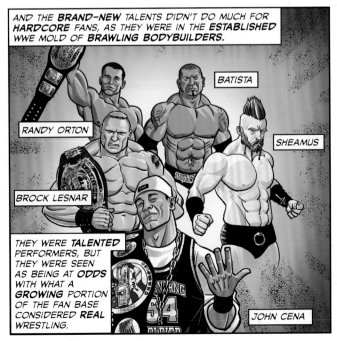

RANDY ORTON

BATISTA

SHEAMUS

BROCK LESNAR

JOHN CENA

THEY WERE **TALENTED** PERFORMERS, BUT THEY WERE SEEN AS BEING AT **ODDS** WITH WHAT A **GROWING** PORTION OF THE FAN BASE CONSIDERED **REAL** WRESTLING.

THEN, IN AN EFFORT TO COURT MORE **LUCRATIVE** ADVERTISERS, WWE WENT **TV-PG** IN 2008. THEY WERE MOVING **AWAY** FROM THE **CRASSNESS** OF THE **ATTITUDE ERA.**

BUT MANY **HARDCORE** FANS SAW THIS AS A CLEAR STATEMENT OF **INTENT:** THE WWE DIDN'T MAKE **WRESTLING** FOR **REAL FANS,** THEY MADE **SPORTS ENTERTAINMENT** FOR **CHILDREN.**

PROFESSIONAL WRESTLING WAS IN A **COMPLICATED** STATE, WITH **HARDCORE** FANS **CLAMORING** FOR A CHANGE FROM WHAT WWE'S **GENERAL** AUDIENCE HAD GROWN **ACCUSTOMED** TO.

IT WAS THIS **MILIEU** THAT GREETED FORMER ROH WORLD CHAMPION **CM PUNK** WHEN HE JOINED WWE'S RELAUNCHED **ECW** BRAND IN 2006.

INITIALLY, **PAUL HEYMAN** WAS IN CHARGE, AND WHILE IT WAS A **TONED-DOWN** VERSION OF THE ORIGINAL, HE STILL DISPLAYED HIS **KNACK** FOR IDENTIFYING AND **PROMOTING** TALENT.

**NOT** SURPRISINGLY, HE TOOK AN INTEREST IN THE **TATTOOED**, HARDCORE **STRAIGHTEDGE** GRAPPLER, AND BY **2007** PUNK HAD BECOME **ECW CHAMPION.**

THOUGH PUNK DIDN'T **LOOK** LIKE A **TYPICAL** WWE WRESTLER, HIS YEARS IN **ROH** AND OTHER **INDEPENDENT** PROMOTIONS LEFT HIM **FULLY** PREPARED TO SUCCEED ON WRESTLING'S **BIGGEST** STAGE...

...WHILE ALSO MAKING HARDCORE FANS EVEN **MORE** LIKELY TO CHEER HIM. IN 2008, HE WON THE **MONEY IN THE BANK**, A MATCH TYPICALLY USED TO **ELEVATE** NEW STARS.

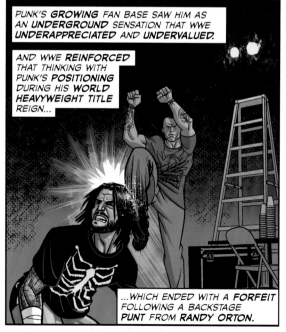

PUNK'S **GROWING** FAN BASE SAW HIM AS AN **UNDERGROUND** SENSATION THAT WWE **UNDERAPPRECIATED** AND **UNDERVALUED.**

AND WWE **REINFORCED** THAT THINKING WITH PUNK'S **POSITIONING** DURING HIS **WORLD HEAVYWEIGHT** TITLE REIGN...

...WHICH ENDED WITH A **FORFEIT** FOLLOWING A BACKSTAGE **PUNT** FROM **RANDY ORTON.**

THE **FOLLOWING** YEAR, PUNK USED HIS **STRAIGHTEDGE** LIFESTYLE TO MAKE A **VILLAINOUS** TURN, DRAWING **RAVES** FROM FANS WHO FELT HE WAS **UNDERUTILIZED** OR EVEN **IGNORED.**

PUNK WAS DOING WHAT PURVEYORS OF THE **ONE TRUE SPORT** HAD **ALWAYS** DONE--BLURRING THE LINES BETWEEN **FACT** AND **FICTION.** AND HE WAS JUST GETTING **STARTED.**

EVERYTHING ABOUT CM PUNK FELT **DIFFERENT**. HE WAS TALL, BUT NOT A **BODYBUILDER**, AND HIS WRESTLING WAS **RAWER**, MORE INFLUENCED BY **ECW** AND **PURORESU** THAN THE WWE.

FANS SAW PUNK GETTING **LEFT BEHIND,** JUST AS **THEY** FELT LEFT BEHIND BY THE WWE PRODUCT. AND ON JUNE 27, 2011, THEIR FRUSTRATION **EXPLODED** WITH PUNK'S **PIPE BOMB** PROMO.

DELIVERED ON THE **RAW** ENTRANCE RAMP IN A **STONE COLD** SHIRT, PUNK TOOK AIM AT **JOHN CENA** BY PLAYING UP THE **DISTINCTION** BETWEEN **WRESTLING** AND **SPORTS ENTERTAINMENT**.

IT WAS A **PLANNED** SPEECH, BUT PUNK WAS **IMPASSIONED** AND **VITRIOLIC** AS HE CALLED OUT NOT ONLY THE WAY WWE WAS **RUN,** BUT **TRIPLE H'S** ROLE WITHIN THE COMPANY.

I AM THE BEST **WRESTLER** IN THE **WORLD!**

IT WAS **CATNIP** TO HARDCORE, CASUAL, AND EVEN **LAPSED** FANS WHO **AGREED** WITH PUNK'S **DAMNING** WORDS.

THEY HAD CAPTURED **LIGHTNING** IN A **BOTTLE,** AS PUNK EMBARKED ON A **FEUD** WITH **CENA,** WHO PUNK'S FANS SAW AS A **SYMBOL** OF EVERYTHING **WRONG** WITH WWE.

THE NIGHT PUNK WAS SCHEDULED TO **DEPART** THE COMPANY, HE **BEAT** JOHN CENA FOR THE **WWE CHAMPIONSHIP** AND LEFT WITH IT.

BUT UNLIKE **RIC FLAIR** OR **ALUNDRA BLAYZE,** PUNK LEAVING WAS ALL PART OF THE **PLAN,** AND NATURALLY, IT BUILT TO HIS **RETURN** A MONTH LATER.

PUNK WENT ON TO HOLD THE **WWE** TITLE FOR **434 DAYS,** MAKING HIM THE **LONGEST** REIGNING CHAMP SINCE **HOGAN'S** 1984 RUN.

BUT PUNK'S REIGN WAS **ENDED** BY A **BODYBUILDING** SUPERHERO, **THE ROCK,** WHO PUNK HAD **CALLED OUT** IN HIS **PIPE BOMB** PROMO, SEEMINGLY PROVING THAT **NOTHING** HAD CHANGED.

**ONE** YEAR LATER, IN EARLY 2014, PUNK, **FRUSTRATED** BY HOW HE WAS **USED** AS WELL AS BY THE **QUALITY** OF WWE **MEDICAL CARE,** STOPPED SHOWING UP FOR **EVENTS** AND WAS OFFICIALLY **FIRED** IN JUNE.

PUNK'S **DEPARTURE** MADE IT **EASY** FOR FANS TO BELIEVE WHAT THEY'D BEEN TOLD FOR **FIFTEEN YEARS**: THE MCMAHONS WERE **EVIL BILLIONAIRES** THAT DIDN'T **CARE** WHAT FANS **WANTED**.

BUT **ANOTHER** ROH ALUMNI, FOUNDING FATHER BRYAN DANIELSON, RECAST AS **DANIEL BRYAN**, WOULD UPSET THAT **TRADITIONAL** WISDOM...

...THROUGH HIS **EXEMPLARY**, ONCE-IN-A-LIFETIME TALENT AND THE **GROUNDWORK** LAID BY **CM PUNK**.

THOUGH A **SENSATION** ON THE **INDIES**, BRYAN WAS THE **ANTITHESIS** OF A **WWE SUPERSTAR**. HE WAS **SHORT**, SMALL, **PALE**, AND BELIEVED TO BE **UNINSPIRING** ON THE MICROPHONE.

HE WAS ALSO A **VICIOUS** SUBMISSION-BASED **GRAPPLER**. BUT HIS **FINISHER** WAS CALLED **CATTLE MUTILATION**, AND IT OBSCURED BOTH HIS **AND** HIS OPPONENT'S **FACES**!

BRYAN WAS A WRESTLER **WITHOUT A GIMMICK**, OR MORE **ACCURATELY**, LIKE **LOU THESZ**, HIS GIMMICK **WAS** WRESTLING.

HIS FANS WERE **CONVINCED** THAT WWE WOULDN'T KNOW **WHAT** TO DO WITH HIM, AND THEIR **SUSPICIONS** WERE CONFIRMED BY HIS **TREATMENT** ON THE FIRST SEASON OF **NXT**.

FROM HIS **2010** DEBUT, BRYAN WAS **BERATED** AND **MOCKED** AS AN UNCHARISMATIC **NERD** BY COMMENTARY AND FORMER REALITY STAR **THE MIZ**.

LATER THAT YEAR, BRYAN WAS **FIRED** FOR A **PLANNED** ATTACK ON AN **ANNOUNCER** THAT WAS DEEMED **TOO** VIOLENT.

BUT ALL THAT **MISTREATMENT?** IT JUST MADE PEOPLE LOVE HIM **MORE** UPON HIS 2011 **RETURN**. HE SOON BECAME **WORLD HEAVYWEIGHT CHAMPION**...

...AND AN ARROGANT **BULLY**. BUT LIKE **PUNK**, BRYAN WAS A **VILLAIN** THAT PEOPLE **LOVED**, GIVING **LIE** TO THE BELIEF THAT HE WAS **UNCHARISMATIC**.

THEN, IN **2012**, DANIEL BRYAN LOST HIS TITLE TO **SHEAMUS** IN THE EIGHTEEN-SECOND **OPENING MATCH** OF **WRESTLEMANIA XXVIII**.

THOUGH **PUNK** WAS STILL IN THE MIDST OF HIS **HISTORIC** REIGN, HARDCORE FANS FELT **BETRAYED**. NOT ONLY DID BRYAN LOSE THE **TITLE**, BUT THEY DIDN'T EVEN GET TO SEE HIM **WRESTLE**.

THE LOSS **GALVANIZED** BRYAN'S FANBASE, WHO BEGAN USING HIS TRADEMARK **"YES!"** CHANT TO SUPPORT HIM.

AND **NATURALLY**, IN A WAY **BEFITTING** THE ONE TRUE SPORT, THIS **REALITY**--A **SWELL** OF SUPPORT FOR BRYAN--WAS **COOPTED** AND TURNED INTO A **STORYLINE**.

AND **BEST** OF ALL? TRIPLE H **EMBRACED** THE ROLE THAT **FANDOM** HAD ALREADY PLACED HIM IN: THAT OF A CONNIVING, **NEPOTISTIC**, CORPORATE **VILLAIN**.

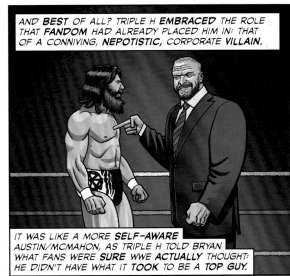

IT WAS LIKE A MORE **SELF-AWARE** AUSTIN/MCMAHON, AS TRIPLE H TOLD BRYAN WHAT FANS WERE **SURE** WWE **ACTUALLY** THOUGHT: HE DIDN'T HAVE WHAT IT **TOOK** TO BE A **TOP GUY**.

**MORE** THAN EVER, BRYAN WAS SEEN IN **OPPOSITION** TO WWE. AND, JUST AS WITH **PUNK**, THAT WAS PART OF THE **STORY** BEING **TOLD**.

IN TRUTH, BRYAN, WITH **FEWER**, MORE VISUALLY **RECOGNIZABLE** MOVES AND TAMPED DOWN **BRUTALITY**, HAD **EMBRACED** THE **CAMP** AND **SPECTACLE** OF WWE...

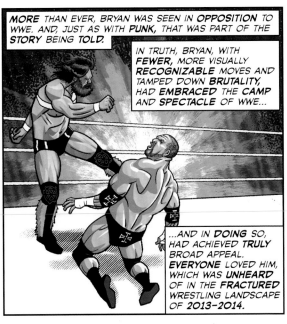

...AND IN **DOING** SO, HAD ACHIEVED **TRULY BROAD** APPEAL. **EVERYONE** LOVED HIM, WHICH WAS **UNHEARD** OF IN THE **FRACTURED** WRESTLING LANDSCAPE OF 2013-2014.

AT **WRESTLEMANIA XXX**, DANIEL BRYAN BEAT **TRIPLE H** IN THE OPENING CONTEST, EARNING A SPOT IN THE **WWE CHAMPIONSHIP** MATCH WITH **RANDY ORTON** AND **BATISTA**.

AND HE **WON**. BRYAN, THE UNDERSIZED **INDIE WRESTLER**, BEAT ONE OF THE **HEADS** OF WWE AND HIS **PROTÉGÉS**, IN THE **SAME** NIGHT TO WIN THE **WWE TITLE**.

A **DECADE** AFTER WRESTLEMANIA XX ENDED WITH **EDDIE GUERRERO** AND **CHRIS BENOIT** STANDING TALL, WWE **ELEVATED** ANOTHER **FAN-FAVORITE** UNDERDOG.

AND IT HAD BEEN IN THE MOST **PROFESSIONAL WRESTLING** WAY IMAGINABLE: TAKE WHAT FANS **THINK** THEY KNOW, **ENCOURAGE** THEM TO THINK IT, COMPLETELY **UPEND** IT, THEN **CHARGE** THEM FOR THE **PRIVILEGE**.

IT WAS AN **EXQUISITE** PIECE OF WRESTLING **STORYTELLING**, EMBODYING SO MUCH OF WHAT'S TRULY **TRANSCENDENT** ABOUT THE MEDIUM.

EVEN OUTSIDE OF THE **WRESTLEMANIA** VICTORY, THERE'S AN **IMPORTANT** COMPARISON TO MAKE BETWEEN **BRYAN** AND NOT ONLY **BENOIT**...

...BUT A MAN THAT BENOIT EMULATED, **DYNAMITE KID**, WHO ALSO **FAMOUSLY** USED THE **DIVING HEADBUTT**, A MOVE **INDICATIVE** OF ALL THREE'S **UNFORGIVING** STYLES.

BRYAN'S **BELIEVABILITY** AND WILLINGNESS TO **SOAK** UP **PUNISHMENT** ARE **HUGE** PARTS OF WHY PEOPLE **FELL IN LOVE** WITH HIM.

BUT SADLY, ITS **EFFECTS** CAUGHT UP WITH HIM, JUST AS THEY DID **BENOIT** AND **DYNAMITE** (WHO WAS LEFT **DISABLED** FROM **CONCUSSIONS** AND INJURIES TO HIS **SPINE**).

ON FEBRUARY 8, 2016, BRYAN, AT THE **PEAK** OF HIS FAME AND ABILITIES, **RETIRED.**

HE HAD EXHIBITED SIGNS OF **CTE** AND SUFFERED POST-CONCUSSION **SEIZURES**, WHILE AN EEG REVEALED A **LESION** ON HIS **BRAIN.**

SHOCKINGLY, IN EARLY 2018, BRYAN WAS **CLEARED** BY WWE DOCTORS AND ALLOWED TO RETURN TO **IN-RING** COMPETITION.

BRYAN AND CM PUNK'S IMPACT **CAN'T** BE OVERSTATED, AS THEY **CHANGED** HOW WWE **HIRED** AND **PROMOTED** TALENT.

WITHOUT THEM, WWE MIGHT **NEVER** HAVE LOOKED **TWICE** AT A SLEW OF **INDEPENDENT** STARS.

A.J. STYLES

SETH ROLLINS

DEAN AMBROSE

SAMI ZAYN

KEVIN OWENS

THIS CHANGE **ALSO** AFFECTED THE WWE'S **DEVELOPMENTAL** TERRITORY, A **REWORKED** NXT, WHICH BEGAN HIRING **TOP** WRESTLERS FROM THE **INDIES**, **JAPAN**, AND **MEXICO.**

RODERICK STRONG

KASSIUS OHNO (CHRIS HERO)

SHINSUKE NAKAMURA

HIDEO ITAMI (KENTA)

ANDRADE ALMAS (LA SOMBRA)

THE LATE 2010s SAW A **MASSIVE** CHANGE IN WWE'S **ON-SCREEN** PRODUCT, WITH AN **INFLUX** OF **NEW** AND **VARIED** TALENTS.

AND SO TOO DID THE COMPANY'S **INTERNAL** WORKINGS UNDERGO A **SEISMIC** SHIFT, WITH THE COMING OF THE **WWE NETWORK**.

FOR **YEARS**, WWE HAD **TALKED** ABOUT CREATING THEIR **OWN** NETWORK, BUT COULDN'T GET **CABLE OPERATORS** TO SIGN ON.

SO IN **2014**, THEY CUT CABLE COMPANIES OUT OF THE EQUATION, CREATING THEIR OWN **STREAMING** NETWORK...

...WHICH INCLUDED **ALL** WWE PAY-PER-VIEW EVENTS, INCLUDING **WRESTLEMANIA XXX**, FOR A **FRACTION** OF THE PRICE OF PURCHASING THEM **INDIVIDUALLY**.

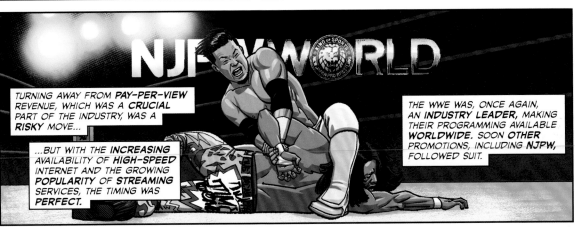

TURNING AWAY FROM **PAY-PER-VIEW** REVENUE, WHICH WAS A **CRUCIAL** PART OF THE INDUSTRY, WAS A **RISKY** MOVE...

...BUT WITH THE **INCREASING** AVAILABILITY OF **HIGH-SPEED** INTERNET AND THE GROWING **POPULARITY** OF **STREAMING** SERVICES, THE TIMING WAS **PERFECT**.

THE WWE WAS, ONCE AGAIN, AN **INDUSTRY LEADER**, MAKING THEIR PROGRAMMING AVAILABLE **WORLDWIDE**. SOON **OTHER** PROMOTIONS, INCLUDING **NJPW**, FOLLOWED SUIT.

THE WWE NETWORK **CHANGED** HOW PEOPLE **CONSUME** PROFESSIONAL WRESTLING. SHOWS WERE NO LONGER **EPHEMERAL**--WATCHED, **CHEERED**, THEN **FORGOTTEN**.

NOW FANS COULD DIVE **HEADFIRST** INTO EVERY WWE, WCW, AND ECW PAY-PER-VIEW IN EXISTENCE...

...AS WELL AS CONTENT FROM THE **TAPE LIBRARIES** OF THE RIVAL PROMOTIONS THAT WWE HAD **COLLECTED** FOR **DECADES**.

WWE BEGAN PRODUCING **MORE** CONTENT FOR THE **NETWORK**, INCLUDING **NON-WRESTLING** PROGRAMMING.

WITH MORE **CONTENT** CAME MORE **VARIETY**, INCLUDING SPECIAL TOURNAMENTS FOR **CRUISERWEIGHTS**, **BRITISH** WRESTLERS, AND **WOMEN**. **SPEAKING OF WOMEN'S** WRESTLING...

IT'S **UNFORTUNATE** WE HAVEN'T GIVEN WOMEN'S WRESTLING MORE **ATTENTION**, BUT THE **SAD TRUTH** IS THAT IN AMERICA IT HAS **LONG** BEEN **MARGINALIZED**...

...EVEN THOUGH IT'S **ALWAYS** BEEN A DRAW, AND THE **ATTITUDE** AND **RUTHLESS AGGRESSION** ERAS SPECIFICALLY FEATURED A NUMBER OF **SUPREMELY** TALENTED **FEMALE** WRESTLERS.

CHYNA

TRISH STRATUS

BETH PHOENIX

LITA

MICKIE JAMES

VICTORIA

NATALYA

BUT WHILE THESE WOMEN AND **OTHERS** PUT ON **GREAT** MATCHES, THE **FOCUS** GIVEN TO THE DIVISION WAS **HAPHAZARD**, AND IT **ALWAYS** TOOK A **BACKSEAT** TO THE MEN.

ADDITIONALLY, WWE WOULD REGULARLY **PRIORITIZE** SWIMSUIT MODEL **PHYSIQUES** OVER **IN-RING** PROWESS AND **CHARISMA**.

BUT THE **AUDIENCE** WAS BECOMING **VOCAL** IN THEIR DESIRE FOR A MORE **DIVERSE** WRESTLING PRODUCT, **ESPECIALLY** REGARDING **WOMEN**.

HARDCORE FANS HAD SEEN WOMEN'S WRESTLING TREATED **SERIOUSLY** IN JOSHI WRESTLING, TNA'S **KNOCKOUTS** DIVISION, AND WOMEN-SPECIFIC INDIES LIKE **SHIMMER**...

...WHERE FUTURE NXT CHAMPION **ASUKA** SQUARED OFF WITH FUTURE NXT TRAINER **SARA DEL REY**.

NOT **SURPRISINGLY**, CHANGE IN WWE BEGAN ON THE DEVELOPMENTAL PROGRAM, **NXT**, WHERE **CHARLOTTE, SASHA BANKS, BAYLEY,** AND **BECKY LYNCH** STARTED TURNING HEADS.

NXT GENERALLY GAVE WOMEN MORE **FOCUS** THAN **RAW** OR **SMACKDOWN** AND THESE FOUR WERE ITS **BREAKOUT** STARS.

IN 2015, **STEPHANIE MCMAHON** ANNOUNCED A **WOMEN'S REVOLUTION**, AND FANS **BOUGHT** IN AS THE FOUR WERE CALLED UP TO THE **MAIN ROSTER**.

WWE **DITCHED** THE PATRONIZING "**DIVAS**" NAME AND BEGAN TREATING THE WOMEN WITH MORE **RESPECT** ON A MORE **CONSISTENT** BASIS.

THEN, AT THE 2016 **HELL IN A CELL**, CHARLOTTE AND SASHA BANKS BECAME THE **FIRST WOMEN** TO MAIN EVENT A WWE PAY-PER-VIEW.

GETTING AMERICAN WOMEN'S WRESTLING THE **RESPECT** IT DESERVES HAS PROVED TO BE A **SLOW** PROCESS, BUT **THANKFULLY**, THERE'S STEADY **PROGRESS** BEING MADE.

AS **WWE** DIVERSIFIED, **OTHER** PROMOTIONS CONTINUED EXPLORING THE **OUTER REACHES** OF THE **ONE TRUE SPORT**, LIKE LOS ANGELES'S **PRO WRESTLING GUERRILLA**...

...THE **ALL-STARS** OF THE INDIES, THIS **AMERICAN LEGION** HALL PACKED WITH A **RIOTOUS** CROWD BECAME MANY WRESTLERS' **LAST STOP** BEFORE BEING **SIGNED** BY WWE.

AND FOR FANS WHO WANT WRESTLING THAT LEANS MORE INTO **STORY** AND CARTOONISHLY **WACKY** CHARACTERS? THERE ARE PROMOTIONS LIKE **CHIKARA, KAIJU BIG BATTEL**...

...AND **LUCHA UNDERGROUND**, FOR A **BILINGUAL**, STORY-BASED APPROACH TO **LUCHA LIBRE**.

AT THE **OTHER** END OF THE WRESTLING **SPECTRUM** ARE MORE **SPORT-BASED** PROMOTIONS, LIKE THE EAST COAST'S **EVOLVE**.

THERE, FANS CAN EXPECT **MORE** GRAPPLING, **LONG** TITLE REIGNS, AND AN **EMPHASIS** ON **WIN/LOSS** RECORDS.

MEANWHILE, THE **SECOND** LARGEST PROMOTION IN THE WORLD, **NJPW**, IS MAKING MOVES **INTERNATIONALLY** VIA THEIR **STREAMING** SERVICE AND SHOWS HELD **ABROAD**.

AND IN 2017, AT A **TOURNAMENT** IN **LONG BEACH**, KENNY OMEGA BECAME THE FIRST-EVER **IWGP UNITED STATES CHAMPION**.

AND SINCE **HIGH TIDES** RAISE **ALL** SHIPS, **REGIONAL** INDEPENDENT PROMOTIONS ARE ON AN **UPSWING** AS WELL, HIGHLIGHTING **LOCAL** WRESTLERS AND **FLYING IN** TOP INDIE **STARS**.

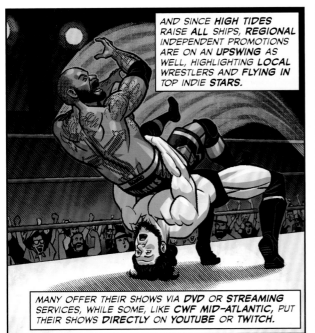

MANY OFFER THEIR SHOWS VIA **DVD** OR **STREAMING** SERVICES, WHILE SOME, LIKE **CWF MID-ATLANTIC**, PUT THEIR SHOWS **DIRECTLY** ON YOUTUBE OR TWITCH.

WITH SO MUCH **ARCHIVAL** MATERIAL ON THE **WWE NETWORK**, LIVE SHOWS TAKING PLACE **EVERY** WEEKEND ALL **OVER** THE WORLD, AND A **WEALTH OF STREAMING** OPTIONS...

...IT'S **EASIER** TO WATCH **MORE** WRESTLING THAN **EVER**, MAKING IT A BETTER TIME TO BE A **FAN** OF THE **ONE TRUE SPORT** THAN AT ANY POINT IN **HISTORY**.

FROM ITS ORIGINS IN THE TRAVELING *CARNIVALS* OF THE 1880S, WHEN *PROMOTERS*, *WRESTLERS*, AND *BOOKIES* BANDED TOGETHER...

...CREATING A FORM OF *ENTERTAINMENT* THAT WAS MOST *EFFICIENT* AT SEPARATING AUDIENCES FROM THEIR *MONEY*...

...TO THE BIGGEST *ARENAS* AND *STADIUMS*, PACKED WITH *TENS* OF *THOUSANDS* AND WITH *MILLIONS* WATCHING AROUND THE WORLD...

...PROFESSIONAL WRESTLING *ENDURES* BECAUSE OF *TWO* KEY THINGS THAT HAVE *ALWAYS* HELD TRUE, THAT HAVE *NEVER* CHANGED:

IT'S BECAUSE OF THE WAY THE MEDIUM *FORCES* US TO *CONFRONT* THE NATURE OF *STORIES* AND *ENTERTAINMENT*...

...BLURRING THE LINES BETWEEN *FACT* AND *FICTION*, BETWEEN WHAT WE *KNOW* AND WHAT WE *THINK* WE KNOW. AND JUST AS *IMPORTANTLY*...

...IT'S BECAUSE OF THE *SIMPLE*, UNAVOIDABLE, *PRIMAL* FACT THAT *EVERYONE*, NO MATTER *WHO* THEY ARE OR *WHERE* THEY COME FROM...

...*LOVES* A GOOD FIGHT, ONE WHERE THE *BAD* GUYS *ALWAYS* GET WHAT'S *COMING* TO THEM...

...AND THE *GOOD* GUYS ALWAYS *WIN* IN THE END.

ALL *HAIL* PROFESSIONAL WRESTLING. ALL HAIL THE *ONE TRUE SPORT*.

## ACKNOWLEDGMENTS...

### AUBREY:

Thanks to Excalibur for his invaluable notes and corrections on
the script. To Dustin Spencer for his input on the book's structure.
To Dominic Griffin for his feedback on the book's tone and approach.
To Roderick Strong for talking me through so much wrestling.
And most of all, to my STRAIGHT SHOOT fans, whose support,
friendship, and enthusiasm made this project possible.

### CHRIS:

A big thanks to everyone who pitched in to help put this book together:
Dee, and Juan, Brad, and Allen for their assistance on color, my studio
mates at Garage Art Studios, notably Dennis Culver, for page
support, Luke Malone, for helping close the gaps, and my brother,
Jay "Zees" Moreno (together again!) for coming through in the clutch.
Most importantly, thanks to Aubrey for being a big supporter of mine,
a great collaborator, and for suggesting I do the book with him
in the first place.

We'd both like to thank the team at Ten Speed for their work on
the book, including our editor Patrick Barb, designer Chloe Rawlins,
as well as Serena Sigona from production and Eleanor Thacher
and Natalie Mulford from marketing and publicity.

# INDEX

## A

Abdullah the Butcher, 65, 104
Abyss, 152
Adams, "Gentleman" Chris,
    77, 94
Adonis, Adrian, 108
Akeem, 122
Albano, Captain Lou, 109
Ali, Muhammad, 34, 89, 110
all-in wrestling, 69–72
All Japan Pro Wrestling
    (AJPW), 87–89, 92, 97
All Japan Women's Pro-
    Wrestling (AJW), 96
All Star Wrestling, 79
Almas, Andrade, 166
Ambrose, Dean, 166
American Wrestling Association
    (AWA), 47, 103, 106, 108, 113
Anderson, Arn, 116
Anderson, Karl, 100
Anderson, Ole, 116
Andre the Giant, 50, 86, 92,
    106, 119
Angelico, 67
Angle, Kurt, 134, 141, 152
Arena México, 54
Aries, Austin, 160
Arquette, David, 144
Asistencia Asesoría y
    Administración (AAA), 63
Assirati, Bert, 75
Asuka, 96, 168
The Attitude Era, 139–41, 153
Austin, "Stone Cold" Steve, 101,
    132, 135, 138, 140, 149, 153
Awesome Kong, 151

## B

Baba, Giant, 37, 41, 50, 68, 86–89,
    92, 97
Backlund, Bob, 47, 107
Baker, Ox, 52
Balor, Finn, 100
Banks, Sasha, 168
Barthes, Roland, 68
Bartoletti, Basilio, 8
Batista, 153, 155, 161, 165

Bauer, Thiebaud, 55
Baumann, Max, 29
Bayley, 168
Belzer, Richard, 111
Benoit, Chris, 98, 135, 142, 153,
    156–57, 166
Bibby, Edwin, 82
Big Daddy, 75–78, 79, 80
Bigelow, Bam Bam, 135
Big Japan Pro Wrestling, 95
The Big Show, 68, 86
Billington, Tom. See Dynamite Kid
Bischoff, Eric, 127–28, 131, 132, 137,
    143, 147, 152
Black Shadow, 58
Black Tiger, 78, 93, 98
Blackwell, "Crusher" Jerry, 106
Blanchard, Tully, 37, 115, 116
Blassie, Freddie, 36, 46, 105
Blayze, Alundra, 96, 128
Blue Demon, 58
Blue Demon, Jr., 67
Bockwinkel, Nick, 106
Booker T, 149, 152
Brisco, Gerald, 105
Brisco, Jack, 41, 88, 105
The Briscoe Brothers, 160
The British Bulldogs, 32, 72
Brody, Bruiser, 65, 92, 141
Brookside, Robbie, 79
Brown, Orville, 35, 38
Bryan, Daniel, 68, 158, 164–66
The Bullet Club, 99–100, 129
Bundy, King Kong, 101
Bunkhouse Stampede, 118
Burke, Mildred, 43, 44
Burns, Martin "Farmer," 6–7, 10,
    12, 19, 20, 82
Bushi, 100

## C

Cactus Jack, 132
Caddock, Earl, 7, 19
Campbell, A. B., 71
Capitol Wrestling
    Corporation, 49
Caras, Dos, 58
Caras, Dos, Jr., 58

Carpentier, Édouard, 37, 46, 47
Carter, Dixie, 152
Casas, Negro, 98
Cassandro, 59, 63
Castle, Dalton, 160
catch-as-catch-can (catch
    wrestling), 6, 9, 69, 72,
    78, 80
Cena, John, 154–55, 161, 163
Cesaro, 160
Chambers, J. G., 69
Charlotte, 168
Chono, Masahiro, 97, 142
Choshu, Riki, 91
Christian, 141
Chyna, 139, 168
Cole, Adam, 160
Colón, Carlito, 64
Colón, Carlos, 36, 64, 65, 70,
    84, 104
Colón, Epico, 64
Colón, Primo, 64
Consejo Mundial de Lucha Libre
    (CMLL), 54, 58, 60, 63
Cooper, Alice, 119
Corgan, Billy, 152
Crabtree, Max, 73, 75
Crabtree, Shirley, 73. See also
    Big Daddy
The Crash, 63
Crockett, Jim, Jr., 110, 113, 115, 117
Curley, Jack, 30–32, 34

## D

El Dandy, 60
Daniels, Christopher, 151, 158
Danielson, Bryan, 158, 164. See
    also Bryan, Daniel
Del Rey, Sara, 168
Del Rio, Alberto, 58
Dempsey, Jack, 72
D-Generation X, 139
DiBiase, "The Million Dollar
    Man" Ted, 108, 131
Dick the Bruiser, 37, 47
Diesel, 129, 130
Dillon, J. J., 116
Ding Dongs, 123

Douglas, Shane, 133
Dragon Gate, 63
Dreamer, Tommy, 135
Dudley, Bubba Ray, 141
Dudley, D-Von, 141
Dunn, Roy, 29
Duprée, Emile, 37
Dusek, Rudy, 7, 32
Dynamite Kid, 32, 72, 77, 78, 92,
    93, 166

**E**

Ebersol, Dick, 112
Edge, 141, 153, 161
Elephant Boy, 43
Elizabeth, Miss, 119, 124
Emelianenko, Fedor, 89
Empresa Mexicana de Lucha
    Libre (EMLL), 54, 60, 63
Evil, 100
Exbroyat, Jean, 8
Extreme Championship
    Wrestling (ECW), 95,
    132–35, 147, 149–50, 158, 162

**F**

Fabiani, Ray, 30, 32
The Fabulous Freebirds, 114
The Fabulous Moolah, 109
Fenix, 67
Ferrara, Ed, 144
Ferrigno, Lou, 105
Finkel, Howard, 110
Finlay, Fit, 77, 79
Flair, Ric, 37, 41–42, 47, 64, 68,
    81, 88, 104, 115, 116, 117, 118,
    123–24, 128, 130, 141, 153
flat hand wrestling, 8
Foley, Mick, 68, 95, 132, 139, 143
The Four Horsemen, 116
The Four Pillars of Heaven, 97
The French Angel, 43
Frontier Martial Arts Wrestling
    (FMW), 95
Fujinami, Tatsumi, 91, 105
Funk, Dory, Jr., 36, 41, 88
Funk, Terry, 36, 41, 88, 123,
    134, 135

**G**

Gagne, Greg, 113, 124
Gagne, Verne, 36, 46–47, 52, 103,
    106, 107, 113
Gallows, Luke, 100
Gangrel, 139

Gaona, Octavio, 56
Garvin, Ronnie, 120
Gedo, 98, 99
George, Paul "Pinkie," 35
Georgia Championship
    Wrestling (GCW), 51,
    102, 115
The Giant, 131
Gilbert, "Hot Stuff" Eddie, 133
gimmicks, 101, 122
The Godfather, 139
Goldberg, Bill, 137, 143, 144
Gold Dust Trio, 20, 22–29, 34, 50,
    121, 124
Goldust, 139
Gomez, Pepper, 36
González, José, 65
Gordon, Tod, 133, 134
Gordy, Terry "Bam Bam," 114
Gorgeous George, 34, 39, 45
Gotch, Frank, 7, 10–12, 13, 15, 17,
    21, 26, 31, 57, 70, 111
Gotch, Karl, 72, 89–90, 105
Graham, "Superstar" Billy,
    105, 107
The Great Kabuki, 94
The Great Muta, 94, 97, 105,
    123, 142
The Great Sasuke, 98
Greco-Roman wrestling, 8–9
Guerrera, Juventud, 63, 66
Guerrero, Chavo, 61, 67
Guerrero, Eddie, 62, 93, 98, 122,
    135, 137, 142, 153, 156, 157, 158
Guerrero, Gory, 61, 66
Guerrero, Hector, 61
Guerrero, Mando, 61

**H**

Hackenschmidt, George "The
    Russian Lion," 8, 9–12, 13, 21,
    31, 69, 70, 111
Hall, Scott, 130
Hansen, Stan, 50, 92
Hardy, Jeff, 141, 152, 161
Hardy, Matt, 141, 152
Hart, Bret "The Hitman," 32, 78,
    80, 124, 126, 132, 136–38, 144
Hart, Jimmy, 119
Hart, Owen, 32, 78
Hart, Stu, 32, 36, 78, 93, 114,
    126, 156
Hart, Teddy, 32
Hashimoto, Shinya, 97
Hayabusa, 95, 98

Hayes, Michael "P.S.," 114
Haystacks, Giant, 75–76, 79
Hebner, Earl, 136
Heenan, Bobby "The Brain," 101,
    108, 124
Helmsley, Hunter Hearst, 129,
    132, 139. See also Triple H
Henderson, Mort, 55
Hennig, Curt, 47, 142, 157
Henry, Mark, 68
Herd, Jim, 123–24
Hero, Chris, 166
Heyman, Paul, 133, 134, 135, 162
Hogan, Hulk, 47, 92, 105–11, 117,
    119, 121, 124, 125, 128, 130,
    143, 152, 154, 163
The Hunchbacks, 123

**I**

Ibushi, Kota, 93
Impact Wrestling, 152
Los Ingobernables de
    Japon, 100
Inoki, Antonio, 37, 86–87, 89,
    90, 105
Inoue, Kyoko, 96
International Championship
    Wrestling, 43
The Iron Sheik, 47, 107
Irslinger, Henry, 69, 70
Itami, Hideo, 166
Ivelisse, 67

**J**

Jackson, Matt and Nick, 100
Jado, 99
James, Mickie, 168
Jannetty, Marty, 126
Japan, wrestling in, 82–100
Japan Pro Wrestling Alliance
    (JWA), 85, 87–88
Jarrett, Jeff, 151, 152
Jarrett, Jerry, 43, 113, 114, 151
JBL, 153, 161
Jenkins, Tom, 9, 10
Jericho, Chris, 135, 137, 142, 161
Jim Crockett Promotions (JCP),
    103–4, 108, 115–20
Johnson, Dwayne. See The Rock
Johnson, Rocky, 140
Joint Promotions, 73, 75, 79
joshi puroresu, 96, 168
Jumping Bomb Angels, 96
Junkyard Dog, 108

## K

Kajiwara, Ikki, 93
Kane, 139
Kansai, Dynamite, 96
Kasaboski, Larry, 37
Kaufman, Andy, 111
Kawada, Toshiaki, 97
Kenta, 166
Kidd, Tyson, 32
Kim, Gail, 151
Kimura, Masahiko, 85
"King's Road" wrestling, 86, 88, 91
Kiniski, Gene, 36, 41, 50
The Kliq, 129
Kobashi, Kenta, 97
Kohler, Fred, 45, 47
Koloff, Ivan, 50, 66, 122
Koloff, Nikita, 117
Kong, Aja, 96
Konnan, 63, 142
Kowalski, Killer, 42, 46, 50
Kudo, Megumi, 95

## L

Lancashire wrestling, 72
Lashley, Bobby, 155
Latino World Order, 142
Lauper, Cyndi, 109, 110
Lawler, Jerry, 37, 43, 111, 113, 138
Lee, Sammy, 93
Lesnar, Brock, 150, 161
Lethal, Jay, 152
Lewis, Ed "Strangler," 17–20, 22–23, 25–29, 35, 38, 39
Lewis, Evan "Strangler," 6, 7, 82
Liberace, 110
Liger, Jushin Thunder, 68, 93, 98, 128
Lita, 141, 168
Loch Ness Monster, 75
Londos, Jim "The Golden Greek," 30–31, 35
The Loose Cannon, 132
Lopez, Tarzan, 57
Low Ki, 158
lucha libre, 53–67
luchas de apuestas, 56
Lucha Underground, 67, 169
Luger, Lex, 117, 123, 128
Lutteroth, Salvador, 54, 55, 57, 58
Lynch, Becky, 168

## M

Madison Square Garden, 9, 13, 34, 107, 110, 129
Madusa, 128, 136
Magnum T.A., 115, 117, 118
Maivia, Ata, 140
Maivia, "High Chief" Peter, 36, 140
Malenko, Dean, 98, 156
Mankind, 132, 143
Mantel, Dirty Dutch, 65
La Maravilla Enmascarada, 54–55
Marshall, Everett, 29
Martel, Rick, 108
masks, 53, 54–56, 93
El Matador, 122
Matsuda, Hiro, 105
Matsuda, Sorakichi, 82
Matsumoto, Dump, 96
McGillicutty, Beulah, 134
McGuinness, Nigel, 80, 160
McMahon, Jess, 32, 49
McMahon, Linda, 155
McMahon, Shane, 149
McMahon, Stephanie, 149, 153, 168
McMahon, Vincent James, 49, 50, 51, 105, 106, 121
McMahon, Vincent Kennedy, 51, 79, 102–3, 107, 110–12, 117, 120, 121, 125–26, 136, 138–39, 145, 147, 155, 164
Meltzer, Dave, 135
Mendoza, Ray, 60, 63
Mexico, wrestling in, 53–64
Michaels, Lorne, 112
Michaels, Shawn, 124, 126, 129, 136, 139, 155, 161
midget wrestling, 43
Mid-South Wrestling, 103, 108
Mil Mascaras, 58, 88
Misawa, Mitsuharu, 93, 97
The Miz, 164
modern freestyle, 71–72
Momota, Mitsuhiro. See Rikidōzan
Mondt, James Ervin "Toots," 7, 20–23, 26, 27, 29–32, 34, 49, 50, 51, 121
The Montreal Screwjob, 136–38
Moolah, 43
Moose, 160
Morales, Pedro, 50, 66
Morishima, Takeshi, 160

Morrell, Norman, 71
The Motor City Machine Guns, 152
Mountevans, Admiral-Lord, 71, 73, 74
Mr. Perfect, 124
Mr. T, 106, 110
Muchnick, Sam, 35, 38, 40
Muldoon, William, 82
Munn, Wayne, 28, 30, 41, 136
El Murciélago Enmascarado, 56
Mutoh, Keiji, 94, 97
MVP, 156
Myers, Sonny, 38

## N

Nagai, Go, 93
Nagasaki, Kendo, 76, 79, 80
Nagata, Yuji, 89
Naito, Tetsuya, 94, 100
Nakamura, Shinsuke, 99, 166
Nakano, Bull, 96
Nash, Kevin, 130, 143, 152
Natalya, 168
National Wrestling Alliance (NWA), 35–49, 51, 60, 64, 69, 73, 84–85, 88, 102, 104, 108, 113, 115, 117, 133, 151
National Wrestling Association, 35
The Necro Butcher, 160
Neidhart, Jim "The Anvil," 32, 78, 126
Neidhart, Natalya, 32
Neville, 80
The New Age Outlaws, 139
New Japan Pro-Wrestling (NJPW), 87, 89–90, 92, 93, 94, 97–100, 167, 169
New World Order (NWO), 100, 130–31, 137, 139, 142, 143, 149
Nitro, 128, 130–31, 137, 143, 144, 149
Nomellini, Leo, 46
NXT, 164, 166, 168

## O

Oakeley, Sir Edward Atholl, 69, 70
O'Connor, Pat, 47
ODB, 152
Ohno, Kassius, 166
Okada, Kuzuchika, 94, 100
Okerlund, "Mean" Gene, 108
Omega, Kenny, 100, 169

One Man Gang, 108, 122
Onita, Atsushi, 95
Orndorff, Paul, 110
Orton, "Cowboy" Bob, 108
Orton, Randy, 153, 161, 162, 165
Ospreay, Will, 80
Owens, Kevin, 160, 166

**P**

Page, Diamond Dallas, 137
Paige, 80
La Parka, 63
Patera, Ken, 108
Peña, Antonio, 63
Pentagón, Jr., 67
Pfefer, Jack, 30–31, 32, 43, 111
Phoenix, Beth, 168
Pillman, Brian, 123, 128, 132, 157
Piper, Roddy, 68, 104, 108,
   109, 110
Poffo, Angelo, 43
Pons, Paul "Colossus," 8, 9
Prince Puma, 67
professional wrestling
   appeal of, 170
   caricature, stereotype, and
      representation in, 122
   fixed nature of, 5, 13, 22, 31
   magic of, 16
   masculinity and, 146
   menace in, 68
   morality play aspect of, 52
   origins of, 2–5
   slang of, 33
   time limits for, 24–25
Promo Azteca, 63
Pro Wrestling USA, 113
Psicosis, 63, 135
Puerto Rico, wrestling in, 64–65
Punk, CM, 159, 162–64, 166
puroresu, 82–100
Putski, Ivan, 50
Pytlasinski, Wladislaus, 8

**Q**

Quinn, Eddie, 46

**R**

Race, Harley, 37, 41, 88, 108
The Radicalz, 156
Ramon, Razor, 129, 130
Raw, 126–27, 128, 131, 139, 143, 144,
   147, 149, 150, 152
Reed, "The Natural" Butch, 108
Regal, William, 77

Rey Mysterio, 62–63, 68, 135,
   153, 161
RF Video, 158
Rhodes, Cody, 160
Rhodes, Dusty, 37, 41, 68, 104,
   116, 123, 139, 151
Rich, Tommy, 41
Richter, Wendi, 109
Ricochet, 67
Rikidōzan, 37, 83–87, 88, 105
Riley, Billy, 72, 90
Ring of Honor (ROH), 158–61
The Road Warriors, 68, 92,
   123, 124
Roberts, Buddy "Jack," 114
Roberts, Jake "The Snake,"
   108, 119
Robinson, Billy, 72, 107
Rocca, Antonino, 32, 39, 86
Rocco, Mark "Rollerball," 78,
   79, 93
The Rock, 140, 143, 148, 149, 153,
   154, 163
The Rockettes, 110
The Rock 'n' Roll Express, 101
Rocky III, 106, 110
Rodman, Dennis, 137
Rogers, "Nature Boy" Buddy, 39,
   48, 49–50, 81, 90, 117
Roller, Dr. Ben, 10, 11
Rollins, Seth, 160, 166
Romero, Rocky, 93
Roode, Bobby, 152
Rose, "Playboy" Buddy, 36
Ross, Jim, 138
rough and tumble duels, 3
Royal Rumble, 118, 119
Rude, Rick, 142, 157
Russo, Vince, 144, 152
Ryan, Joey, 67

**S**

Sabre, Zack, Jr., 80
Sabu, 95, 134
Sammartino, Bruno, 37, 50, 51,
   117, 122, 154
Samoa Joe, 151, 159
Sanada, 100
The Sandman, 134
Sandow, Billy, 18–20, 27, 29
Sandow, Eugen, 18
Santana, Tito, 122
Santel, Ad, 12, 39, 55
El Santo, 37, 57–58, 60, 61
Saturday Night's Main Event

(SNME), 112
Saturn, Perry, 156
Savage, "Macho Man" Randy,
   43, 101, 112, 119, 124, 130,
   131, 137
Sayama, Satoru, 78, 93
Schiavone, Tony, 143
Schultz, David, 111
Schwarzenegger, Arnold, 105
Scurll, Marty, 80
Sgt. Slaughter, 124
Sheamus, 80, 161, 164
The Sheik, 37
Shibata, Katsuyori, 99
Shikat, Dick, 30
Shockmaster, 127
Silkin, Cary, 160
Singh, Tiger Jeet, 92
SmackDown, 148, 150
Smith, Davey Boy, 72, 77, 78,
   80, 157
Smith, Davey Boy, Jr., 32
The Snake Pit, 72, 86, 90
La Sombra, 166
Son of Havoc, 67
Starrcade, 104, 118, 120, 143
Steamboat, Ricky "The Dragon,"
   47, 108, 119, 123
Stecher, Joe, 15, 19, 29
Steiner, Rick, 123
Steiner, Scott, 123, 142
Sting, 94, 115, 117, 120, 123, 128,
   131, 152
Stossel, John, 111
Stratus, Trish, 141, 168
Strong, Roderick, 160, 166
strong style wrestling, 86, 87,
   89–91, 99
Styles, A. J., 100, 151, 166
submissions, 81
SummerSlam, 119, 141
Super Crazy, 135, 158
Super J-Cup, 98, 156
Survivor Series, 118, 119, 136
The Swedish Angel, 43, 86
Syxx, 131

**T**

Tajiri, 95, 135
Takahashi, Hiromu, 100
Tanahashi, Hiroshi, 99
Tanaka, Masato, 95
Tateno, Noriyo, 96
Taue, Akira, 97
Taz, 135

Tenzan, Hiroyoshi, 142
Thesz, Lou, 12, 37, 38–41, 46, 48, 49, 84, 164
Thornley, Peter, 76
The Three Musketeers, 97, 99
Tiger Mask, 92–93, 97
Tokyo Pro Wrestling, 87
Toryumon, 63
Total Nonstop Action (TNA), 151–52
Toyota, Manami, 96
Triple H, 139, 150, 153, 161, 163, 165
Trump, Donald, 155
Tsuchiya, Shark, 95
Tsuji, Naoki, 93
Tsuruta, Jumbo, 92, 97
Turner, Ted, 120, 123, 128, 145
2 Cold Scorpio, 133
Tyler, Tarzan, 87

**U**

The Ultimate Warrior, 120
Último Dragón, 63, 94
Umaga, 155
The Undertaker, 68, 126, 139, 153, 155, 161
United Kingdom, wrestling in, 69–80
United States Wrestling Association (USWA), 114
Universal Wrestling Association, 63
Universal Wrestling Federation (UWF), 103

**V**

Valentine, Greg "The Hammer," 104, 108
Vampiro, 60
Van Dam, Rob, 135, 153
Venis, Val, 139
Ventura, Jesse "The Body," 105, 108
Victoria, 168
Von Erich, David, 114
Von Erich, Fritz, 103, 113, 114
Von Erich, Kerry, 113–14
Von Erich, Kevin, 114
The Von Erichs, 37, 114

**W**

Wagner, Dr., 60
Waltman, Sean, 129, 131, 139
Wanalaya, Kimona, 134
Watson, Whipper Billy, 37
Watts, Bill, 37, 87, 108, 113
Webb, Maurice, 71
Wepner, Chuck, 106
Wild Pegasus, 98, 156
Williams, Douglas, 160
women's wrestling, 70, 74, 95–96, 141, 151, 168
World Championship Wrestling (WCW), 62, 63, 120, 123–24, 127–32, 137, 142–45, 147–50
World Class Championship Wrestling (WCCW), 103, 114
World of Sport, 74–77, 79, 93

World Wide Wrestling Federation (WWWF), 49–51, 66
World Wrestling Council (WWC), 64–65
World Wrestling Entertainment (WWE), 66, 147, 150–51, 153–57, 161–69
World Wrestling Federation (WWF), 51, 79, 102–13, 117–21, 124–29, 132, 136–41, 143, 145, 147–50
WrestleMania, 110, 112, 118, 119, 129, 132, 142, 153, 155–56, 164, 165, 167

**X**

X-Pac, 139

**Y**

Yamazaki, Itsuki, 96
Yamazaki, Yoshihiro, 93
The Young Bucks, 100, 160

**Z**

Zahorian, George, 125
Zayn, Sami, 160, 166
Zbyszko, Larry, 137
Zbyszko, Stanislaus, 10, 28–29, 30, 41, 44, 124, 136